DALLAS COWBOYS

DALLAS
COWBOYS

★

THE AUTHORIZED PICTORIAL HISTORY

BY
JEFF GUINN

THE SUMMIT PUBLISHING GROUP

THE
SUMMIT
PUBLISHING
GROUP

One Arlington Centre,
1112 East Copeland Road, Fifth Floor
Arlington, Texas 76011

Printed in the United States of America.

00 99 98 97 96   010   5 4 3 2 1

Library of Congress
Cataloging-in-Publication Data

Guinn, Jeff.
    Dallas Cowboys : the authorized
    pictorial history / by Jeff Guinn
        p. cm.
        ISBN 1-56530-231-1 (cloth).–
        ISBN 1-56530-235-4 (pbk.)
        1. Dallas Cowboys (Football team)–History.
        2. Dallas Cowboys (Football team)–
    Pictorial works. I. Title
    GV956.D3G85 1996
    796.332'64'097642812–dc20   96-25336
                                        CIP

Photo Credits–page 222

                Photo Editor: Ron Ennis

        Cover design by John Baird & David Sims

        Book design & layout by Bill Maize
                    DUO Design Group

        Production Manager: Ken Dunaway

            Research: Andy Grieser

                Editor: Mark Murphy

CONTENTS

ACKNOWLEDGMENTS

For help above and beyond the call, thanks go out to George Hays, Len Oszustowicz, Marilyn Love, Rich Dalrymple, Brett Daniels, Kelli McGonagill Finglass, Regina Tucker, Cindi Burck, Christy Van Meter, Russ Russell, Jim Browder, Barbara Goodman, Emily Cruz, Ed Shipman of Happy Hill Farm, Roz Cole, Greg Aiello, Carlton Stowers, Pam Minick, Mark Murphy, Jill Bertolet, Amy Grieser, Patti Ennis, Ty Benz, Joy Nguyen, Julie Heaberlin, and Robert Philpot. We also recognize the late Al Panzera for his photographic contributions. Special thanks to all the Cowboys players and coaches—past and present—who have shared their memories. We also appreciate former Dallas opponents Ray Nitschke and Rocky Bleier for their contributions.

The Dallas Cowboys wish to thank the Fort Worth Star-Telegram for generous use of its photographs.

Photo Credits–page 222

FOREWORD

Let me welcome you to *Dallas Cowboys: The Authorized Pictorial History*. Many books have been written about our team, and, as we continue to set standards in the National Football League, I'm sure many more will follow. This one is different because it's *our* book. No other stories could come from closer to the source.

Even before I was fortunate enough to join the Cowboys family in 1989, I was well aware of the team's fabulous history. Since our first days as an expansion franchise in 1960, no other organization has succeeded so well for so long. As we like to say in this part of the country: That ain't brag. It's just fact. Name all the NFL franchises where every head coach has won at least one Super Bowl. We're a one-team list.

That kind of success reflects the hard work of many, many people over a considerable period. Recent Cowboys' achievements reflect the present generation of coaches and players, but the lengthy traditions and winning heritage of the team are because of the efforts of others. We've never forgotten that.

I'm so proud that our book goes all the way back to the very beginning. I've been fascinated to read the words of Tex Schramm and Coach Landry, of Bob Lilly and Walt Garrison, of Jethro Pugh and Bob Breunig and Tony Dorsett and many, many others. What they've got to say isn't rehashed material from old interviews. Everything you read here is fresh, contributed just for this authorized history.

This is an interesting time for the NFL. Salary caps and free agency are designed to bring about parity. That doesn't mean every team will end up every season with a .500 record. It just means there are new rules to follow, with all the teams starting even. As always, the most innovative, hard-working organizations will find ways to win. I promise you this: Every member of the Dallas Cowboys organization is committed to nonstop excellence. We've always found ways to be the best before, and, whatever it takes, that will not change.

Just after the 1978 season, the Dallas Cowboys were nicknamed "America's Team." We're still known that way, and it makes us proud. As Tony Dorsett pointed out in an interview for this book, it's a title we've earned. It also means we've earned special attention from every other team in the NFL and the fans of those teams. Good, hard, entertaining competition is what professional football is all about. Maybe, if they read this book, the folks who've loved to hate us during all these years might actually start liking us a little. That would be nice.

But I want my last message here to go out to the ultimate heroes in this team's history: you true fans who've been behind the Dallas Cowboys every step of the way. Mostly, we do our best to thank you by putting the very finest teams we can on the field and by trying to make our organization a vital part of our community through participation in as many worthy causes as possible.

This book is another way of thanking you. We love being America's Team. But, most of all, we love being *your* team.

Jerry Jones

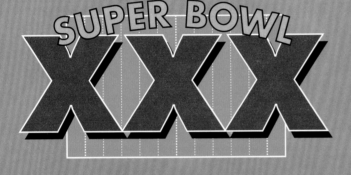

SUPER BOWL XXX

Once in awhile, a Super Bowl is special.

Too often, the game matching the NFC and AFC champions is a bore. One team proves far superior to the other, and, by midway through the second quarter, all that's left to wonder about is how long the halftime show will last.

The occasional upsets—the Jets over the heavily favored Colts in Super Bowl III, the Chiefs over the Vikings in Super Bowl IV—are pleasant distractions giving momentary prominence to teams that aren't going to make another Super Bowl appearance for a long, long time—if ever.

Super Bowl XXX, though, might have been the most special of all.

The Dallas Cowboys had overcome almost unprecedented adversity to make their third Super Bowl appearance in four years. Their opponents, the Pittsburgh Steelers, had won both previous Cowboys-Steelers Super Bowl matchups two decades earlier, thus earning the team from the Steel City the nickname of "Team of the '70s"—a title the Cowboys had hungered for themselves.

The teams hadn't liked each other then, and 17 years later they still didn't. After the squads had arrived to prepare for their 1996 Super Bowl clash at Sun Devil Stadium, the media made much about how the Cowboys were styling their way in limousines around Phoenix's hottest nightspots, while the Boy Scout-like Steelers stayed in their rooms to study game films. That was never the case—few teams prepare more intensely for any games

Fans gathered at the Phoenix airport await Cowboys' arrival

· · · · · · · · · · · · · · · · ◆ · · · · · · · · · · · · · · · ·

"The media benefits from writing there's controversy. When things occur, like in the case of Troy and me, they embellish and perpetuate and enhance. I understand that, I accept it. Being the head coach is like the ocean. Some days the water gets rough; it can't be smooth. Troy Aikman is the best player in the NFL, in my opinion. He'll never lead the league in passing yardage or touchdown passes because our style of offense is run, run, give the ball to Emmitt. But what heritage Troy will leave is that he was the winningest quarterback during his playing time. He can win more Super Bowls than any other quarterback, and that will put him where he belongs, in the Hall of Fame."

—BARRY SWITZER

· ·

Chad Hennings celebrates sack of Neil O'Donnell

than the Cowboys, let alone for a Super Bowl. But the horde of television, radio, magazine, and newspaper personnel who had followed the Cowboys through their tumultuous '95 season was already in the habit of crafting stories casting almost everyone on the team, from head coach Barry Switzer to flamboyant defensive back Deion Sanders, in the worst possible light. Bad news makes headlines, and the Cowboys were in for more than their fair share. A particularly hot topic during the week before the Super Bowl was whether Dallas quarterback Troy Aikman and Switzer were getting along so badly that one or the other might have to go.

So on that Sunday afternoon in Phoenix, the Cowboys were out to prove themselves both as football players and as men.

Historically, much was riding on the game as well. If Dallas came out on top, the Cowboys would have won three Super Bowls in four years, something that had proved beyond the ability of the Steelers, the Green Bay Packers, the San Francisco 49ers, the Miami Dolphins, or any other team that had earned its way into the ultimate game since Super Bowl I in January 1967.

Vanessa Williams sang the national anthem; Joe Montana, representing all previous Super Bowl most valuable players, tossed the coin; Norm Johnson of the Steelers kicked off, and the Cowboys faced their destiny.

At first, it seemed almost too easy. On the second play from scrimmage, Dallas quarterback Troy Aikman connected with receiver Michael Irvin for a 20-yard gain. The Cowboys drove to

Emmitt Smith powers his way to second touchdown

the Steelers 24-yard line; stopped there by a gritty Pittsburgh defense, they took a 3-0 lead when Chris Boniol booted a 42-yard field goal. The Steelers couldn't move the ball, and they punted. Dallas charged back down the field on the strength of a 47-yard pass from Aikman to the controversial Sanders, who was playing on offense as well as defense. Moments later, Aikman tossed a 3-yard lob to tight end Jay Novacek and it was 10-0.

Midway through the second quarter, Boniol split the uprights from 35 yards out. It was 13-0 Dallas, and it appeared a rout might be under way.

It wasn't. If the 1995 Cowboys were going to establish themselves as belonging on a list of all-time great

teams, they'd have to do it against a Steelers club that was worthy of its own distinguished heritage. Pittsburgh's defense stiffened, and just 13 seconds before halftime, Neil O'Donnell pitched a 6-yard scoring pass to Yancey Thigpen. The teams headed for their respective locker rooms with Dallas on the high end of a 13-7 score. As with the two previous Cowboys-Steelers Super Bowl clashes, at halftime this was still anybody's game.

Almost an hour later, when halftime star Diana Ross had finally changed costumes for the last time before being whisked out of Sun Devil Stadium by helicopter, Dallas and Pittsburgh went at it again. The only

⸻ ◆ ⸻

"It's numbing to play in a Super Bowl. You have to quiet your emotions because you've got a job to do. The spectacle is unbelievable."

—JASON GARRETT
Dallas Cowboys quarterback
1992-

Diana Ross stars in halftime show

Larry Brown sets up a touchdown with this interception

third-quarter scoring came from the Cowboys. Emmitt Smith dove 1 yard into the end zone, and Boniol's extra point made it 20-7. Larry Brown's interception of an O'Donnell pass had given his team possession on Pittsburgh's 18-yard line. Again, it seemed the game might have been decided.

But heroes truly earn their accolades only by defeating other heroes. The Steelers, it was clear, lacked the superior athletic ability possessed by the Cowboys; but they were just as determined to win.

Pittsburgh moved grimly down the field toward the Dallas goal line. The Cowboys' defense tightened, and the Steelers settled for a 46-yard field goal by Norm Johnson, making it 20-10.

Part of the enduring rivalry between the franchises was based on a perception of their contrasting philosophies of play. Supposedly, Dallas was historically a "finesse team," a club often relying on gadget plays and other trickery to win. Pittsburgh, it was believed by many fans and media pundits, had always exemplified "blue-collar football," with a willingness to fight games out in the trenches until opponents were simply too worn down to stop them.

But now, in Super Bowl XXX, the Steelers had their own surprise—an onside kick that was successfully recovered by Deon Figures. From their 48, the Steelers pounded at the Cowboys. With a little more than 6 minutes left in the game, the aptly nicknamed

Larry Brown's two key interceptions earned him Most Valuable Player honors in Super Bowl XXX

Bam Morris bulled over from the 1, and Johnson's extra point cut the Cowboys' margin to 20-17.

Dallas could have folded. Their season had been plagued by injuries, controversial officiating, and sniping by the media. Losing a seemingly safe Super Bowl lead might have confirmed all the jibes by the critics. But these players had rallied before. They still believed in themselves after a midseason pasting by the San Francisco 49ers, and they loudly supported Switzer when two consecutive tries at a fourth-and-one conversion fell short and resulted in a heartbreaking loss to the Philadelphia Eagles. They had survived those shaky moments. Now they would not only hold off the Steelers, they would go back on the attack.

The Cowboys offense couldn't score; the Steelers regained possession. O'Donnell had the time to win the game but not the skill. Larry Brown, once a twelfth-round draft choice from Texas Christian University, made his second interception of the game. Fittingly, Emmitt Smith scored a final Dallas touchdown on a 4-yard run 2 plays after Brown's heroics.

When the final gun sounded, the Cowboys had made Super Bowl histo-ry—the three championships in four years, never accomplished by any other team; five Super Bowl titles in all, which tied the 49ers. During the presentation of the Super Bowl trophy, Switzer screamed, "We did it our way, baby!" to beaming Cowboys owner Jerry Jones.

And they had. In Super Bowl XXX, the Cowboys won for the untold millions of fans who love the team, and in spite of the millions of others who always hope to see the best-known, most controversial franchise in professional football history lose.

They won for Jerry Jones, who had been ridiculed as an egomaniac far more often than he had received well-deserved credit as a dynamic, innovative businessman who had rebuilt a proud dynasty from football ashes. They won for Barry Switzer, whose laid-back demeanor perhaps masked too well his competitive, roll-the-dice nature.

Of course, the players won for themselves—for all the household names such as Aikman, Smith, Irvin, Sanders, and Daryl "Moose" Johnston; but also for Larry Allen, Bill Bates, Mark Tuinei, and Tony Tolbert, and all the other immensely talented athletes

"There are three levels to being a consistent winner as a football team. First is the level that when you line up against the other team, you know you're gonna win. And the best level is when you know they know you're gonna win. That's the level where we intend to keep the Dallas Cowboys."

—JERRY JONES

"Everybody loves or hates the Cowboys. We need more of that. I'll tell you a story: I went to a Super Bowl XXX party in the East Bay area, and everybody there was rooting for Pittsburgh. I thought, 'Nobody else in this room can name five of the Pittsburgh players.' But you see, they were all 49ers fans, and so they were rooting against the Cowboys. It's a compliment to the team that when you talk about the Cowboys, there is no neutral corner. Everyone's either red or blue. You love or hate them."

—JOHN MADDEN

Steelers linebacker Kevin Green walks off the field in defeat

◆

*"There's no question.
Super Bowl XXX was the sweetest."*

—JERRY JONES

Coach Switzer endures traditional dunking after the win

whose skills helped the better-known stars achieve their more-publicized heroics.

And they won for Tex Schramm, Tom Landry, and Jimmy Johnson. For Clint Murchison and Gil Brandt. For Roger Staubach and Tony Dorsett, who

enjoyed Super Bowl championships, and for Don Meredith and Don Perkins, who deserved to win them but never did.

Each Super Bowl victory for the Cowboys has been sweet in its own way. The 24-3 romp over the Dolphins in Super Bowl VI was memorable as the first championship for a team that had been molded from the unwanted players of existing NFL squads in 1960. Super Bowl XII, 27-10 over Denver, might have been the high point of Tom Landry's 29-year coaching tenure, when a powerhouse club featuring Staubach, Dorsett, Drew Pearson, Randy White, and many more looked invincible and was dubbed "America's Team" not long afterward. Super Bowl XXVII was a

Barry and Jerry share the Super Bowl trophy as sportscaster Greg Gumbel watches

52-17 blowout of the Buffalo Bills and an emphatic announcement that the Jerry Jones-era Cowboys had arrived to dominate the NFL. Super Bowl XXVIII, a 30-13 win over the same opponent, proved that the latest edition of the Cowboys could snuff out a talented opponent even when Dallas wasn't having one of its better days.

But Super Bowl XXX was perhaps the true culmination of everything from 1959 on, 36 years of hard work, sacrifice, victories, and disappointments. It

was a cry of triumph for the football ages, achieved by a team founded as a National Football League stepchild, a maneuver by existing NFL team owners to grab a piece of a new market before an upstart professional league could snatch Dallas for itself.

And to understand the real meaning of the Cowboys' Super Bowl XXX victory, it's necessary to go all the way back to 1959, and to meet the Dallas Steers—that's right, the Steers—at their moment of birth.

Deion Sanders relaxes before the big game

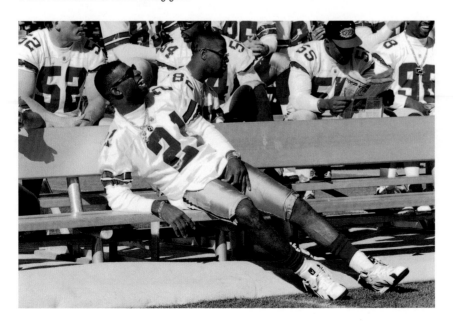

SUPER BOWL XXX STATISTICS

SCORING

Dallas	10	3	7	7	**27**
Pittsburgh	0	7	0	10	**17**

FIRST QUARTER:
Cowboys, Boniol 42-yard field goal
Cowboys, Novacek 3-yard pass from Aikman

SECOND QUARTER:
Cowboys, Boniol 35-yard field goal
Steelers, Thigpen 6-yard pass from O'Donnell

THIRD QUARTER:
Cowboys, Smith 1-yard run

FOURTH QUARTER:
Steelers, Johnson 46-yard field goal
Steelers, Morris 1-yard run
Cowboys, Smith 4-yard run

TEAM:	DALLAS	PITTSBURGH
First downs	15	25
Net yards	254	310
Fumbles lost	0	0
Interceptions	0	3
Penalty yards	25	15

INDIVIDUAL:
RUSHING:
Dallas: Smith 49, Johnston 8, K. Williams 2, Aikman 3
Pittsburgh: Morris 73, Pegram 15, Stewart 15, O'Donnell 0, J. Williams 0

PASSING:
Dallas: Aikman 15-23, 209 yards, 1 touchdown
Pittsburgh: O'Donnell 28-49, 239 yards, 1 touchdown

RECEIVING:
Dallas: Irvin 5-76, Novacek 5-50, K. Williams 2-29, Sanders 1-47, Johnston 1-4, Smith 1-3
Pittsburgh: Hastings 10-98, Mills 8-78, Thigpen 3-19, Morris 3-18, Holliday 2-19, J. Williams 2-7

IN THE BEGINNING

★

In 1959, owners of the existing 12 franchises in the National Football League (NFL)— the Chicago Bears, Chicago Cardinals, Green Bay Packers, New York Giants, Detroit Lions, Washington Redskins, Philadelphia Eagles, Pittsburgh Steelers, Los Angeles Rams, Cleveland Browns, San Francisco 49ers, and Baltimore Colts—were talking about expansion. Two new teams to begin play in 1961 would be just right, they decided. Dallas was one of the cities being considered for an expansion team; so were the Twin Cities of Minneapolis-St. Paul.

Any plans for orderly expansion were discarded after the announcement that a rival, eight-team professional football league would be formed and begin play in 1960. The new American Football League (AFL) planned to place teams in New York, Boston, Buffalo, Denver, Los Angeles, Minneapolis-St. Paul, Houston, and Dallas.

The NFL owners decided to take the offensive. First, the Cardinals were allowed to move from Chicago to St. Louis, giving the NFL a stronger mid-America base. Second, Pete Rozelle, the 33-year-old general manager of the Los Angeles Rams, was named NFL commissioner, replacing the late Bert Bell. Third, NFL expansion play would begin in 1960, not 1961—and in a market otherwise wide open to the AFL.

Max Winter and William Boyer, the businessmen planning a Minneapolis-St. Paul team in the AFL,

opted instead for the established NFL. Their expansion Vikings, though, wouldn't begin play until 1961. AFL organizers filled the eighth franchise slot vacated by Minneapolis-St. Paul with a team based in Oakland.

Most NFL owners thought it necessary to put an expansion team in Texas; the AFL was coming to Houston and Dallas, so one of those cities would also get an NFL squad.

While NFL owners got ready to meet, Bud Adams, who would own the AFL franchise in Houston, approached the man he wanted as the Oilers' first head coach. But Tom Landry, an assistant coach for the NFL's New York Giants, turned down the offer. Landry, a native of Mission, Texas, and a college star with the University of Texas Longhorns, was a natural for the helm of a pro franchise in his home state. But during his playing career, Landry had spent a year with the old New York Yankees of the All-American Football Conference, another upstart pro league that soon folded when matched against the better-established, better-financed NFL. He decided not to risk his coaching career with another league that might collapse overnight.

Crusty George Halas, founder, owner, and then still coach of the Chicago Bears, was impressed with the businessman who would own the Dallas franchise if that city was granted an NFL expansion team. Clint Murchison, 36, was heir to one of Texas's largest family oil fortunes and had been trying to acquire an NFL team for a half-dozen years. In 1954, he had come close to buying the San Francisco 49ers, and, more recently, Murchison had made unsuccessful overtures to the owners of the Washington Redskins and the Chicago Cardinals.

Dallas had failed to support an NFL franchise once before. In 1952, the league moved its New York Yanks to Dallas. *The Football Encyclopedia* describes the fiasco this way:

It was a promising venture that ended as a joke. The league transferred the New York Yanks franchise to Dallas, but after four echo-filled games in the Cotton Bowl, the club owners threw in the sponge and turned the operation over to the league. For the second half of the season, the Yanks-Texans traveled the country as a road team, using Hershey, Pennsylvania, as their home base for loosely organized practices. With morale lower than the floor, the Texans shocked the world by beating the Bears 27-23 on Thanksgiving Day in Akron, Ohio, before a rousing throng of three thousand paid customers, for the only win in their existence.

Thirteen players from that 1-11 team stayed with the franchise in 1953 when the NFL tried again in another city. The sad-sack Dallas Texans became the Baltimore Colts, who would win their first NFL title in 1958.

But in 1959, Halas believed enough in Murchison to help get the prospective Dallas owner in touch with Tex Schramm, who had served as general manager of the Los Angeles Rams until 1957, when he resigned to become an executive of CBS Sports. In fall 1959, Murchison hired Schramm as Dallas's first general manager, though there was no team yet for Schramm to take over. Schramm contacted Landry, who wanted to return to Texas. Landry didn't expect to last long as the Dallas coach—it was obvious to him that an expansion squad wouldn't win many games for a long time and that the team's first coach would be lucky not to be fired after two or three seasons. Schramm offered Landry a five-year contract; in his autobiography, Landry recalled it paid $34,500 a year. And on December 28, 1959, Schramm introduced Landry to the media as the first head coach of the Dallas Rangers, who until then had been the Dallas Steers.

Eventually, Schramm announced that the Dallas franchise would be known as the Cowboys instead. A minor league baseball team from Dallas was already named the Rangers, a fact that had escaped the brain trust of the new NFL club until then.

Only one thing prevented Murchison, Schramm, and Landry from putting together the first Cowboys roster: The NFL owners had not yet formally approved a Dallas franchise. In late January 1960, the owners met in Miami Beach. They wrangled long and hard over Bell's successor as

"I knew about Tom Landry as a defensive coach for the New York Giants. I worked for CBS, I lived up there, I saw their games. I was so impressed by the morale he built up in that defensive team. I thought it would be the best thing for an expansion team to have a coach with a defensive background. I called Tom and asked if he'd be interested in talking with me. He said he and his wife would like to go home to Texas. He came over and had dinner, and we talked through the meal and just kept on talking. The Giants had to meet Baltimore in the playoffs, then after that we flew down to Dallas, and I introduced him as the team's head coach. We horned in on a Cotton Bowl press conference to announce that. We weren't really important enough then to have a press conference on our own."

— **Tex Schramm**

9

Don Meredith, when he was the SMU quarterback

commissioner before choosing Rozelle in desperation as a compromise candidate. Then they turned their attention to expansion. George Marshall, owner of the Washington Redskins, was especially reluctant to enlarge the existing league. Owner debate over expansion went on for almost two days.

Cowboys' fans should thank the Washington fight song, *Hail to the Redskins*, for their beloved team. Not long before the owners' meeting, Marshall had fired his team's music director. The ex-director, who had composed *Hail to the Redskins*, retaliated by selling the song's copyright to an attorney who chose to deny Marshall and the Redskins the right to play it. That lawyer had purchased *Hail to the Redskins* on behalf of Clint Murchison. Learning this, Marshall offered to vote in favor of NFL expansion to Dallas if Murchison would give *Hail to the Redskins* back to Washington.

So it was that on January 28, 1960, the NFL owners voted to place a league franchise in Dallas and to have the Cowboys begin play in the

1960 season. Murchison and partner Bedford Wynne paid $50,000 as a league entry fee. The Minnesota Vikings franchise was approved at the same time, but the Vikings had an extra year to prepare for entry into the NFL.

It wasn't until after the vote that the owners came up with a plan to stock the new Dallas team with players. The Cowboys had an immediate problem—they couldn't participate in the annual NFL draft of college players that was traditionally held in the spring. To prevent the rival AFL owners from signing up all the best college graduates first, the NFL had held its draft in November, well before the Cowboys could have taken part.

George Halas tried to help Murchison and Schramm work around that dilemma. On Halas's advice, before the NFL owners began dividing up college players in November, Murchison signed star University of New Mexico running back Don Perkins to a "personal services contract." Murchison informed the other owners of his action before the draft so none of them would take Perkins.

Halas then used the draft to help the Cowboys acquire their second player. He used his own third-round pick in the November 1959 draft to select Don Meredith, a star quarterback from Southern Methodist University in Dallas. Halas then traded Meredith to the Cowboys in exchange for Dallas's third-round pick in the 1962 college draft. Murchison hoped that Meredith, a hometown hero who originally hailed from the small Texas town of Vernon, would draw a lot of fans into Dallas's Cotton Bowl during the Cowboys' first few losing seasons.

The rest of the NFL owners then ensured that the Cowboys would begin play with a deficient roster by having the team complete its squad through a draft of players from lists provided by the 12 existing teams. Each established NFL club could protect 25 of its 34 players. The Cowboys would choose one of the 9 players left; after they did, that team's owners could remove one player from those remaining on the list. Dallas had to choose 3 players from each team, no matter how bad some clubs' lists of 9 players might be. Worst of all, Landry was given just 24 hours to study the picks and make his selections.

Landry chose primarily from among the NFL dregs, who collectively still cost Murchison and Wynne $550,000. A few decent choices were made available, especially linebacker Jerry Tubbs, an outspoken player whom the 49ers simply wanted off their roster. Receiver Frank Clarke became a useful Cowboys player. But most of the 36 failed to survive the first Dallas training camp. Eventually, the desperate Landry and his coaching staff gave tryouts to almost 200 would-be players of every size, shape, and degree of athletic ability.

THIRTY-SIX PLAYERS SELECTED IN EXPANSION DRAFT BY COWBOYS

denotes drafted players who actually made the first Cowboys team

Charlie Ane, center, from Detroit Lions
Al Barry, guard, from New York Giants
Dick Bielski,* tight end, from Philadelphia Eagles
Leroy Bolden, halfback, from Cleveland Browns
Nate Borden,* defensive end, from Green Bay Packers
Tom Braatz,* linebacker, from Washington Redskins
Bill Butler,* safety, from Green Bay Packers
Frank Clarke,* tight end–flanker, from Cleveland Browns
Gene Cronin,* linebacker, from Detroit Lions
Bobby Cross, tackle, from Chicago Cardinals
Gerry DeLucca, tackle, from Philadelphia Eagles
Jim Doran,* split end, from Detroit Lions
Fred Dugan,* split end, from San Francisco 49ers
L.G. Dupre,* halfback, from Baltimore Colts
Ray Fisher,* defensive tackle, from Pittsburgh Steelers
Tom Franckhauser,* defensive back, from Los Angeles Rams
Bob Fry,* tackle, from Los Angeles Rams
John Gonzaga,* defensive end, from San Francisco 49ers

Melwood "Buz" Guy,* guard, from New York Giants
Don Healy,* defensive tackle, from Chicago Bears
Don Heinrich,* quarterback, from New York Giants
Ed Husmann,* defensive tackle, from Chicago Cardinals
Jack Johnson, defensive guard, from Chicago Bears
Pete Johnson, defensive back, from Chicago Bears
Ray Krouse, defensive tackle, from Baltimore Colts
Bobby Luna, defensive back, from Pittsburgh Steelers
Ray Mathews,* flanker, from Pittsburgh Steelers
Don McIlhenny,* halfback, from Green Bay Packers
Ed Modzelewski, fullback, from Cleveland Browns
Joe Nicely, guard, from Washington Redskins
Doyle Nix, defensive back, from Washington Redskins
Jack Patera,* linebacker, from Chicago Cardinals
Duane Putnam,* guard, from Los Angeles Rams
Dave Sherer,* punter, from Baltimore Colts
Bill Striegel, guard, from Philadelphia Eagles
Jerry Tubbs,* linebacker, from San Francisco 49ers

SIXTIES

1960 For their inaugural season, the Cowboys were placed in the NFL's Western Conference with the Baltimore Colts, Chicago Bears, Detroit Lions, Green Bay Packers, Los Angeles Rams, and San Francisco 49ers.

The first Cowboys training camp was held at Pacific University in Forest Grove, Oregon. Tom Landry assembled his ragtag crew and put them through their paces, which were notably slow. Even prized rookie running back Don Perkins was a temporary disappointment. He couldn't complete a mile run under the 6-minute limit Landry required of his running backs. When Perkins failed to complete the "Landry Mile," he was discouraged enough to quit the squad, but Landry talked him out of leaving.

The Dallas coaching staff was impressed with Don Meredith, but they believed the rookie would need a few seasons of apprenticeship before he could completely grasp the intricacies of play in the NFL. Landry wanted to sign Eddie LeBaron, a short (5 feet 8 inches) quarterback who had retired from the Washington Redskins after the 1959 season. In return for LeBaron, the Redskins demanded—and got—the Cowboys' first-round draft choice in 1961.

Before training camp was over, the Cowboys lost Perkins for the season because of a leg injury he suffered while playing in a preseason all-star game. This meant LeBaron would have to shoulder most of the offensive burden himself.

Dallas managed to win 1 of 4 exhibition games, but during the regular season established NFL clubs took turns beating the expansion team. The Cowboys' first two losses, both at home in the Cotton Bowl, were respectable—35-28 to the Steelers and 27-25 to the Eagles. (Tom Franckhauser returned the season-opening kickoff from Pittsburgh to become the first ballcarrier in Dallas Cowboys history.) Tubbs and defensive back Jim Mooty anchored the defense, and LeBaron was always capable of outsmarting opponents whenever his offensive line gave him sufficient protection.

Cowboys vs. Eagles

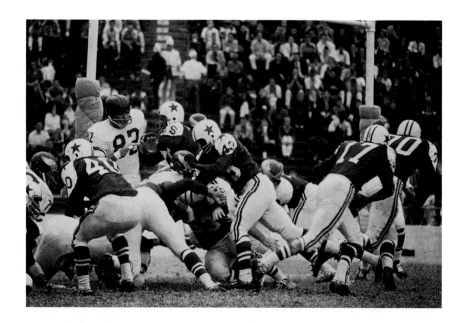

Tom Landry, the young Cowboys coach

Later in the season, perennial league powers Cleveland, Baltimore, and Green Bay thrashed the Cowboys. With an 0-10 record on December 4, the Cowboys played on the road in New York and stunned the Giants by battling to a 31-31 tie. LeBaron provided most of the offensive spark with 3 touchdown passes. When the team arrived back in Dallas, Landry recalled, they were met at the airport by a crowd of two fans, one of whom waved a homemade sign.

Buoyed by a non-loss, the Cowboys played their final game in Detroit a week later. The Lions spanked the visitors 23-14, and the Cowboys' first season ended with an 0-11-1 record. No NFL team had stumbled to a worse record in 18 years. Defensively, the Cowboys had given up 369 points, the most in the league; on offense, they had scored just 177, one point less than the Redskins' second-worst 178.

Postseason scrutiny centered on Cowboys fan support, or rather the lack of it. Dallas management had hoped for regular crowds of 40,000 in the cavernous Cotton Bowl. But the largest home game attendance for Dallas in 1960 was 30,000 for the opening game against Pittsburgh; by midseason the average home crowd had dwindled to 10,000. It didn't help the Cowboys' cause that the crosstown rival Dallas Texans managed an 8-6 record in their first season.

LeBaron finished 1960 with 111 completions in 225 passing attempts. Meredith, relegated to backup duty, completed just 29 of 68. The Dallas ground attack had been pitiful; L.G. Dupre led all Cowboys rushers with 362 yards. (League leader Jim Brown of Cleveland rushed for 1,257 yards.) LeBaron, often running for his life, managed 94 yards on the ground himself. But with Perkins scheduled to return in 1961, the Cowboys could hope for a more balanced offense.

1961

The Cowboys opened their second season by holding training camp at St. Olaf College in Northfield, Minnesota. They had spent the off-season struggling with a draft dilemma. Their own No. 1 pick had gone to the Redskins in return for LeBaron, but the Cowboys coveted defensive lineman Bob Lilly, who had been a standout at Texas Christian

Don Meredith passes in Vikings game

University in Fort Worth. Besides wanting Lilly on his own merits, Dallas knew he'd already been drafted by the archrival Texans of the AFL. Lilly made it clear to scouts for other NFL teams that he intended to stay in his native Texas. If the Cowboys drafted him, he'd consider signing with them. If his rights went to any other NFL club, he'd become a Dallas Texan.

But Schramm had hired draft wizard Gil Brandt, who helped engineer two preseason trades that would solidify Dallas's defense for years to come. First, the Cowboys traded their first-round pick in 1962 to Cleveland for the Browns' first pick in 1961. With that choice, Schramm drafted Lilly and signed him soon afterward.

Dallas also sent future draft choices to Chicago in return for the rights to linebacker Chuck Howley, who played briefly for the Bears in 1959 before being sidelined for 18 months with an injury.

Those trades accomplished, Landry turned his attention to the Cowboys offense. Painfully aware that his team had trouble blocking defenders, he designed a series of plays involving frequent last-minute shifts in position by halfbacks and receivers. He hoped the resulting confusion might cause opposing defenses to give Dallas quarterbacks an extra second to pass or running backs an additional moment to pick their way through holes in the line. Eventually, the Dallas "multiple offense" would evolve into a high-powered scoring juggernaut.

The NFL had realigned itself to make room for the first-year Minnesota Vikings in its Western Conference. The Cowboys were now an Eastern Conference team, along with the Giants, defending NFL champion Eagles, Browns, Cardinals, Steelers, and Redskins.

Cowboys vs. Vikings

The Cowboys bench

. . . . ◆ . . . .

"They hired a bunch of high school coaches to come over to their first office, which was off Knox Street. We'd go down there at night and watch films from college teams, fill out forms about the players they were interested in. We were supposed to rate the players one, two, three, four or else R for 'reject.' We weren't supposed to give anybody a one, but I gave a one to Lee Roy Jordan. Gil Brandt gave me hell for that, but it turned out I was right. The Cowboys also had on the payroll an assistant coach or somebody from all the major college teams and most of the small ones. Brandt did a super job organizing it. It was fun. I think we only got paid two dollars an hour, but the experience was worth more than the money."

—JOHN NAYLOR
High school football coach and part-time Dallas Cowboys scout 1960-65

. . . .

Perkins's presence paid big dividends as the season began. On opening day at the Cotton Bowl, the Cowboys shocked the Steelers 27-24 for the franchise's first NFL victory. It took a 10-point scoring spurt in the game's last 56 seconds for Dallas to secure the upset. Afterward, Steelers players described themselves as embarrassed.

With Perkins giving opponents something to think about besides pass defense, the Cowboys won again on the next Sunday, a 21-7 victory at home over the Vikings. The Vikings were no pushovers; in fact, they had won their first regular-season game a week earlier against the Bears.

Dallas football fans weren't convinced the Cowboys had become an overnight powerhouse. In fact, only 23,500 bothered to attend the game against the Steelers. But after the Browns beat the Cowboys 25-7, Dallas shut out the Vikings 28-0 for a 3-1 mark.

The rest of the season was less distinguished: The Cowboys beat the Giants in New York, tied the Redskins in the Cotton Bowl, and lost all the rest of their games to finish 4-9-1. Still, that record was a substantial improvement. Dallas actually finished ahead of the Redskins in the Eastern Conference standings, and they would have been ahead of Minnesota and the Rams if they had played in the Western Conference.

Almost all of the team's season statistics were better; they had given up 380 points but had scored 236. Perkins led the team with 815 rushing yards, sixth-best in the NFL. Shuttling in and out of the Cowboys lineup after each offensive series of downs, LeBaron completed 120 of 236 passes, and Meredith completed 94 of 182. Receiver Frank Clarke gained 919 yards on 41 receptions and scored 9 touchdowns.

Clearly, the Cowboys were on their way.

1962 Once again, the Cowboys were without a No. 1 draft choice. But Schramm and Brandt had been hard at work perfecting a scouting system that could track thousands of college football players, including many at tiny backwater schools. They hit pay dirt in the sixth round of the 1962 draft. Marquette defensive end George Andrie would play a big part in Dallas's future success. Defensive back Cornell Green was signed as a free agent; he'd been a basketball player at Utah State.

Quarterback Eddie LeBaron

But it was the Dallas offense that propelled the team to the next level. In 1962, the Cowboys scored 398 points. The New York Giants, who won the Eastern Conference with a 12-2 record, also racked up 398 points. The only NFL team scoring more points than the Cowboys was Green Bay, storming to a total of 415 while going 13-1. The Cowboys finished 5-8-1 because their defense allowed 402 points, second only to Minnesota's rock-bottom 410.

There were moments, such as a 45-21 pounding of Cleveland and Jim Brown, when the Dallas offense was a thing of beauty. Landry's multiple options sometimes left defenders helpless. At the end of the season, several Dallas players were among league leaders in various offensive categories, something that had never happened before. Perkins was fifth in rushing with 945 yards. LeBaron ranked third among NFL passers with 95 comple-

tions in 166 attempts. Meredith completed 105 of 212 passes and compiled 15 touchdown tosses. LeBaron had 16. The happy recipients in the end zone included Frank Clarke with 14 touchdown catches and Billy Howton with 6.

Cowboys kicker Sam Baker booted the season's longest field goal of 53 yards. The Cowboys also led in another "longest" category, this one less desirable. Against the Steelers, LeBaron launched a 99-yard scoring pass to Clarke, only to see the play called back. The penalty was offensive holding in the end zone, so the Cowboys ended up surrendering a 2-point safety instead. That proved to be the margin of defeat; the Steelers won 30-28. No NFL team has ever suffered a longer penalty.

As the Cowboys continued to improve, their crosstown rivalry with the Dallas Texans ended. Neither team had drawn as well as its respective

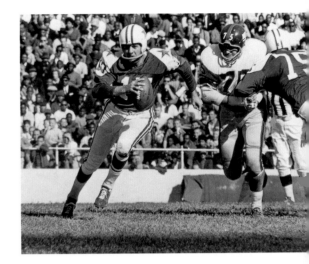

Cowboys vs. Giants

Cowboys vs. Giants

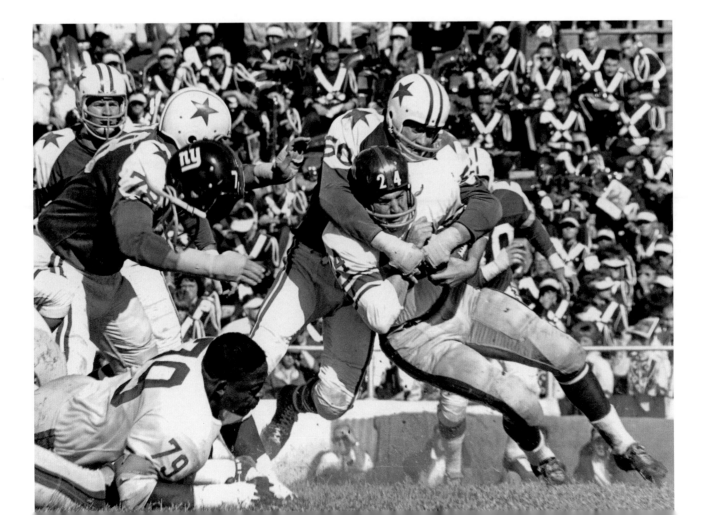

"When I was doing the Winter Olympics for CBS, the CBS office in Squaw Valley was in the basement of the IBM building. IBM did all the scorekeeping for our broadcasts; this was my introduction to computers. I got to know the IBM people and thought of them when I had concerns about the Cowboys' scouting. We were supposed to sift through the scouts' reports and give each player a grade, but personal prejudices always affected the grading. I loved speed; if a guy had speed, then as far as I was concerned all his other grades were great, too. Landry, with him all they had to do was write, 'This player has great character.' If he saw that, he wanted the guy. I called IBM and said, 'I've got to have an objective way of grading players. Could that be done?' They said it could, though nobody'd ever done it before. One of their subsidiaries, Service Bureau Corporation, I think it was, was interested, so I made a deal with them. Do it for us, but not for any other team. It took a while for us to work out the system, but afterward we had computerized scouting and no other team did for a long time."

—TEX SCHRAMM

ownership had expected, but the Texans' Lamar Hunt was especially vexed. While the Cowboys had suffered through the inevitable growing pains of an expansion team, the Texans had started out even with the other seven AFL clubs and prospered. In 1962, the Texans beat the Houston Oilers in a dramatic overtime game to win the third AFL championship game. Afterward, Hunt announced that his club would move to Kansas City and be renamed the Chiefs. The Cowboys had Dallas all to themselves.

1963 As the Cowboys finished up training at their new camp at California Lutheran College in Thousand Oaks, California, *Sports Illustrated* shocked everyone,

including the team itself, by picking Dallas to win the NFL Eastern Conference title. Landry's explosive offense plus an improving Cowboys defense were supposed to add up to the championship. It didn't turn out that way.

A crowd of 36,432 turned out at the Cotton Bowl on September 14 to see the Cowboys, featuring exciting rookie linebacker Lee Roy Jordan, open the season against St. Louis. The Cardinals sent everyone home unhappy by clobbering Dallas 34-7. A week later, the visiting Browns made the Cowboys' season record 0-2, with Cleveland racking up 41 points to 24 for the home team. After two more losses on the road, Dallas was winless four games into the schedule.

HIGH-TECH SCOUTING

★

By 1962, the Cowboys had established a wide-ranging college football scouting network. At most major schools, Dallas scouts quietly would offer an assistant coach a stipend to keep them up to date on the progress of his team's best pro prospects. There were full-time Cowboys scouts who spent most of the year on the road evaluating college players in person. In addition, many high school coaches in the Dallas area were hired to spend evenings and weekends grading players in game films sent to the Cowboys by colleges.

Eventually, there was too much information and no way to sort it out objectively. Before draft day, hundreds of players had to be ranked by skill and position; Schramm, Brandt, and Landry had to have a system that would organize scouting reports better.

The ever-inventive Schramm solved the problem. At his request, IBM sent Salan Querishi, a representative from Service Bureau Corporation, a subsidiary company, to develop a computer system and programming to collect reports from all the Cowboys scouts and break the information down into a series of categories. Other NFL clubs would later copy the Cowboys' high-tech scouting operation, but by then Schramm's ingenuity had given Dallas a tremendous head start in effectively evaluating and drafting top college talent.

TEX SCHRAMM

BY GALYN WILKINS

Imagine the arched eyebrows, the giggles, the barroom derision around the National Football League when a native of India named Salan Querishi was hired for a scientific project in Dallas.

You might say Querishi was the top draft choice that year of a guy named Texas E. Schramm, inspiring the same mirthful skepticism heard when the Wright Brothers hauled their new-fangled contraption to the top of a North Carolina sand dune. But then Schramm, in his third year as the orchestrator of the Dallas Cowboys, feared neither the skeptics among the peerage of the NFL nor unique leaps of faith.

If the name and playing position don't linger in the memories of even the most encyclopedic Cowboys worshipper-historians, Querishi was a computer programmer.

Imagine that: A computerized operation in a pro football era in which Bobby Layne and Johnny Unitas, who had recently beaten the Cowboys, still lingered. Computer was still a far-out science yet to be discovered and appreciated by other team owners and general managers, who would sooner have hired witch doctors.

So here was Schramm, a 1960s Lindbergh, taking off for the wild blue age of Aquarius with a computer whiz who promised to distill information on 3,000 college players into hard and fast bytes that would help the Cowboys catch up to the Packers. Obviously, it worked, because the Cowboys eventually had 20 consecutive winning seasons, 5 winning trips to the Super Bowl (so far), and Schramm has his name on the gilded roster of the Pro Football Hall of Fame.

But then everything that tumbled out of Schramm's unique vision seemed to work. Yet it was not only an eagerness to take other wild leaps—how soon do you think Paul Brown or Vince Lombardi would have thought of cheerleaders?—but also the work experience of a guy who worked his way up from the sports desk of the Austin newspaper, to general manager of the Los Angeles Rams, to New York City as a CBS sports producer putting together the 1960 Winter Olympics broadcasts.

Though they were distinctly different personalities, the odd couple of high-tech football—Schramm and the owner who hired him, Clint Murchison—were a blockbuster combination from the day they opened the first team offices above a Dallas auto store. Tex had the ideas and Clint had the money. And they had Schramm's choice as head coach.

No matter how many other people get credit for turning the Cowboys from an 0-11-1 first year in 1960 into a two-decades-long space shot, Tom Landry points to one person.

"Tex," says the only coach Schramm ever had or ever wanted. "Tex was the architect of the Cowboys."

Let's search through the files for a key move by Schramm and his scouts, who dug through computer printouts with the diligence of archeologists rummaging through hidden tombs. It could be—

probably should be—the 1964 gamble on heroic Naval Academy quarterback Roger Staubach, or it might be the clever trade 13 years later that allowed the Cowboys to draft Tony Dorsett.

Or it could be the computer programmer, or, rather, the revolutionary idea to hire one. Yet Schramm remembers it as evolutionary, not revolutionary, a natural move, given the way the NFL was advancing into the television age and becoming a Sunday afternoon phenomenon.

"Years ago, scouting wasn't very sophisticated," Schramm says whenever someone tries to pin the pioneer label on him. "But when I was with the Rams, teams were beginning to develop well-organized scouting systems. In other words, they were no longer picking names out of college football magazines."

Still, the Cowboys had jumped far ahead with their computer-aided shrewdness. Without Schramm's electronic brainchild, don't you wonder if the Cowboys' bird dogs would have discovered on footwork alone Rayfield Wright at Fort Valley State College in 1967, or Larry Cole at Hawaii the next year? But no one, and certainly not fast, large, aggressive players, could elude the computer's attention.

So much for the futuristic Schramm. What about the persona, the human framework of the man? You'd think a guy with a head full of computer chips might be, if not dull, at least withdrawn and uneasy in the public glare. A banker type. A no-comment type.

But Tex Schramm? He was as quiet and withdrawn as a rock band blasting away at full volume. If he had an opinion—no, make that when he had an opinion—it was yours for the asking, and often you didn't even have to ask.

There was the evening in 1973, for example, when Schramm and his wife, Marty, were sitting down to dinner in a fashionable cafe with NFL Commissioner Pete Rozelle and his wife, Carrie. The afternoon had not gone well for the Schramms, particularly Mr. Schramm, because the Cowboys had lost a playoff game to the Vikings. Before the soup arrived, Schramm launched a seismic lecture on the game officials, Rozelle's officials, and how their incompetence had ended the Cowboys' season. In so many words, Schramm said the men in the striped shirts should be locked up without hope of ransom.

It didn't matter—nothing else mattered when the Cowboys lost, especially with the Super Bowl in sight—that Schramm and Rozelle had formed a respectful bond while both worked for the Rams. Schramm spoke his piece, shooting with both barrels.

"Isn't he one of your closest friends in football?" Carrie Rozelle asked her husband later, after the verbal shelling had ceased. "And if he is, what are the others like?"

Schramm usually kept a highly focused eye on the refs from the second row of the Texas Stadium press box, as well as press boxes on hostile soil. There, on purpose, he kept himself almost, but not quite, out of earshot of friends and the gentry in the luxury boxes. Often he would leap out of his seat, necktie flying, machine-gunning the distant refs with partisan accusations. In time, the other press box occupants grew accustomed to Schramm shattering the otherwise-professional silence. After all, it was his territory. If Texas Stadium wasn't named for him, it should have been. And, of course, it was his team. His vision. His legacy.

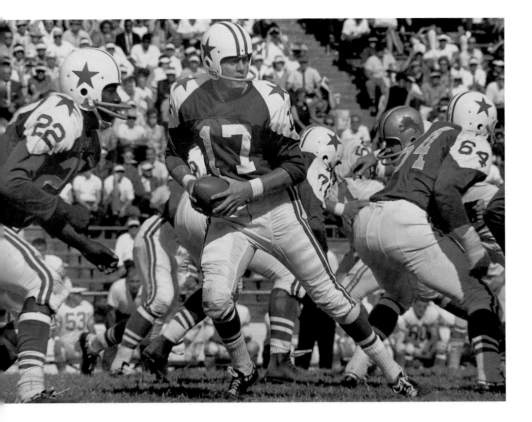

Things improved slightly over the next six weeks. The Cowboys managed a 3-3 record during that span. But their season, and their image around the rest of the country, were shattered on Friday, November 22, when President John F. Kennedy was assassinated in Dallas. NFL Commissioner Pete Rozelle ordered the full schedule of Sunday, November 24, to be played. The Cowboys, matched against the powerful Browns in Cleveland, were jeered throughout the game by the huge crowd of 55,000.

Shaken, Dallas lost its next two games at home, then won the final game of the year 28-24 in St. Louis, despite being booed throughout. Cowboys players said later they were especially upset by players on opposing teams belittling the city of Dallas during those games.

Hometown fans were booing, too, but because of the team's disappointing record. Some sports columnists

called for Landry to resign or be fired. Team owner Clint Murchison responded by granting Landry an unprecedented 10-year extension on his original five-season contract, which still had a year to go.

In terms of statistics, the Cowboys did major backsliding in 1963. The offense scored 305 points; the defense gave up 378, third-worst in the NFL. Perkins managed just 614 yards rushing. Meredith, who had mostly supplanted LeBaron at quarterback, completed 167 of 310 passes for 17

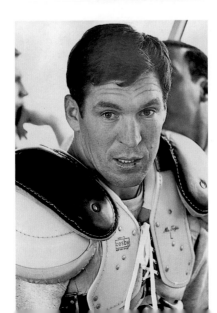

Lee Roy Jordan, linebacker, 1963

"When I played at the Naval Academy, I wasn't thinking about turning pro. Abilitywise I knew I could do it, but I'd made a commitment to spend four years in the service. Then I got drafted late by the Cowboys. It was unexpected, and there really wasn't much press to-do about it. It was a non-event. But the Cowboys stayed in touch, even when I was in Vietnam. Gil Brandt would send letters, footballs for me to practice with, films for me to study. My third year in the Navy, I took two weeks' leave and worked out at training camp as a rookie. I was excited. My adrenaline was pumping. During those two weeks, I made up my mind to quit the Navy after my commitment and try to play for the Cowboys."

—**ROGER STAUBACH**
Dallas Cowboys quarterback
1969-79

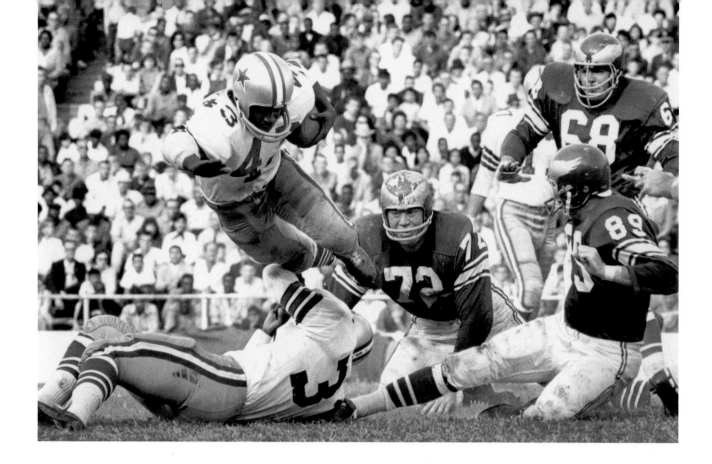

Cowboys vs. Eagles, 1964

· · · · · · · · · · · · · ◆ · · · · · · · · · · · · ·

"Don Meredith was outstanding.
He was one of the toughest players
ever on our team. Sometimes I don't
think the fans realized what he
was sacrificing, the pain he was
playing in."

—TOM LANDRY

· ·

touchdowns. No Cowboys ranked among league leaders in any offensive or defensive category.

The team needed some sort of energizing. The next college draft would provide long-term solutions for some of Dallas's woes.

1964 It had never been against the rules for NFL teams to draft college underclassmen; they simply had to designate those players as "futures" and not sign them to contracts until after they had used up their four years of college football eligibility. Until 1964, drafting "futures" was a luxury the Cowboys couldn't afford. They needed help immediately.

But in the 1964 draft, the Cowboys gambled. First-round pick Scott Appleton, a defensive tackle from the University of Texas, was a wasted selection. He signed with the rival AFL. But the Cowboys took Oregon defensive back Mel Renfro in the second round, and Renfro enjoyed a sparkling 14-year career with Dallas that culminated with his election to the Hall of Fame.

The addition of Mel Renfro alone would have made the 1964 draft memorable. But in the seventh round, the Cowboys brain trust tapped Florida A&M receiver Bob Hayes, who was better known for his championship exploits in the hundred-yard dash. In the tenth round, Dallas really rolled the dice by selecting quarterback Roger Staubach of Navy. Staubach owed the Navy four years of military service before he would be available to play professional football.

And the 1964 season found the Cowboys short by one quarterback. Eddie LeBaron had decided to retire, leaving Don Meredith as the undisputed starter. But Meredith's first full season at the offensive helm didn't go smoothly. He completed just 49 percent of his passes, and his 9 touchdown tosses were more than offset by 16 interceptions. Cotton Bowl crowds decided Meredith was a convenient subject for jeering. They didn't know Meredith played the entire schedule with badly torn knee cartilage, an injury he couldn't have repaired during the season because the Cowboys had no adequate backup quarterback.

Meredith's offensive line wasn't much help; he was sacked so often one writer suggested a new statistical category: "Yardage lost attempting to live."

A midseason winning streak of three games enabled Dallas to finish with a 5-8-1 mark. Perkins climbed back to fifth place among NFL rushers with 768 yards, and Clarke was third among the league's receivers with 65 catches good for 973 yards and 5 touchdowns. Still, the Cowboys finished next to last in offensive points scored, with 250. It was lost on many fans that the defense had improved significantly, allowing just 289 points, almost 100 fewer than in 1963.

This improvement wasn't accidental; rather, it stemmed from Landry. In 1964, most NFL teams used the 4-3 basic defense—four defensive linemen straight across the line of scrimmage, supported by the three linebackers. Landry had helped craft the 4-3 during his years as a defensive coach for the New York Giants. But now, Landry

believed, his 4-3 defense in Dallas gave up too many long runs by opposing backs when overpowering offensive lines simply drove the Cowboys back and out of position to make tackles.

So, in 1964, Landry invented what would be called "the flex." The Cowboys' right defensive tackle and left defensive end were moved slightly

Cleveland great Jim Brown eludes Cornell Green, 34

Coach Landry on sidelines before 1964 game with Chicago

Bob Hayes, 22, terrrorized defenses with his speed

◆

"Bob Hayes changed the chemistry of the National Football League, really. He'd won that gold medal in the Olympics, and when he lined up for us the other teams would go right into a zone defense. They were not able to run with him. Oh, he was exciting."

—TOM LANDRY

Quarterback Craig Morton, 1965

back from the line of scrimmage. This allowed them extra time to watch offensive plays develop. The disadvantage was that it proved difficult to ever stop opposing runners for no gain, but that was offset by the vastly increased chances of holding those gains to 1 or 2 yards. Suddenly, the Cowboys' opponents found themselves continually facing third-and-long dilemmas.

And because of that, Dallas's first postseason appearance was only a year away.

1965 The Cowboys were in the habit of presenting quality rookies every season, but in 1965 they pushed the talent envelope far enough to achieve full respectability.

The 1965 draft brought quarterback Craig Morton from California in the first round. Morton's selection was an obvious signal to Don Meredith. Healthy for a change, with five full NFL seasons to learn the Landry offense, the former college star was due to put up some big numbers.

Morton was fated to ride the bench, putting in his apprentice time behind Meredith as Meredith had done behind Eddie LeBaron. But the Cowboys' second-round choice, center Malcolm Walker of Rice, was an instant addition to the steadily jelling Dallas offense. Walker was joined on the team by rookie defensive lineman Jethro Pugh, whom the ubiquitous Cowboys scouts had discovered at tiny Elizabeth City State. Taken together, Walker and Pugh alone would have made the latest group of Cowboys rookies a distinguished bunch.

But even more help had arrived for the offense. The Cowboys landed tackle Ralph Neely of Oklahoma after a lengthy legal tussle with the Houston Oilers of the AFL. Neely's addition guaranteed that Meredith's life would be in far less danger than in 1964.

The Cowboys also had signed a free agent running back named Dan Reeves. In his first season, Reeves wouldn't see much action, occasionally spelling Perkins or being used as an extra receiver on obvious passing downs. It would take the Dallas coaching staff almost the entire 1965 season to realize fully Reeves's ability and to keep him on the field regularly.

Everybody expected big things from rookie receiver Bob Hayes, and the youngster delivered. There had never been another lightning-swift receiver like Hayes in professional football, and Landry was ecstatic to discover his new star could catch the football as well as run extremely fast to get under it. The man nicknamed "The World's Fastest Human" after winning the hundred-meter dash in the 1964 Olympics was immediately the NFL's most dangerous wide receiver. Hayes's presence on the field meant opposing defenses had to worry on every play whether he'd blow by them and catch a bomb from Meredith. As a result, Perkins had some great days running the ball and Frank Clarke had another fine season with a lot of catches, while opponents were double-teaming Hayes on the other side of the field.

But even with all their new talent, the Cowboys gave every indication during the season's opening weeks that they weren't much better than in 1964. Two schedule-opening wins at home against New York and Washington were followed by five straight losses. Meredith played badly. In desperation, Landry finished some games by shuttling rookie quarterbacks Morton and

Jerry Rhome in and out while Meredith brooded on the sidelines.

The fifth consecutive loss, on the road to the Steelers, was the final straw. Meredith had completed just 12 of 34 passes as the Cowboys lost 22-13. In the locker room afterward, Landry broke down, telling the players that perhaps it was all his fault.

Before the team's next game, at home against the 49ers, Landry told Meredith he would be the team's starting quarterback for the rest of the season. Meredith responded by leading Dallas to a 39-31 victory. Dallas fans weren't convinced a corner had been turned. After turning out in near-record numbers—about 60,000 for the opening game against the Giants and then 61,500 strong for the second home game against the Redskins—just 39,677 came to see the Cowboys beat San Francisco. The following Sunday, the Cowboys played at home again and beat Pittsburgh 24-17. Hayes was in full tilt, Perkins was running hard, Meredith was completing

George Andrie, 66, in 1965 49ers game

Coach Ernie Stautner

most of his passes, and the defense was finally standing firm. More than 57,000 people witnessed the win over the Steelers, and on the next Sunday fans filed into the Cotton Bowl until the Cowboys had recorded their first-ever sellout—76,251. Unfortunately, the tough Cleveland Browns pinned a 24-17 loss on the home team.

The lowly Redskins clipped Dallas 34-31 in Washington, but then the Cowboys ensured the team's first .500 season record by winning their last three games to finish at 7-7.

There was significant cause for optimism. Some of Meredith's numbers weren't impressive—just 141 of 305 passes completed, with 13 interceptions—but his 22 touchdown passes were another thing entirely. Twelve of those scoring strikes went to Hayes, whose average of 21.8 yards gained per catch led the league by a huge margin. Perkins ran for 690 yards, and, for a change, some of Dallas's backup runners contributed substantially. In all, the offense scored 325 points, which fell about in the middle

of the league pack. But the defense allowed just 280 points, third-fewest in the NFL. This was the first season that the Dallas offense scored more points than the Cowboys defense allowed. Dallas's 7-7 record didn't come close to matching the 11-3 mark achieved by Cleveland to win the Eastern Conference, but it did put the Cowboys into a tie with the Giants for second place in the division. After some tiebreakers were applied, Dallas had qualified for its first postseason game.

As a snack before the main course, at that time the NFL scheduled a meeting between the second-place finishers in its two divisions a week before the division leaders met to decide the league championship. The contest between the two second-place teams was played in Miami and called "The Playoff Bowl." Many teams disdained the game, believing it was humiliating to participate. Packers coach Vince Lombardi once described the Playoff Bowl as "a rinky-dink game for rinky-dink teams." Still, the Cowboys were thrilled to go. Several thousand Dallas fans made the trip to Florida, where their heroes played the always-menacing Baltimore Colts.

Baltimore players, however, were in a surly mood. The Colts had finished with a 10-3-1 record, tying Green Bay, but the Packers edged the Colts 13-10 in a playoff game at season's end and advanced to the NFL Championship, which Green Bay won 23-12 over the Browns.

The Colts came to Miami without star quarterback Johnny Unitas, who was out for the season with a knee injury. He wasn't needed. Baltimore walloped Dallas 35-3 in a game that wasn't as close as the final score. Afterward, Landry called the loss "a team effort." It was impossible for anyone to be too disappointed. The

Pete Gent reaches for a Craig Morton pass

Cowboys' goal for 1966 was also postseason play—but not in the Playoff Bowl.

1966

Beginning in 1966, nothing was ever the same again for the National Football League or for the Dallas Cowboys.

On June 8, representatives of the NFL and AFL held a news conference in New York to announce that the two feuding leagues had agreed to merge. Ironically, the architects of the agreement were the Cowboys' Tex Schramm and the Kansas City Chiefs' Lamar Hunt, who had pulled his club out of Dallas after the 1962 season because of poor fan support.

Pete Rozelle, who would serve as commissioner for the combined leagues, had more to announce: Teams from the NFL and AFL would engage in interconference play after 1969. The conferences would be called the National Football Conference and the American Football Conference; together they would form the National Football League. And in January 1967, the respective conference champions would meet in a world championship contest eventually known as the Super Bowl. There would also be a combined collegiate draft beginning in 1967, ending the desperate days of fighting over draftees that had gained youngsters such as Joe Namath of Alabama an unheard-of $400,000 contract when the New York Jets won a bidding war over the St. Louis Cardinals.

Almost as startling was the transformation of the Dallas Cowboys into an NFL power. Schramm and Landry had worked hard to lay the organizational groundwork and to get the right players in place. Now the old NFL teams that had treated the new franchise roughly were about to get bloodied themselves.

Dan Reeves runs against the Packers

As always, the Schramm/Landry/ Brandt draft troika had brought in top new talent. Guard John Niland of Iowa and defensive end Willie Townes of Tulsa made big contributions in their rookie seasons. A third rookie, running back Walt Garrison of Oklahoma State, had a quiet first year after being drafted in the fifth round. He'd have a greater impact in seasons to come.

But the players already in place were ready to shine. The Cowboys defense, led by Lilly, Howley, Jordan, and Renfro, was formidable. At season's end the Cowboys had given up just 239 points, fewest among the NFC's Eastern Conference teams.

On offense, Don Meredith stepped forward as team leader. Meredith's 177 completions in 344 attempts, with 2,805 yards gained and 24 touchdown passes to just 12 interceptions, ranked fourth in the NFC. For the first time since 1960, a Cowboys back other than Don Perkins led the team in rushing. Dan Reeves

Lee Roy Jordan

Bob Hayes in 1966 Pittsburgh game

Bob Lilly, 74, Cowboys defense, move in on
Packers' Bart Starr, 15

racked up 757 yards and 8 touchdowns; Perkins wasn't far behind with 726 yards and 8 touchdowns of his own. Even Meredith, far from fleet, did well on the ground. He managed 242 yards rushing and 5 touchdowns. In preseason camp, Landry had tried moving Renfro from defense to running back, hoping to exploit Renfro's speed. When Reeves emerged, though, Renfro was returned to the Dallas defense and was a stalwart there as always.

Bob Hayes was brilliant. The track-star-turned-receiver caught 64 passes for 1,232 yards and 13 touchdowns. Washington's Charley Taylor caught more balls, 72; Detroit's Pat Studstill gained a few more receiving yards, 1,266. But Hayes's 19.3 yards gained per catch outpaced everyone. His longest scoring play, 95 yards, was also tops in the NFL.

A hint of great things to come was Dallas's 21-3 win over the Packers in an exhibition game. That victory wouldn't count in the 1966 standings, but the Cowboys had come out on top of Green Bay for the first time.

Dallas opened the regular season at home and thrilled a Cotton Bowl crowd of 60,000 with a 52-7 stomping of the New York Giants. All season long the home folks embraced the Cowboys, with game attendance never falling below 58,000.

The Cowboys next steamrolled Minnesota, Atlanta, and Philadelphia. Unwilling to settle for a championship season, some Cowboys fans began wondering out loud if Dallas might finish 14-0. A 10-10 tie with the Cardinals in the season's fifth week scuttled that; a 30-21 loss to the Browns a week later brought the almost-delirious fans down to earth. But Dallas went 7-2 through the season's final nine games, and their 10-3-1 mark won the Eastern Conference by 1 1/2 games over Cleveland and the Eagles.

That meant the Cowboys would meet Green Bay for the NFC championship and the right to play in Super Bowl I. Like Dallas, Green Bay was loaded with talent. On defense, luminaries such as Ray Nitschke, Herb Adderley, and Willie Wood were dominant. While Cowboys defenders had given up just 239 points, the fewest among Eastern Conference teams, the veteran Packers had allowed only 163. On offense, quarterback Bart Starr, running backs Donny Anderson and Elijah Pitts, and receiver Boyd Dowler hadn't matched the glittering statistics of their Dallas counterparts. The Packers' 335 points scored in 1966 paled against the 445 amassed by the Cowboys. The NFC championship seemed to boil down to the Dallas offense versus the Green Bay defense, and Tom Landry matching wits against Vince

Dan Reeves, 30, follows Ralph Neely, 73, in 1966 title game against Green Bay

Lombardi—an especially interesting confrontation since the men were good friends and had served as assistant coaches together under former New York Giants coach Jim Lee Howell.

The game was played before a sellout Cotton Bowl crowd, and early on Cowboys fans hid their eyes. Green Bay marched straight down the field and scored on a 17-yard pass from Starr to Pitts. Renfro fumbled the subsequent kickoff; Packers rookie fullback Jim Grabowski picked up the ball and scored. Dallas was behind 14-0 before they'd touched the ball on offense.

The Cowboys came back, but midway through the fourth quarter Green Bay had an apparently insurmountable lead of 34-20. Throughout the game, the Green Bay defensive strategy had been to deny Bob Hayes the ball. Hayes was well bottled up; he caught just one pass for a 3-yard gain. But all the attention directed toward Hayes freed Frank Clarke, and with only minutes left to play he scored on a 68-yard bomb from Meredith.

Trailing just 34-27, the Cowboys forced Green Bay to punt and took the

ball for one last drive with 2:11 to go. After Meredith moved his team to the Packers' 26, a Green Bay defensive back was called for pass interference, and Dallas had the ball on the 2-yard line.

A running play got Dallas inside the one. An offsides penalty pushed the Cowboys back to the 6. Meredith and Reeves missed connections on a pass: third and goal. Meredith completed a pass to Pettis Norman that moved the ball to the 2-yard line: fourth and goal. Meredith rolled back to pass; a mixup left relatively small Bob Hayes as a blocker. Green Bay

Vince Lombardi

"Our offense moved the ball all day, but they moved it also. I can still see Don Perkins running up and down the field. Willie Woods called the defensive signals for whatever offensive formations they went into, but I swear Landry could anticipate our coverage. Lombardi thought Landry was reading his mind. Those games said so much about Tom Landry."

—RAY NITSCHKE
Green Bay Packers linebacker
1960-72

Don Meredith

Linebacker Chuck Howley watches 1967 championship loss to Green Bay

defenders blew past Hayes, and Meredith was intercepted in the end zone by the Packers' Tom Brown.

Green Bay went on to Super Bowl I, where they whipped the Kansas City Chiefs 35-10. The Cowboys went home, many players feeling oddly content that they had matched up to mighty Green Bay and played well. Next season, certainly, they'd bring down the Packers dynasty and begin to establish their own.

1967

Before the season began, the NFC realigned its divisions and changed its postseason playoff format. The Western Conference was split into Coastal and Central divisions, the Eastern Conference into Capitol and Century lineups. After the regular season, the champions in each division would meet to determine the confer-

ence champions. Those two teams would then clash, with the winner going on to the Super Bowl to face the AFC kingpin.

The Cowboys found themselves placed in an otherwise weak Capitol group; the Eagles, Redskins, and expansion Saints would all end 1967 with losing records. It was obvious Dallas could play at a level well below its superlative 1966 performance and still win its division easily. That, in fact, was what happened.

As always, new talent arrived. Receiver Lance Rentzel came via trade, and defensive end Rayfield Wright was a steal in the seventh round of the draft. Wright played tight end at first; later, he'd be shifted to the offensive line and become a fixture there.

But talent couldn't overcome injuries. Various nicks plagued Dan Reeves all season, center Dave Manders missed the whole year, and Don Meredith was battered beyond belief. Among other injuries, Meredith suffered two cracked ribs, a broken nose, and a sprained knee. Backup Craig Morton had a gun for an arm, but not Meredith's experience. Both Meredith and Morton had as many interceptions as they did touchdown passes—16 and 10 respectively.

Still, the season opened with convincing wins over the Browns and Giants. An ecstatic crowd of 75,000 crammed into the Cotton Bowl on the next Sunday to see the Cowboys beat visiting Los Angeles, but the Rams prevailed easily, 35-13. It was a particularly galling win because Schramm had accused Los Angeles head coach George Allen of spying on Cowboys practices. This wasn't the last time the Cowboys and Allen would be at odds.

Dallas bumbled through the remainder of the season. Solid wins were followed by inexplicable defeats at the hands of obviously inferior

teams. By Dallas's last home game, attendance was back down to 55,000. Only the receiving combination of Rentzel and Hayes had offensive seasons worth noting. Dallas ended up scoring 342 points while allowing 268, both declines from 1966. So was the Cowboys' final 9-5 record.

Still, Dallas had won its division and next faced Cleveland for the right to advance to the NFL championship game. Playing before a substantial home crowd of nearly 70,000, the Cowboys roared to a 52-14 win and had, apparently, gotten healthy again just in time finally to knock off their nemesis. Green Bay had emerged again as Western Conference champs, eliminating the Rams 24-7 in their division matchup.

This was a different Packers team. Most key players were older veterans, many struggling with declining skills. The most exciting Green Bay player was rookie Travis Williams, who set an NFL record by running back four kickoffs for touchdowns.

The Cowboys went north to meet the Packers at Lambeau Field in Green Bay on December 31. They arrived two days before the game and were pleasantly surprised by sunshine and a temperature in the upper 20s. Practice sessions at Lambeau went well. Lombardi, the Green Bay general manager as well as team coach, had even installed a heating system under the playing field, which was supposed to ensure ice-free conditions in the coldest weather.

However, at game time, the temperature was 15 degrees below zero. Lambeau Field was coated with ice, particularly in one end zone. The Dallas players did everything they

Don Meredith confers with Tom Landry

◆

"Before that game we wrapped our feet in Saran wrap. But during the game we had a feeling of, 'Why are we here?' It hurt to breathe. On the first play of the game the ref blew his whistle, and when he pulled it out of his mouth afterward part of his lip came along with it. Water had settled on the field and turned into ice, especially in that end zone where we lost the game."

—**BOB LILLY**

Warming up for the Ice Bowl

. . . . ◆ . . . .

*"That Ice Bowl was the greatest
game I ever played in. We never
quit, even though we hadn't moved
the ball for the whole game. But we
knew on that one play Bob Lilly
would follow the pulling guard.
There was such a huge hole, it
made Chuck Mercein look like
Jimmy Brown. I had frostbite on
all my toes. To this day, the nerves
on the ends of my toes are all shot."*

—RAY NITSCHKE

. . . .

could to bundle up; Meredith even cut
two slits in the front of his jersey so he
could warm his hands in a sweatshirt
pocket between plays.

Not surprisingly, the home team
adjusted more quickly to the polar conditions. Green Bay scored the only
touchdown of the first quarter and
scored again early in the second quarter for a 14-0 lead. But the Cowboys,
believing for the first time that they
were the superior team, turned two
Packers fumbles into points. George

Andrie lugged a Starr fumble 7 yards
for a touchdown, and kicker Danny
Villanueva booted a 21-yard field goal
to make the halftime score 14-10.

The cold worsened. As the third
quarter began, it was 20 degrees
below zero with a windchill factor of
40 below. Neither team could score in
that period.

In the fourth quarter, the Cowboys
stunned Green Bay with a halfback
option pass. Reeves connected with
Lance Rentzel for a 50-yard score;

Packers fans at the Ice Bowl

after Danny Villanueva kicked the extra point, Dallas led 17-14 with 4:50 left on the clock.

Beginning in 1968, the Green Bay Packers would fall into NFL oblivion. But now Vince Lombardi's team reasserted itself for the last time against top-notch opposition.

Running back Chuck Mercein, a castoff acquired from the Giants, ran for several good gains, once when Lilly followed a pulling guard and left a huge hole in the Dallas defensive line.

Starr tossed short passes to Donny Anderson, whose 6- and 7-yard gains ate up the frozen field. On almost every play, Cowboys defenders were in position to shut down the Packers only to slip on the ice and watch helplessly while Green Bay ballcarriers skidded by.

On a first-down call from the Dallas 11, Mercein ran for 8 yards when George Andrie slipped on the ice and missed the tackle. The Cowboys defenders found themselves backed into the very end zone that was iced over the worst. Between plays, they desperately ground their cleats into the rock-hard ice, trying somehow to gouge out footholds. They couldn't. Another Green Bay running play moved the ball to the Dallas 1-yard line; it was first and goal from there.

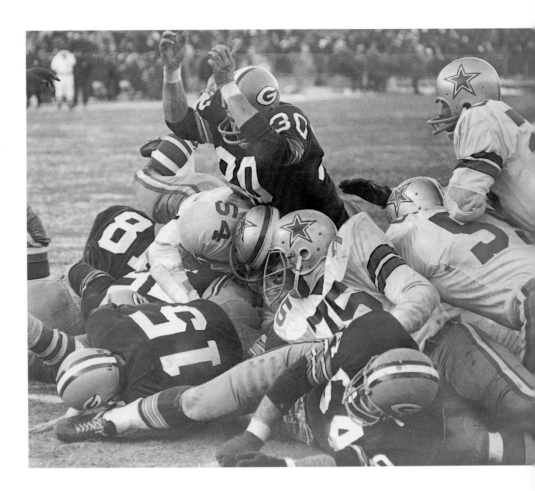

George Andrie at rain-soaked Cotton Bowl game

Two more running plays netted Green Bay 2 feet. With 16 seconds left, Starr called time and conferred with Lombardi. Sportswriters would speculate later that Dallas expected the Packers to attempt a pass; if that fell incomplete, there would still be time for the Packers to kick a field goal, tie the game, and move into overtime. Most Cowboys players disagreed, recalling that they expected Green Bay to run right up the middle, where Dallas defenders had little chance to hold their ground on sheer ice for a third straight play.

Green Bay center Ken Bowman and guard Jerry Kramer double-teamed Jethro Pugh. Cowboys players, coaches, and fans viewing replays would always believe Kramer was offside. Game officials didn't agree. Starr kept the ball himself on a quarterback sneak and barely fell into the end zone.

Bart Starr, 15, sneaks in for the deciding touchdown in the 1967 Green Bay-Dallas title game.

◆

"We were standing in ice. My feet were numb; it felt like they were in buckets of concrete. I personally didn't think it would be a quarterback sneak. I thought they would try a short pass. From what I understand, Starr didn't even tell anyone on his side he was going to keep the ball."

—JETHRO PUGH
Dallas Cowboys defensive lineman 1965-78

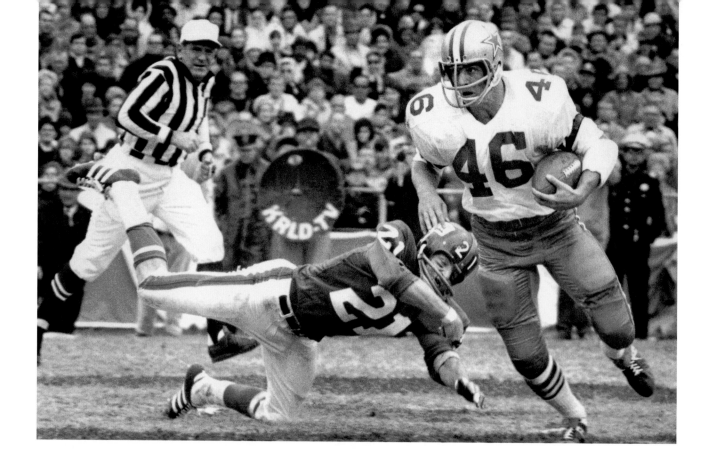

Craig Baynham carries for a gain in 1968 Giants game

Dave Edwards

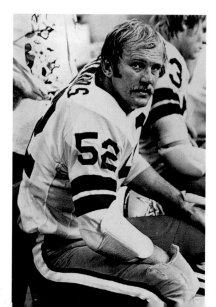

The extra point ended the game: Green Bay 21, Dallas 17. Green Bay eventually defeated Oakland in Super Bowl II, but the Packers haven't returned to the Super Bowl since.

Once again, the Cowboys went home in defeat. The first newspaper headlines and magazine stories began to hint that maybe, just maybe, this Dallas team wasn't up to winning the big games. Meredith inexplicably blamed himself for the loss. After the game, he inadvertently pinned an unfortunate label on the Cowboys when he said, "I guess we can do everything but win the big one."

1968 In retrospect, it seems ludicrous that the Cowboys ended the 1968 season feeling ashamed after a 12-2 record and a trip to the Eastern Conference championship game. In almost every way, 1968 was a banner season other NFL teams would have been proud to experience. But the Cowboys and their fans had almost reached league championship heights for two consecutive years, only to come up short under heartbreaking circum-

stances. For Dallas, anything short of a trip to the Super Bowl would now seem unacceptable and a sign of character deficiency.

All the usual stars remained with the team. The Cowboys' draft moguls brought in flanker Dennis Homan, guard Blaine Nye, linebacker D.D. Lewis, and, on a gambling pick in the sixteenth round, defensive end Larry Cole from the University of Hawaii.

For a change, every key player was healthy. The Cowboys stormed through the first six games on their schedule, winning by an average score of 36-10. But for many fans, any perception that things were really different vanished when a tottering Green Bay team handed Dallas its first loss, 28-17 before 75,000 fans at the Cotton Bowl. The defeat shook the Cowboys. They beat the lowly New Orleans Saints the next week, then lost 27-21 to the Giants.

Yet this team was too talented to lose any more regular-season games. Wins in the final five games gave the Cowboys a record of 12-2. Dallas was awesome statistically. On offense, the Cowboys rolled to 431 points, by far the best among NFL teams. On defense, Dallas allowed a miserly 186 points. Only the 13-1 Baltimore Colts in the Western Conference did better.

Baltimore's own superlative season had football fans drooling over the prospect of a Cowboys-Colts championship game matchup, with the winner surely going on to a crushing Super Bowl III win over the lucky-to-be-there New York Jets and their mouthy quarterback, Joe Namath. But to play the Colts, the Cowboys first had to beat Cleveland to determine the Eastern Conference winner.

Going into the game, Dallas seemed like a sure thing. Meredith had enjoyed a superb season, with 171 pass completions in 309 attempts, 2,500 passing yards, 21 touchdowns, and only 12 interceptions. Rentzel and Hayes were an unbeatable combination of wide receivers. Rentzel had 54 catches, 1,009 receiving yards, and 6 touchdowns; Hayes's 1968 regular season totals were 53 catches, 909 yards receiving, and 10 touchdowns. Though Dan Reeves had suffered some injuries, the Cowboys still had a crushing ground attack led by Don Perkins with 836 yards, Craig Baynham with 438, and Walt Garrison with 271.

The Browns just didn't measure up. They had finished 10-4, scoring 394 points and allowing 273. Running back Leroy Kelly, who had the tough task of replacing Jim Brown, did lead the league in rushing with 1,239 yards. But it seemed obvious that the Cowboys defenders—now nicknamed the Doomsday Defense—would shut Kelly down. Best of all, to Dallas fans, was the Cowboys' easy 28-7 win over the Browns during the regular season.

On December 21, the teams met. Meredith had a poor first half; when the teams headed to their respective locker rooms after the second quarter, the score was 10-10. In the third quar-

Don Meredith passes against the Eagles

ter, Cleveland took advantage of 2 Meredith interceptions to go ahead 24-10. Landry pulled Meredith and sent in Craig Morton, who managed to lead a scoring drive, but it was too late. The Browns won 31-20 in a game Landry called "one of the worst days in Cowboys' history."

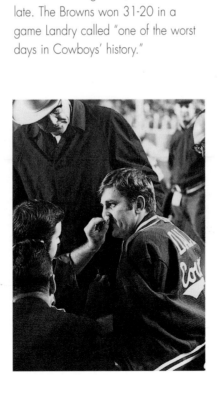

Meredith sidelined with nose injury against Green Bay, 1968

35

Don Meredith announces his retirement

Instead of the Super Bowl, the Cowboys made their second trip to Miami for the Playoff Bowl. They beat Minnesota 17-13, but it made no difference. Players, coaches, and fans were all frustrated. Meredith decided he'd had enough, and he retired just before the 1969 season.

Dallas still hadn't won the big one, and more hard times were ahead.

1969 Don Meredith wasn't the only Cowboy who chose to retire. He was joined by gutty Don Perkins, meaning that the two were forever linked as the first Cowboys in 1960, and the two stars who retired before the '69 season.

Though Landry valued Perkins greatly, his loss was less critical than Meredith's. For a ground attack, the Cowboys still had Dan Reeves and Walt Garrison. In addition, Schramm and Brandt confounded observers again by drafting a player from Yale in the first round. Few sportswriters covering the Cowboys had heard of Calvin Hill. They would soon become very familiar with him.

But Meredith's retirement left Craig Morton as the only experienced Dallas quarterback. Morton had paid his dues—four seasons as a backup—and no one doubted the strength of his arm. Still, Dallas had traded its third-string veteran quarterback, Jerry Rhome, just before Meredith made his bombshell announcement. The Cowboys were left with only a rookie to back up Morton. Roger Staubach had joined the club fresh from four years of duty with the U.S. Navy. Already 27, Staubach was impatient to show what he could do on a football field again, but Landry had no intention of letting him compete with Morton for the starting job.

Another roster addition was tight end Mike Ditka, acquired via trade. Ditka's presence was considered less crucial to the Dallas offense than to team morale. Schramm and Landry hoped his competitiveness would rub off on some of his new teammates.

All through the regular season, it seemed the Cowboys could survive the losses of Perkins and Meredith and still have a good chance to participate in Super Bowl IV. Only the Western Conference's Minnesota Vikings, whose offense scored more points— 379 to 369—and whose defense allowed fewer points—133 to 223— looked capable of keeping the Cowboys from their first NFC title.

Dallas beat St. Louis 24-3 to open the 1969 schedule; Calvin Hill threw a halfback option pass for a touchdown. Dallas edged the Saints 21-17 in their second game. Hill set a team individual game record with 138 yards rushing in that one, as well as scoring two touchdowns. Hayes and Rentzel were catching a lot of passes, as usual. Walt Garrison provided hard-nosed counterpoint to Hill in the Cowboys backfield. Morton was throwing a few too many interceptions, but Dallas's

Calvin Hill runs against the Cardinals in 1969, next page

- - - - - - - - - - - - - ◆ - - - - - - - - - - - - -

"Calvin Hill was a great athlete. And he was so smart. In those days we were always in the position of drafting late, so we had to pick some players who looked like gambles. Boy, Calvin Hill sure paid off."

—TEX SCHRAMM

- -

Landry and Schramm ponder a future without Meredith

Calvin Hill carries against the Jets

Bob Hayes with the ball vs. Cleveland

defense bottled up the opposition and negated most of the turnovers.

Dallas didn't lose until the seventh game of the season; ominously, Cleveland administered a 42-10 thrashing at Memorial Stadium. Still, the Cowboys eased through the rest of their schedule with 5 wins, a 24-24 tie with San Francisco, and a hard-fought 24-23 loss to the Rams in Los Angeles.

Again, Dallas's statistics at season's end were glittering. In his rookie year, Hill notched 942 rushing yards, second in the league only to Gayle Sayers of the Bears and his 1,032. Morton was fifth among league passers; he had 162 completions in 302 attempts, with 21 touchdowns and 15 interceptions. Rentzel snagged 43 passes for 960 yards and 12 touchdowns; Hayes suffered a performance drop-off with 40 catches good for 746 yards and just 4 touchdowns. On defense, Mel Renfro was a particular standout; he intercepted 10 passes and doubled on punt returns with Hayes.

As their reward for winning the Capitol Division for three straight years (and the old NFL Eastern Conference the year before that), the Cowboys got to play the Browns again for the NFC East title. This time the teams met at the Cotton Bowl; 69,000 Dallas fans hoped for the best.

They got the worst. The Browns' defense stifled Hill, holding the rookie star to 17 rushing yards. Morton was completely ineffective, completing just

7 of 24 passes. By the time Dallas finally scored on a 2-yard sneak by Morton in the third quarter, the Browns already had 24 points. Before the hopeful fans in the stands could even imagine a comeback, Cleveland drove back for a touchdown, then returned a Morton interception 88 yards for another score. Morton was booed unmercifully; Landry put Staubach in the game. He completed 3 of 5 passes, including a touchdown toss to Rentzel, but it was much too late. Dallas was soundly defeated, 38-14. After the game, the retired Meredith went to Landry's house to console his former coach.

The hapless Cowboys went back to the Playoff Bowl, where the Rams humiliated them, 31-0. Adding insult to injury, the Kansas City Chiefs, once chased out of Dallas by the Cowboys,

upset the Minnesota Vikings to win Super Bowl IV.

Dallas finished the 1960s with a regular season record of 67-65-6. (The Minnesota Vikings, voted in as a league expansion franchise with the Cowboys but joining the NFL one season later, were 52-67-7. But the Vikings, at least, played in Super Bowl IV.) In league playoff games, including league championship matchups, the Cowboys were 1-4, their lone win coming against Cleveland in 1967 for the Eastern Conference title. In league championship games, both against Green Bay, they were 0-2.

The Dallas Cowboys, a team that hadn't even existed before 1960, entered the 1970s labeled as a vastly talented team that always failed, somehow, to live up to its potential.

◆

"By the time we lost those two playoff games to Cleveland, we had become the bridesmaids of the NFL. We began to doubt ourselves. That Green Bay game in the ice set us back, and it showed up for years. We started thinking that maybe we couldn't win the big one. Maybe everybody else was right about us."

—Bob Lilly

◆

"I was pretty upset after those playoff losses to the Browns. It had looked like we were on our way to Super Bowls, and all of a sudden we just couldn't do it. I never did figure out what went wrong then."

—Tex Schramm

John Niland, left, and Blaine Nye

SEVENTIES

1970 On Monday night, November 16, in their ninth game of the 1970 season, the Dallas Cowboys took the first step toward erasing forever their image as talented losers. They did this by losing disgracefully.

Before that fateful night, it had already been an odd year for Dallas. Many players had spent the winter seething over the second consecutive playoff loss to the Browns; others brooded that they might never get to the Super Bowl. But when training camp opened, there were enough talented newcomers to foster hope that maybe 1970 might be the Cowboys' season.

Just one year after acquiring unknown Calvin Hill for their backfield, Schramm and Brandt took West Texas halfback Duane Thomas with their top pick. Thomas was undeniably talented and undeniably trouble. He'd been a discipline problem in college, and Landry wanted no part of him. But Schramm and Brandt were convinced Thomas had the kind of rare talent that would offset any difficulties he might cause the Dallas coaching staff.

The same draft yielded Charlie Waters, a cornerback from Clemson who became a longtime star for the Cowboys; Boston College's John Fitzgerald, a plugger at center; Pat Toomay from Vanderbilt, whose quirky personality brought humor to the team and whose tackling skills wreaked havoc on opponents; and Morgan State's Mark Washington, another cornerback, who contributed for nine seasons.

The Cowboys didn't draft defensive back Cliff Harris from tiny Ouachita State, but nobody else did, either. Dallas signed Harris as an undrafted free agent. He would team with Waters to make a formidable duo of backfield defenders.

All those players, plus the returning nucleus of proven veterans, again made Dallas a prohibitive favorite to win the newly minted Eastern Division of the National Football Conference (NFC). Only the name had changed—the Cowboys were still paired with the Giants, Cardinals, Redskins, and Eagles.

Dallas sputtered from the beginning of the season. Morton was the starting quarterback, but Staubach hounded Landry for a chance to win the position. Landry refused, telling Staubach he still didn't have the necessary experience.

41

But Morton suffered a shoulder injury, and Staubach led the club to a pair of wins to open the schedule. Morton then presided over a 20-7 loss to the Cardinals in St. Louis, a team that suddenly seemed capable of top-pling the Cowboys from their perennial division championship perch.

The Cowboys bounced back to beat Atlanta 13-0; then, in a road game against Minnesota, they fell to the Vikings 54-13. It was the most points ever scored against the Cowboys, even during their early years as a patchwork expansion team. Two more wins, both shaky, were fol-lowed by a 23-20 road loss to the Giants.

So when they faced the Cardinals in a rematch at the Cotton Bowl, Dallas was 5-3. Monday Night Football had made its debut in the 1970 season, and on this particular Monday untold millions of Americans tuned in to the new, explosively popu-lar show to watch the game.

Dallas lost 38-0. The offense was flat, and the defense was listless. Don Meredith, once reviled by Cowboys fans, was part of the Monday Night Football announcing crew along with Keith Jackson and Howard Cosell. As the trouncing on the field grew more emphatic and Morton stumbled around helplessly, a large segment of the crowd stood, turned to face the ABC-TV broadcast booth, and began chanting, "We want Meredith!" He declined to leave retirement. On the air, Meredith, Jackson, and Cosell debated whether the Cowboys were a team on the decline. Dallas's stock had never been lower.

Chastened, the team gathered for practice. The players asked the coach-es to leave while they held a private

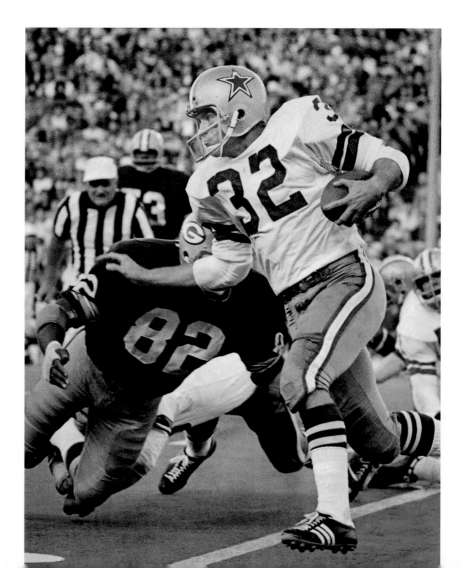

Walt Garrison carries the ball in 1970 game with the Packers

meeting. Afterward, when his staff was allowed to return, Landry spoke. Some players say it was their idea; Landry remembers that he made the suggestion. In any event, instead of a hard afternoon spent sweating through drills and lamenting the St. Louis loss, the Dallas Cowboys played a laughter-filled, rollicking game of touch football.

On Sunday, Dallas crushed the Redskins 45-21, the first of five straight wins to close the season. Along the way, the Cowboys beat the Packers for the first time in the regular season, 16-3. They won the Eastern Division.

Some numbers for the regular season weren't impressive. The offense scored 299 points, about in the middle of the league pack, and the defense allowed 221, a little better but still not superlative. Morton's pass-completion rate was dreadful—102 of 207. At least he had only 7 interceptions; Staubach, who'd passed just 82 times, had 7.

The Dallas ground game had been solid, not spectacular. Thomas finished his rookie year with 803 yards rushing. Hill had 577 and Garrison had 507. Staubach's penchant for scrambling was already evident: He

picked up 221 yards in 27 carries. Hayes caught just 34 passes but managed 889 yards and 10 touchdowns; Rentzel, who had serious legal problems stemming from an encounter with a minor, totaled 28 catches, 556 yards and 5 touchdowns. He would be gone from Dallas in 1971.

The Cowboys met the Detroit Lions, runners-up in the Central Division, in the first round of the playoffs. The NFC was now split into three divisions, with one wild-card team earning the fourth and final playoff spot. The Lions had been an offensive powerhouse during the season, led by speedy halfback Mel Farr. But against Dallas in the playoffs, Detroit could manage only 7 first downs. The Cowboys offense didn't do much better, but a field goal and a safety gave Dallas a 5-0 win.

The NFC championship game matched the Cowboys against the 49ers, who had upset the Vikings a week before. With Thomas rushing for 143 yards and a touchdown, Dallas won a tight game 17-10. The Cowboys had made it to Super Bowl V, where they would meet the Baltimore Colts.

Teammates hug Dave Edwards, with the ball, in muddy game against the Browns

◆

"In that 38-0 loss, we finally said we would quit trying to please anybody else and just go out and knock some people down. Coach Landry loosened up a little. We started playing touch football in practice."

—BOB LILLY

43

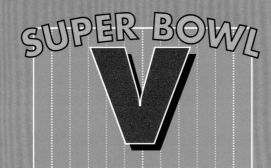

SUPER BOWL V

More than 80,0000 fans packed Miami's Orange Bowl on January 17, 1971. The game promised to be a great one. The Colts, who had switched over to the American Football Conference (AFC) along with the Browns and Steelers as part of the NFL-AFL merger, were eager to erase memories of their embarrassing loss to the Jets in Super Bowl III. The Cowboys just wanted to win.

They got off to a solid start. The only scoring in the first quarter was a 14-yard field goal by Dallas kicker Mike Clark. Clark booted a 30-yard 3-pointer early in the second period and the Cowboys were up 6-0. Their defense was completely shutting down the Colts offense when Johnny Unitas tried to complete a pass to receiver Eddie Hinton. Mel Renfro, defending, jumped for the ball at the same time as Hinton. According to the referees, the ball glanced off Hinton's hands, scraped Renfro's finger-tips, and ricocheted into the arms of Baltimore tight end John Mackey, who rumbled 75 yards for a game-tying touchdown. Renfro screamed that he hadn't touched the ball; under NFL rules at that time, a football rebounding from the hands of one player directly to a teammate without being touched by an opponent could not be ruled a completed pass. If Renfro was right,

Dan Reeves gains yardage against the Colts in Super Bowl V

Mackey's touchdown should have been called back. But the officials ruled in favor of the Colts. Outraged, the Cowboys blocked Colts kicker Jim O'Brien's extra point. The game was tied 6-6.

Dallas couldn't move the football. But on Baltimore's next possession, George Andrie knocked the ball loose from Unitas, and the Cowboys recovered on the Colts' 29-yard line. Morton moved them to the 7; Duane Thomas scored from there. Clark kicked the extra point, and Dallas led 13-6 at halftime. Unitas, injured by Andrie's hit, was out of the game. The Cowboys were in control.

Dallas kicked off to open the second half. Baltimore's Jim Duncan fumbled, and the Cowboys fell on the ball on the Colts' 31.

Five plays later, Dallas had the ball on the Baltimore 2-yard line. The touchdown they were about to score would probably put the game out of

reach and let the Cowboys win the big one at last. Thomas had been gaining steady yardage on the ground; now Landry ordered him to take the ball again. Thomas smashed into the Colts' line, and the football came loose. Dallas center Dave Manders fell on the ball, but the closest officials were screened off from the fumble. Baltimore lineman Billy Ray Smith began screaming that the Colts had recovered. An official on the other side of the field indicated it was Baltimore's ball.

The Cowboys' futile protest wasn't sour grapes. Manders had clearly fallen on the ball. Despite the bad call, Dallas continued to hold off the Colts. Earl Morrall, who replaced Unitas, was largely ineffective. So was Morton, who had completed just 12 of 26 passes in the game. But Dallas still held the 13-6 lead with 8 minutes left to play.

Morton attempted a short pass to Garrison. The ball bounced off the

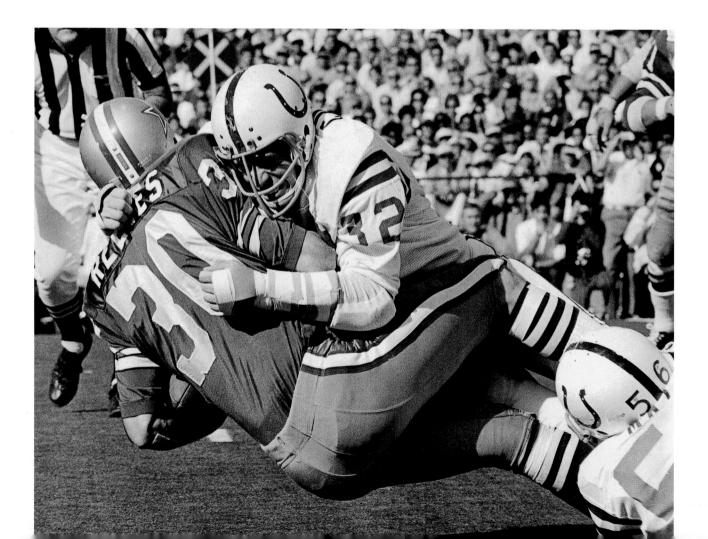

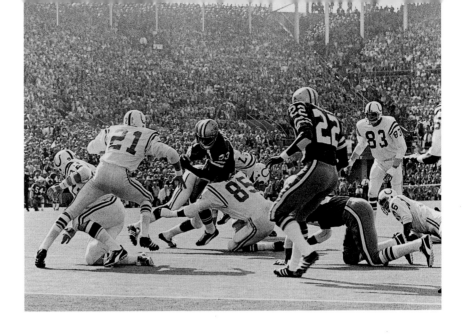

Duane Thomas heads for the end zone in Super Bowl V

SUPER BOWL V STATISTICS

SCORING

Baltimore	0	6	0	10	**16**
Dallas	3	10	0	0	**13**

FIRST QUARTER:
Dallas, Clark 14-yard field goal

SECOND QUARTER:
Dallas, Clark 30-yard field goal
Baltimore, Mackey 75-yard pass from Unitas (kick blocked)
Dallas, Thomas 7-yard pass from Morton (Clark kick)

THIRD QUARTER:
None

FOURTH QUARTER:
Baltimore, Nowatzke 2-yard run (O'Brien kick)
Baltimore, O'Brien 32-yard field goal

TEAM	DALLAS	BALTIMORE
First downs	10	14
Net yards	215	329
Fumbles lost	1	3
Interceptions	3	3
Penalty yards	133	31

INDIVIDUAL:

RUSHING:
Dallas: Garrison 65, Thomas 35, Morton 2
Baltimore: Nowatzke 33, Bulaich 28, Unitas 4, Havrilak 3, Morrall 1

PASSING:
Dallas: Morton 12-26, 127 yards
Baltimore: Morrall 7-15, 147 yards; Unitas 3-9, 88 yards; Havrilak 1-1, 25 yards

RECEIVING:
Dallas: Reeves 5-46, Thomas 4-21, Garrison 2-19, Hayes 1-41
Baltimore: Jefferson 3-52, Mackey 2-80, Hinton 2-51, Havrilak 2-27, Nowatzke 1-45, Bulaich 1-5

fullback's hands, and Baltimore safety Rick Volk intercepted. He returned the ball to the Dallas 3-yard line; Tom Nowatzke scored from there, and the extra point tied the game.

Landry chose not to control the ball for the remainder of the quarter and decide the contest in overtime. Morton went back to pass again. This time Dan Reeves had the ball skip off his fingers, and Colts linebacker Mike Curtis intercepted. His 13-yard return put the Colts on Dallas's 28-yard line, within comfortable field-goal range. Two running plays moved the ball a little closer, and on the game's last play O'Brien kicked a 32-yard field goal to make the Colts 16-13 winners. In frustration, Bob Lilly flung his helmet 40 yards down the field.

Chuck Howley, who had intercepted two Baltimore passes, became the first participant on a losing Super Bowl team to be named the game's Most Valuable Player. That was no consolation. Too many writers and fans decided the Cowboys had choked again.

◆

"Some people say I heaved my helmet 50 yards. All I know is I just threw it. Then some Baltimore rookie ran after it, brought it back to me and said, 'Mr. Lilly, here's your helmet.' It made me feel like a heel."

—BOB LILLY

Bob Lilly throws his helmet in disgust as a Colts field goal wins Super Bowl V

1971 Duane Thomas made the biggest news for Dallas during the off-season. As Landry had feared, the running back from West Texas stirred up trouble. Before training camp, Thomas demanded that Schramm renegotiate his contract. When Schramm refused, Thomas boycotted the first week of training camp at Thousand Oaks. When he finally showed up, he brought along a friend and insisted that Landry give him a tryout. Landry wouldn't. Thomas left immediately for Dallas, where he called a news conference and told the assembled media that the team mistreated him because he was black; that Landry was "a plastic man"; that Gil Brandt had lied to him; and that Schramm was "sick, demented, and completely dishonest." When informed of the insult, Schramm responded with one of the best comeback lines ever: "That's pretty good. He got two out of three."

Dallas traded Thomas to the New England Patriots for running back Carl Garrett and New England's top pick in the 1972 draft. Thomas reported to the Patriots' training camp but was thrown out almost immediately for not following instructions during running drills. Dallas had to return Garrett and the draft pick.

Landry had other things to think about. For the first time in years, the draft hadn't brought any top new players to the Cowboys. Number one pick Tody Smith, a defensive end from the University of Southern California, was a bust. Lance Rentzel was gone; his replacement was former All-Pro flanker Lance Alworth, once a superstar for the

Tom Landry surveys Texas Stadium, spring 1971

Duane Thomas runs free against the Lions in 1970 game

AFC San Diego Chargers and still a quality receiver. Alworth would eventually be inducted into the Hall of Fame.

Since Calvin Hill and Walt Garrison were still around, Landry concluded that the Cowboys would do just fine running the football without Duane Thomas. His offensive dilemma was at quarterback. Morton had led the team to Super Bowl V, but Staubach played well in the preseason and clearly had earned his chance to supplant Morton. As the season began, Landry couldn't make up his mind. Finally, he announced that Morton and Staubach would alternate games as starters, a decision that angered both quarterbacks and didn't sit well with the rest of the team.

Morton started game one on the road against Buffalo. He played well as the Cowboys won a slugfest 49-37. Staubach won the second game of the season over Philadelphia. He played

well, too, and Dallas romped 42-7.

Then it was back to Dallas for the Cowboys' final two games in the Cotton Bowl. Texas Stadium was almost completed. Built in the Dallas suburb of Irving, the structure featured a unique roof that extended beyond the stands below but was open above the playing field. Schramm explained that this would protect fans from the elements but still allow them to enjoy game conditions affected by rain, sleet, or snow.

The Redskins edged Dallas 20-16 in the Cowboys' home opener. Then Duane Thomas showed up before the next week's game with the Giants, announcing he'd play under protest. After that, Thomas refused to talk to the media and, often, to most of his teammates.

Staubach started against New York but wasn't especially effective. Highly competitive, he was insulted

Larry Cole

Craig Morton confers with coaches

············ ◆ ············

"Roger was a great leader, but he wasn't the best quarterback Dallas ever had. Don Meredith was the best as far as reading defenses, and Craig Morton had the strongest arm. But Roger won and did what it took to win. I guess he was the best total package."

—WALT GARRISON
*Cowboys running back
1966-74*

·····························

Lance Alworth, 19, and Craig Morton

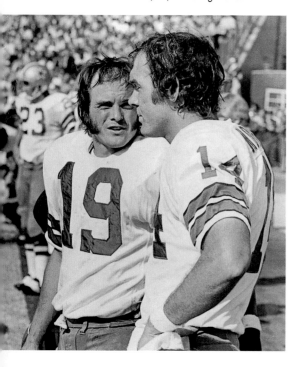

when Landry replaced him with Morton at the half with New York leading 13-6. The Cowboys ended up winning 20-13, but Morton wasn't the catalyst. Thomas hadn't played football, or even worked out, since Super Bowl V. But Calvin Hill was injured in the third quarter, and Landry sent Thomas in. He rushed for 60 yards on just 9 carries.

The Morton-led Cowboys lost to New Orleans 24-14. Staubach started against New England in the first game ever at Texas Stadium, and the Cowboys romped 44-21. Thomas scored the first Texas Stadium touchdown on a 56-yard burst just 2 minutes into the opening quarter.

Pressure mounted on Landry to settle on a starting quarterback. The fans and the press wanted Staubach; pri-

vately, so did most of his Dallas teammates. Instead, in the Cowboys' seventh game of the season against the Bears, Landry alternated Morton and Staubach at quarterback on every other play.

The every-other-play quarterback shuttle was a disaster; the Bears, later to finish the season at 6-8, beat Dallas 23-19. Afterward, Landry finally made his decision—Roger Staubach would be the starting Dallas quarterback for the rest of the season.

It was another benchmark in the Cowboys history. Staubach led the team to seven consecutive victories, clinching another NFC East title and putting Dallas back in the playoffs. Along the way, Staubach performed so well that, despite his part-time status for seven games, he led the NFL in

Roger Staubach brought down by 49ers

passing with 126 completions in 211 attempts. Staubach's touchdown-interception ratio was an amazing 15-4.

Thomas did well for an abbreviated season, too. His 793 rushing yards put him comfortably ahead of Hill's 468 and Garrison's 429. There were some changes among team receiving leaders: Garrison caught 40 passes for 396 yards and a touchdown; Hayes trailed with 35 catches, but for 840 yards and 8 touchdowns; Alworth chipped in 34 catches for 487 yards; and Ditka caught 30 balls for 360 yards.

Overall, the offense was back in gear with 406 points, the most in the league. Detroit was second with 341 points. On defense, Dallas allowed 222 points, third-fewest in the NFL. Best of all, the Cowboys players, with the exception of Thomas, were all friends as well as teammates.

The Cowboys faced Minnesota in the opening playoff round. It wasn't as close as the 20-12 score suggested. Dallas whipped the Vikings in every phase of the game, and only 10 points for Minnesota late in the fourth

quarter, when the game was out of reach, made the final score respectable. Then came the NFL championship game, against the 49ers for the second consecutive year.

With both teams eager for a trip to Super Bowl VI, the game was a tough defensive struggle. Staubach and San Francisco quarterback John Brodie were absolutely stymied. With the contest still scoreless in the second quarter, George Andrie once again forced a big turnover in a playoff game. He intercepted a short pass deep in 49ers territory and lumbered to the San Francisco 1. Hill dived in for the touchdown.

The only third-quarter scoring was a 28-yard 49ers field goal. With a meager 7-3 lead in the final period, Staubach led Dallas on the Cowboys' only prolonged drive of the day. Ditka made a key catch, and Thomas scored from 2 yards out. Clark's extra point made the Cowboys a 14-3 winner. They were on their way back to the Super Bowl, and the AFC champion would have to face Dallas's long-term, frustrated rage.

"We used to have a party every weekend, not getting drunk but getting together after the game. We'd gather at somebody's house. Also on Thursday afternoons, the team got together after practice. Some people came for five minutes and some for five hours. We'd work out our problems then that we couldn't work out on the field."

—WALT GARRISON

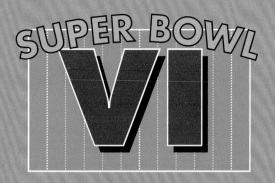

SUPER BOWL VI

In 1971, the Miami Dolphins were just a year away from posting a perfect 17-0 record, rolling undefeated through the regular season, playoffs, and Super Bowl VII. They'd go on to another win in Super Bowl VIII and conclude the Seventies as arguably one of the decade's three dominant teams, along with the Cowboys and Pittsburgh Steelers.

But Super Bowl VI belonged to Dallas, although on paper the Dolphins matched up well against the Cowboys. Miami finished the regular season

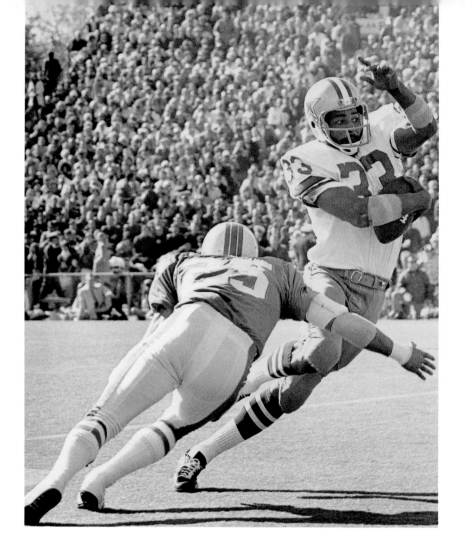

Duane Thomas slips by a Miami defender in Super Bowl VI

at 10-3-1, scoring 315 points and allowing just 174. Dolphins quarterback Bob Griese topped the AFC in passing, just as Staubach led the NFC. Miami's backfield trio of Larry Csonka, Jim Kiick, and Mercury Morris seemed at least the equal of Thomas, Hill, and Garrison. The Dolphins could counter Hayes and Alworth of Dallas with Paul Warfield and Howard Twilley. On defense, Dick Anderson and Nick Buoniconti and Jake Scott could cause any offense headaches. Even legendary Miami coach Don Shula seemed about equal to Tom Landry.

Yet, when the game was over and the Cowboys were world champions, it was clear they'd won easily. Super Bowl VI was no contest.

An unexpected turnover helped the Cowboys get a first-quarter lead. During the regular season, burly Dolphins fullback Larry Csonka just didn't fumble. Early in Super Bowl VI, he did. Dallas recovered on its own 48. Mixing short passes with runs into the outmanned Miami defensive line, the Cowboys moved into Dolphins territory before settling for a 9-yard, chip-shot field goal by Mike Clark.

In the second quarter, Staubach commanded a lengthy drive that concluded with him pitching a 7-yard touchdown pass to Alworth. Clark kicked the extra point. The Cowboys didn't know it yet, but they had just put on the scoreboard all the points they would need to win.

Miami didn't quit. Just before halftime, Dolphins kicker Garo Yepremian got his team 3 points with a 31-yard field goal. But the Cowboys' 10-3 lead looked far more precarious than it really was. Their defense, highlighted by Bob Lilly and Larry Cole chasing Griese seemingly forever before sacking him for a 29-yard loss, had the younger Dolphins well in hand.

SUPER BOWL VI STATISTICS

SCORING

Dallas	3	7	7	7	**24**
Miami	0	3	0	0	**3**

FIRST QUARTER:
Dallas, Clark, 9-yard field goal

SECOND QUARTER:
Dallas, Alworth, 7-yard pass from Staubach (Clark kick)
Miami, Yepremian, 31-yard field goal

THIRD QUARTER:
Dallas, Thomas, 3-yard run (Clark kick)

FOURTH QUARTER:
Dallas, Ditka, 7-yard pass from Staubach (Clark kick)

TEAM	DALLAS	MIAMI
First downs	23	10
Net yards	352	185
Fumbles lost	1	2
Interceptions	0	1
Penalty yards	15	0

INDIVIDUAL:
RUSHING:
Dallas: Thomas 95, Garrison 74, Hill 25, Staubach 18, Ditka 17, Hayes 16, Reeves 7
Miami: Csonka 40, Kiick 40, Griese 0

PASSING:
Dallas: Staubach 12-19, 119 yards, 2 TDs
Miami: Griese 12-23, 134 yards

RECEIVING:
Dallas: Thomas 3-17, Alworth 2-28, Ditka 2-28, Hayes 2-23, Garrison 2-11, Hill 1-12
Miami: Warfield 4-39, Kiick 3-21, Csonka 2-18, Fleming 1-27, Twilley 1-20, Mandich 1-9

The Cowboys had no intention of letting the Dolphins back into the game in the second half. Dallas received the kickoff, then took more than 5 minutes off the clock with a lengthy drive. Duane Thomas barreled into the Miami end zone for a 3-yard touchdown. With the conversion kick, it was 17-3 Dallas.

For the final 25 minutes of the game, the Cowboys calmly throttled Miami. There was seldom reason for Staubach to pass—Thomas, Hill, and Garrison were grinding out all the yards he needed on the ground. Meanwhile, the vaunted Dolphins backfield had only 20 collective carries; successful with a ball-control attack during the regular season, the Dolphins proved woefully inept at playing catch-up.

Staubach iced the victory with a 7-yard touchdown pass to Ditka. At the final gun, it was 24-3 Cowboys. This time, Bob Lilly didn't heave his helmet. Instead, he was one of three Cowboys who hoisted Tom Landry on their shoulders and carried the smiling coach off the field.

In the world champions' locker room after the game, there seemed less outright elation than a sense of heartfelt relief. They had won the big one.

The winning coach, Super Bowl VI

A dejected Landry during a 1972 Raiders game

Cowboys hammer Detroit running back Mel Farr

1972

Dallas began the new season with Schramm and Landry trying to create addition by subtraction. When Duane Thomas showed up at training camp and continued his bizarre behavior, he was promptly traded to the San Diego Chargers for receiver Billy Parks and running back Mike Montgomery. While both were useful players, they clearly weren't worth a well-behaved Thomas. Still, the Cowboys were glad to make the trade. Remembering his futile deal a year earlier with New England, Schramm even insisted on a no-return clause, so that no matter how Thomas might act when he joined his new team, he couldn't be shipped back to the Cowboys.

Besides Parks and Montgomery, the draft strengthened Dallas. First-round pick Bill Thomas, a running back from Boston College, was a mistake. He was gone from the Cowboys' roster in one season. But Brandt and Schramm plucked stocky Houston running back Robert Newhouse in the sec-

ond round, and they added punter Marv Bateman and tight end Jean Fugett later.

But Dallas's chances to repeat as Super Bowl champions were drastically reduced in a preseason game when Staubach separated a shoulder. Surgery was required, and he was lost for the regular season. Craig Morton rejoined the starting lineup and often played well, but the emotional spark provided by Staubach that had been an integral part of the Cowboys' championship season in 1971 was missing.

Dallas was even being challenged for supremacy in its own division. After a typically undistinguished 6-8 season in 1970, Washington had hired former Los Angeles Rams coach George Allen to run the team. Because of the spying spat several seasons earlier, Dallas was already none too fond of the pushy Allen. Still, during his first season he accomplished a Lombardi-like transformation of the Redskins, dealing draft choices like bubblegum cards for seasoned veterans Richie

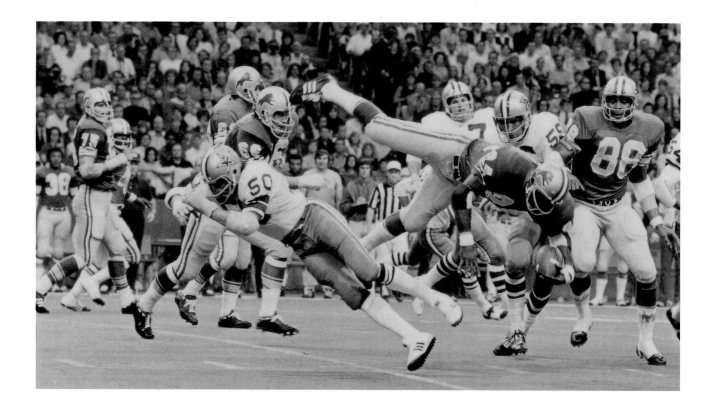

Petibon, Jack Pardee, and others. Allen's war cry of "The future is now!" took Washington by storm, though the long-suffering Redskins fans were even more enamored of the 9-4-1 record their new coach coaxed from his club.

With Morton at quarterback and Reeves, who had played behind center at South Carolina, available as an emergency backup, the Cowboys began the defense of their championship with a 28-6 win over the Eagles. The Giants fell 23-14 a week later in New York, but on the season's third week, old nemesis Green Bay squeezed out a 16-13 win. After two more victories, the Cowboys traveled to Washington for a showdown with the Redskins. Allen's grizzled crew won 24-20.

The Cowboys were still a very good team and proved it by winning their next four games. With Thomas gone, Calvin Hill happily regained his old spot as Dallas's featured running back. Running with abandon—annoying Landry by sometimes unnecessarily leaping over would-be tacklers—Hill eventually became the first Cowboys back to gain a thousand yards in a single season.

But Dallas could only manage a split of its last four games. The Cowboys avenged the earlier loss by beating Washington 34-24 at Texas Stadium, but the Redskins' final season mark of 11-3 was one game better than Dallas's 10-4. Washington also edged Dallas in just about every offensive and defensive category.

The Cowboys' regular season totals were no cause for shame. They scored 319 points and gave up 240. (Washington's numbers were 336 and 218.) Morton had passed for a high percentage of completions, 185 of 339, but he had thrown 21 interceptions to just 15 touchdown passes. Washington's duo of Billy Kilmer and Sonny Jurgenson combined for 159 of 284, with 21 touchdowns and 15 interceptions.

Hill ended up with 1,036 yards rushing, finishing third in the league behind leader Larry Brown of the Redskins (1,216) and the Giants' Ron Johnson (1,182). With Staubach out, Landry had all but abandoned game plans, including long bombs. Hill led Dallas receivers with 43 catches good for 364 yards; Garrison was next with 37 catches for 390 yards.

As the NFC wild-card team, Dallas opened the playoffs in San Francisco against the 49ers, who had won the weak Western Division with a so-so 8-5-1 mark. San Francisco, though, had the always dangerous John Brodie, and fleet Gene Washington had superseded Bob Hayes as the league's most dangerous long-distance receiver.

A positive note for the Cowboys was that Staubach was back on their roster for the playoffs. Landry chose to leave Morton in at quarterback; after being out all season, he theorized, Staubach would be rusty.

Vic Washington welcomed the Cowboys to Candlestick Park by returning the opening kickoff 97 yards for a touchdown. The Cowboys answered with a 37-yard field goal by Toni Fritsch. But San Fancisco scored two touchdowns early in the second quarter to take a 21-3 lead. Dallas refused to

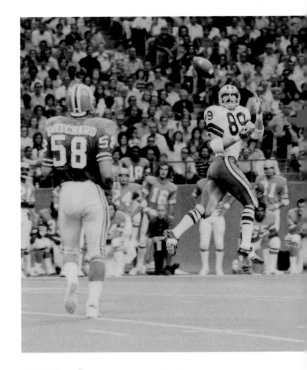

Mike Ditka pulls in a pass against Houston

Ron Sellers

fold; a second Fritsch field goal and a 28-yard scoring pass from Morton to Alworth cut the 49ers advantage to 21-13 at the half.

The 49ers seemed to have a safe lead when they managed a third-quarter touchdown while the Cowboys couldn't score in the period. Even though Fritsch booted another field goal in the fourth quarter, Dallas was still behind by 12 points when the Cowboys got the ball on their own 45-yard line.

Midway through the third quarter, Landry had replaced Morton with Staubach. Morton hadn't played well—7 completions in 21 attempts and 2 interceptions to go with his lone touchdown pass. Staubach hadn't done anything spectacular since his insertion. But now in the game's waning moments he was about to pull out his first spectacular, come-from-behind win.

Staubach calmly moved the Cowboys down the field, throwing short sideline passes to use up as little time left on the clock as possible. With 90 seconds left, he nailed Billy Parks with a 20-yard strike. After the extra point, Dallas trailed 28-23.

Everyone—the 49ers, the fans, the vendors peddling hot dogs—knew the Cowboys would attempt an onside kick. Fritsch dribbled the ball forward, and Mel Renfro recovered for Dallas.

Staubach scrambled for a first down. He threw a pass for a first down. Finally, with seconds remaining, he found Ron Sellers in the end zone for a 10-yard scoring pass. Staubach had worked a miracle. The Cowboys scored 14 points in a minute and a half and moved on to the NFC title game.

On December 31, the Cowboys went to Washington to meet the Redskins for the NFC title. There was no question who Landry would start at quarterback, but Staubach had used up his 1972 allotment of magic in San Francisco. Washington dominated the game, winning 26-3 and moving on to Super Bowl VII, where they lost to the Dolphins. The Cowboys went home, but for a change they didn't have to worry about a reputation for not winning the big one. They had made the playoffs for the seventh straight season, an NFL record. The decade was still young, and there would be more Super Bowls.

Cowboys' drive ends with sack of Craig Morton by the Eagles

THE DALLAS COWBOYS CHEERLEADERS

★

In 1971, the Cowboys wowed the world with Texas Stadium, the first—and by no means last—football-only facility with luxury boxes. In 1972, they introduced an even more glamorous concept—the Dallas Cowboys Cheerleaders.

It wasn't that Dallas was the first pro football team to put pretty girls on the sidelines. But earlier cheerleading squads for Dallas and all the other NFL franchises tried to entertain in the high school and college tradition—urging spectators to join in organized cheers. Pro football aficionados weren't interested in chanting, "Fight, team, fight!" Up to that time cheerleaders at NFL games were duds.

Gigi Pittman, Suzanne Rouse, Tara Rene, and Kimberly Ball, from left

But Tex Schramm decided to change the cheerleading mix. He reasoned that fans enjoyed the sight of attractive young women; they just didn't want to be led in synchronized rooting. So, under Schramm's direction, a troupe of cheerleaders was recruited whose talents included dancing. Dressed in specially designed outfits in traditional Dallas colors of blue and silver, they and their choreographed routines were an instant hit with Cowboys fans.

Their appearance with the Cowboys in Super Bowl X made the Dallas Cowboys Cheerleaders a national phenomenon. They became the subject of two made-for-TV movies. Other sports franchises, and not just NFL football teams, began to incorporate cheerleaders into

"I always felt we had an obligation to put a show on at the game. We'd had the high school bands, the usual things. Teams had cheerleaders before. The Colts cheerleaders would hold up cards to show fans what they were supposed to chant, but nobody ever chanted. Fans at pro games didn't want to cheer college-style. I finally said, 'The hell with it, let's entertain 'em with our cheerleaders instead of trying to lead them in cheers. Dress 'em up pretty and let 'em entertain.' So they were sexy, but they weren't lewd. You had young women who were fun to look at in healthy surroundings. They were loved immediately in Dallas, but what made them nationally popular was that we got in a playoff game and took them with us. I think it was against the Rams in '75. The public just fell in love with them."

—TEX SCHRAMM

Kelli McGonagill Finglass

their own game rituals. But the Dallas Cowboys Cheerleaders had come first, and they have remained by far the best-known and most popular squad.

It's not easy to become a Dallas Cowboys Cheerleader, or to remain one. Applicants, who must be at least 18, go through a rigorous series of tryouts at Texas Stadium. There are far more applicants than positions. Most seasons, there are 36 cheerleaders on the squad, and every year there are always more than 1,000 women competing for the coveted spots.

For many applicants, becoming a Dallas Cowboys Cheerleader has been a lifelong dream. Many who don't make the squad during their first tryouts are back again the next year.

First-time applicants who are successful usually have spent months or even years preparing for their chance. It's not uncommon for women to move to Dallas with the express intention of making the squad, no matter how much hard work it takes.

Good looks, dancing ability, and overall athleticism are requirements, but brains play a part, too. Finalists each year must pass a tough written test, of which topics always include Dallas Cowboys' history, signals by NFL referees, and current events.

Each member of the squad has earned her position only for one season. If she chooses to return, she has to endure tryouts all over again. Sometimes "veterans" tearfully lose their places to talented rookies.

While football seasons last only five months, the cheerleaders are on duty all year. Besides entertaining at Texas Stadium during games, they also visit innumerable hospitals, schools, and nursing homes.

North Korean soldiers appreciate Cowboys Cheerleaders Cara Blackmon Harting and Kelli McGonagill Finglass, from left, at the North-South Korea border

Jo Smith visits patient at a care center

They lend their presence to every conceivable charitable program, from telethons to benefit concerts. Within the main group of cheerleaders, there's a 12-member "show group" that performs at conventions and non-football sports events.

After they've made the squad, members still must pass a weekly current-events quiz. Those who don't succeed face reprimands. Director Kelli McGonagill Finglass, herself a former squad member, explains that the cheerleaders constantly find themselves in every kind of public situation, so it's important they know about subjects other than football.

Night rehearsals are mandatory and may be called every night of the week. These usually last from 7:00 to 10:30 P.M. With performances and rehearsals, few nights are free. In August 1996, squad members had only two days off. That was still better than July, when they had just one.

Each season, almost every cheerleader is either in college or holds a full-time job. Outside income is important because they're paid just $15 per game. Of course, opportunities for extra income are available. Each cheerleader is paid $500 for personal appearances at store openings, car dealerships, and other business locations and events.

Over the years, many cheerleaders have earned graduate degrees, and it's not uncommon for them to spend their workdays as executives in major Dallas-area companies. Squad members believe that the skills they learn as cheerleaders can also benefit them in business.

It's rare for any cheerleader to stay on the squad more than four or five years. Many leave to get married or move on in their business careers. Physically, it's tough to maintain such a constant training regimen.

But those who do last a few seasons rave about their opportunities to travel. Off-seasons find the cheerleaders showing up at American military bases all over the world as they participate in USO shows. Recent stops have included Macedonia, Egypt, Korea, Israel, Japan, and Alaska. Homesick servicemen somehow find it comforting to spend a few minutes with some of the world's most famous women!

After nearly 25 seasons, the popularity of the Dallas Cowboys Cheerleaders shows no sign of slackening. But it takes hard work. A briefing book several hundred pages long is required reading; the squad rules for public behavior are far more stringent than any regulations set for football players by their coaches. To keep game and show programs fresh, it's a constant challenge to develop and master new dance routines, sometimes in as little as a week.

That's fine with the squad members. It's how they can be certain that the special affection of the public for the Dallas Cowboys Cheerleaders will last for generations to come.

◆

"There's more to earning a place on the squad than looking nice. When we take our show out for the USO or whatever, it includes dancing, singing, gymnastics. You've got to be physically fit. And then tryout finalists have to take a written test that's very hard. Its subjects include current events, referees' signals in the NFL, and the history of the Dallas Cowboys. Then if they make the squad, they have to pass weekly tests on current events. These girls have microphones and cameras in their faces all the time, and they need to be prepared to discuss any subject. They are."

—Kelli McGonagill Finglass

Calvin Hilll running against Cincinnati in 1973 game

1973 The draft yielded tight end Billy Joe DuPree, wide receiver Golden Richards, and defensive tackle Harvey Martin. There was also a free agent rookie receiver named Drew Pearson.

When they were added to the talented mix of veterans already on the Dallas roster, it seemed likely the Cowboys could reclaim the NFL East title from Washington and have a good chance to make it back to the Super Bowl.

Landry had just one major decision to make, and it was a relatively simple one. With Staubach healthy again, Landry installed him as the starting quarterback and returned Morton to the bench.

Dallas jumped to an early season 3-0 record, with a 40-3 trouncing of the New Orleans Saints bringing the franchise its one hundredth NFL victory. Then Dallas lost a 14-7 road game to the despised Redskins. The Rams ambushed the Cowboys on the next weekend, dropping Dallas to 3-2. A win over the Giants and a loss to the Eagles left the Cowboys with a 4-3 midseason record. Perhaps training camp optimism had been misplaced.

But Staubach was a fine leader, and he had no intention of letting his comeback season become a disappointment. Dallas won six of its last seven games, losing only 14-7 to the Dolphins in Miami. Both the Cowboys and Redskins finished 10-4, but Dallas won the NFC East because the Cowboys had scored more points in their two regular season matchups.

Dallas had scored a total of 382 points, second only to the 388 racked up by the Rams. The Dallas defense allowed 203, fourth-lowest in the league.

It was a banner statistical year for Staubach. He claimed his second

NFC passing crown by completing 179 of 286 attempts for 23 touchdowns and 15 interceptions. He scattered his passes among several favorite targets—Hill led the team with 32 receptions, followed by DuPree with 29, Garrison with 26, and Pearson and Hayes with 22 each.

On the ground, Hill rumbled for 1,142 yards, losing the league lead by just 2 yards to John Brockington of the Packers. Old reliable Garrison contributed 440 yards, and Robert Newhouse, being carefully groomed as Walt's successor at fullback, gained 436.

The Cowboys met the Rams in the opening playoff round, and they gained revenge for their regular season loss with a 27-16 win that was cemented only in the fourth quarter. Hill

rushed for 97 yards, and Pearson grabbed 2 touchdown passes from Staubach, the second one a late-game, 83-yard bomb that finally gave Dallas a comfortable lead. Many Cowboys fans hoped their heroes would meet the Redskins in a rematch of the 1972 NFC title game, but Washington was upset 27-20 by Minnesota in its first-round game.

That made it Dallas versus Minnesota for the right to go to Super Bowl VIII. The game was played in Bloomington. Both starting quarterbacks—Staubach for the Cowboys, Fran Tarkenton for the Vikings—completed just 10 of 21 passes, but Staubach was intercepted 3 times. Part of the problem was Calvin Hill's absence due to injury; Newhouse and Garrison combined for just 49 rushing

Drew Pearson

Calvin Hill, 35, follows Blaine Nye, 61, through the Redskins

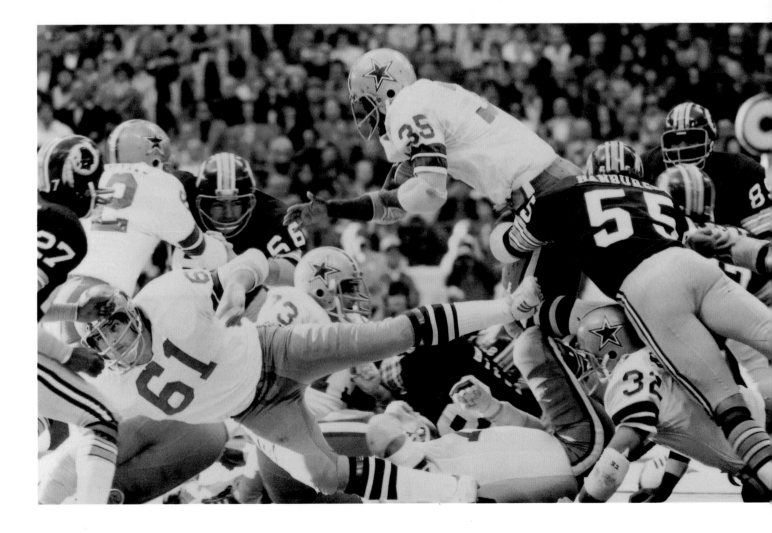

Landry instructs Benny Barnes during NFC title game with the Vikings

yards. Golden Richards's 63-yard punt return was the only touchdown scored by Dallas. Minnesota won easily, 27-10, and had the privilege of being annihilated by Miami in the Super Bowl.

So far, the Dolphins were clearly the glamour team of the seventies with their two Super Bowl titles to the Cowboys' one. There was some suspicion that age was beginning to weaken Dallas. Bob Hayes was no longer a premier receiver, and 1973 was the last season for steady linebacker Chuck Howley. Lee Roy Jordan and Bob Lilly were certainly nearing retirement.

Fortunately, no one knew what was coming in 1974.

1974 Training Camp at Thousand Oaks got off to a slow start. The NFL Players Association had declared a strike. The collegiate draft system and potential free agency were key issues, but the players also wanted smaller concessions from the owners, such as pay for

rookies playing in preseason games and per-diem meal allowances on road trips.

The team owners hung tough, and on August 14 the players came into training camp. They had failed completely to overhaul free agency and the draft; as consolation, they did win rookie preseason pay and per diem.

Landry was impatient to get going. For the first time in team history, the Cowboys had garnered the first choice in the draft's first round, acquired from the Houston Oilers in exchange for '73 draft bust Tody Smith and receiver Billy Parks. Dallas used the pick to select a defensive end from Tennessee State. Though few had heard of him at the time, Ed "Too Tall" Jones would soon be familiar to football fans everywhere.

Jones wasn't the only draft coup. In round three, Dallas drafted Arizona State quarterback Danny White, but he wouldn't join the Cowboys until 1976, after which he would spend three years as Staubach's backup.

There was another distraction. A new NFL rival, the World Football League (WFL), had been formed to begin play in 1974. The WFL made headlines by signing up some of the established league's premier players— Larry Csonka, Jim Kiick, and Paul Warfield being among the most notable. Danny White signed with the WFL, too, but as an unsigned draftee he had no contractual obligations to complete with an NFL club. In the case of veterans, the WFL's strategy was to sign them to future contracts that would begin as soon as the players' current NFL contracts expired.

Calvin Hill shocked Dallas by signing with the WFL for the 1975 season. This meant he'd be gone from the Cowboys roster immediately after 1974. That set back Landry's future plans considerably. Hill was

Cliff Harris, 43, and Charlie Waters, 41, watch action in 1974 St. Louis game

established as a premier runner, a rare commodity, and a player the Cowboys couldn't hope to replace anytime soon.

The Cowboys were distracted and stumbled early in the regular season. After shutting out Atlanta 24-0 in the season opener, Dallas lost four straight games to Philadelphia, the New York Giants, Minnesota, and St. Louis. Dallas hadn't gone four consecutive games without a win since 1965. By mid-October, the playoffs were certainly out of reach.

But pride kept the Cowboys competitive. They won their next four games, lost one, won three more, and lost the season finale 27-23 to the Oakland Raiders. Dallas's 8-6 season record dropped the Cowboys to third in the NFC East, behind St. Louis and Washington.

One game in 1974, though, would live forever in Cowboys fans' memories. On Thanksgiving Day, Dallas played Washington at Texas Stadium. The Redskins swaggered into

Walt Garrison, 32, in 1974 Vikings game

Cliff Harris defending against the 49ers

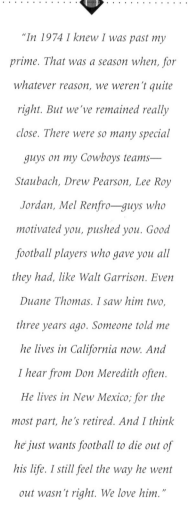

town and began to administer a physical beating to the Cowboys. With the score 9-3 in the third quarter, Redskins defenders knocked Roger Staubach senseless. Just weeks earlier, Schramm had honored Craig Morton's request to be traded, sending Dallas's only veteran backup to the Giants. The lone quarterback on the Cowboys bench was unheralded rookie Clint Longley. With no other option, Landry put the youngster in the game, and Longley led an incredible comeback that concluded with him tossing a 50-yard bomb to Pearson for the winning touchdown with just 28 seconds left to play.

Only two Cowboys had statistically gaudy seasons. Calvin Hill, in apparently his final year in Dallas, still played hard and finished third in NFC rushing with 844 yards. Pearson's first year as Dallas's primary receiver was stupendous. He caught 62 passes for 1,087 yards and 2 touchdowns.

As a team, the Cowboys were in the middle of the league's offensive and defensive standings. They scored 297 points, almost 100 fewer than in 1973 and their fewest for a full season since 1964. The defense allowed 235. Staubach completed 190 of 360 passes, but he had 15 interceptions and only 11 touchdown strikes. Bob Hayes, in his final year as a Cowboy, caught 7 passes for 118 yards and a touchdown.

While the Cowboys stayed at home, Pittsburgh beat Minnesota in Super Bowl IX. Not far down the road, Dallas would be the Steelers' Super Bowl opponent instead.

1975

In 1974, the Cowboys hadn't done as well as expected. In 1975, they exceeded expectations.

There seemed more cause for gloom than optimism. Bob Lilly, Cornell

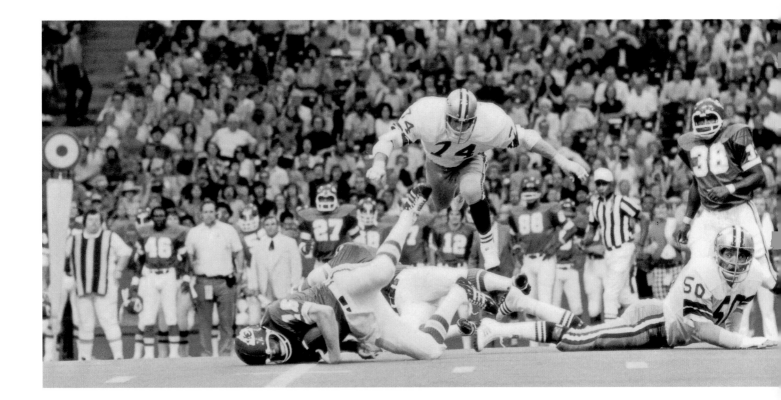

Green, and Walt Garrison retired. Hill was gone to the WFL. To replace him, the best the Cowboys could do was sign a Steelers castoff named Preston Pearson.

The college draft was far more significant than most observers first realized. Everyone had heard of Maryland's Randy White, the defensive end Dallas selected with their initial pick. But it wasn't until White and 11 other draftees made the Dallas roster that it became apparent Schramm,

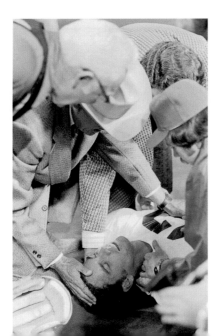

Medical team attends to Staubach in 1975 Kansas City game

Brandt, and Landry might have pulled off the best NFL draft of all time.

Linebacker Thomas "Hollywood" Henderson, guard Burton Lawless, linebacker Bob Breunig, offensive lineman Pat Donovan, defensive back Randy Hughes, cornerback Kyle Davis, defensive back Rolly Woolsey, linebacker Mike Hegman, punter Mitch Hoopes, guard Herb Scott, and running back Scott Laidlaw would all earn a spot on the Cowboys roster. A few—Davis, Hoopes, and Woolsey—would be gone after the season. The rest would make significant contributions for years. They were collectively dubbed "The Dirty Dozen."

On the strength of the 1975 draft alone, the Cowboys had rejoined the NFL elite.

Landry had another surprise for Dallas opponents. During the early

Bob Lilly flies against Kansas City in a 1974 game

◆

"*A lot of players had just retired. It turned out the '75 draft provided a number of outstanding players. Approximately twenty-five percent of the team was rookies. But our youth seemed to add a spark of life to the veteran players. Only one of us was a starter, Burton Lawless, and the rest of us were special teams players. At midseason we all grew beards, so we were dubbed The Dirty Dozen. Our class became the new nucleus.*"

—**BOB BREUNIG**

Robert Newhouse pounds through the Vikings line. John Fitzgerald is number 62, on the ground

Cowboys fans at chilly game against the Jets, 1975

1960s, San Francisco coach Red Hickey had introduced a unique offensive setup known as the "shotgun formation." On obvious passing plays, Hickey had his quarterback set up 5 to 7 yards behind center; the ball was snapped back to him through the air. This maneuver ostensibly saved a precious second in getting the pass off. Landry had previously tried to talk Don Meredith into giving the shotgun a try, but Meredith refused. Now Landry asked Staubach to test the shotgun, and Staubach became an instant convert. Cowboys opponents initially mocked the formation, but within years many teams included the shotgun in their offensive plans.

During the regular season, the Cowboys played steadily if not spectacularly. They opened the season with 4 victories, a squeaker 37-31 win over the Cardinals being especially satisfying since St. Louis was the defending NFC East champ. Old nemesis Green Bay handed Dallas its first 1975 defeat—this would be the last time the Packers remained dominant in the series.

The Cowboys won four of their next six. Newhouse's solid play com-

pensated for the loss of Hill. Preston Pearson was a godsend. The ex-Steeler was only average as a ball-carrier, but Landry discovered his new player was without equal at catching short passes out of the backfield.

There was a late-season loss to St. Louis, and a pair of victories against Washington and the New York Jets ended regular season play. Dallas hadn't quite regained the NFC East crown, but they were at least back in the playoffs as a wild card.

Dallas's end-of-season statistics were a pleasant contrast to those of 1974. The Cowboys were rejuvenated on offense; their 350 points scored was third in the league. Defensively, they surrendered 268; only three teams did better.

Newhouse had proved more than capable of filling Hill's shoes. He accumulated 930 yards rushing, third-best in the NFC, and added 34 receptions for 275 yards. Preston Pearson had 509 rushing yards and 27 catches. Doug Dennison often got the ball near the goal line; he had 383 yards and 7 touchdowns to 2 touchdowns each for Newhouse and Pearson. Drew Pearson, of course, led all Dallas receivers with 46 catches for 822 yards and 8 touchdowns.

After his off-year in 1974, Staubach had returned to top form. He completed 198 of 348 attempts for 17 touchdowns with 16 interceptions. That performance placed him second among NFC passers, behind Fran Tarkenton of Minnesota.

And it was Tarkenton's Vikings the Cowboys faced in the first round of the playoffs. As the wild-card team, Dallas had to travel to Minnesota. The crowd was hostile, and the Vikings, who had finished the regular season with a gaudy 12-2 record, were favored.

It was a tough, close game. A 1-yard plunge by Minnesota running back Chuck Foreman and the subsequent extra-point kick gave the Vikings

a 7-0 halftime lead. Minnesota's rugged defense was containing, if not entirely stopping, Newhouse, Dennison, and Preston Pearson. Staubach was completing more than half his passes, but the Vikings defense always was able to make a key tackle and thwart a Dallas drive.

Finally, in the third quarter, Dennison scored on a 4-yard run. Fritsch kicked the extra point, and the game was tied. In the final period Fritsch put the Cowboys ahead with a field goal, but Tarkenton rallied the Vikings, and they went ahead, apparently for good, on a touchdown and extra point.

Down 14-10, Dallas faced the almost insurmountable dilemma of fourth and 18 on their own 25-yard line with just 44 seconds left to play. Staubach cooly completed a 25-yard pass to Drew Pearson, who fell out of bounds on the 50. As he sprawled

Preston Pearson moves against the Rams

there, a stadium security guard kicked him in the ribs and walked away. Somehow, Pearson returned to the Dallas huddle.

After an incomplete pass to Preston Pearson, Staubach set up again in the shotgun. Drew Pearson tore down the sideline, covered by Vikings defensive back Nate Wright. Wright had Pearson covered, but Staubach had no choice. He threw the ball high and deep. As Pearson and

Wright both went up for the ball, they collided. Wright was knocked down; somehow, Pearson managed to cradle the ball against his hip and tiptoe into the end zone. The Vikings screamed for offensive pass interference, but an official who had been on top of the play signaled a Dallas touchdown.

A whiskey bottle hurtled out of the stands and struck the official in the head, dazing him, but the final gun sounded and Dallas had won 17-14.

Jubilant Cowboys

"After making that catch for the first down, I came back to the huddle on about the 50. Roger said, 'What do you have?' meaning what route did I think I could beat the defenders on. I said, 'Roger, wait a minute. I got no breath.' So he called a pass to Preston Pearson; he threw him a short pass in the middle of the field. Preston, who never dropped a ball, dropped this one. I consider this part of the blessing of the 'Hail Mary' pass. We had no time-outs. If Preston had caught that ball, the clock would have run out. So we got back in the huddle. Roger looked at the clock and said, 'We've got to go. You remember that route you ran last Thanksgiving to beat the Redskins?' I did—we called it the 'turn in and take off' route. I wanted to fake inside, get [Vikings defender] Nate Wright to bite, and then cut downfield. Well, Nate bit a little. As we ran down the field we were about even, and I thought I could beat him with what I thought of as my going-to-the-football gear. I wasn't real fast, but I could kick it in a little to get to a ball. I hoped Roger would throw the ball quicker, but he was putting a fake on [Vikings safety] Paul Krause. When he finally put the ball up I could see that it was underthrown. I was able to plant my outside foot and lean back to it. I used a 'swim move,' bringing one arm over. There was contact between me and Wright, but no deliberate push by either one of us. The ball arrived as we both went up, and I knew I'd dropped the pass. But I came down bent over, and somehow the ball stuck between my elbow and my hip. They say the fans were surprised, but I was surprised, too. I backed into the end zone untouched. I remember that the stadium got so quiet. When you're a player in an opposing stadium that's what you hope for, no noise from the home team's fans. I made a lot of other plays I think were better than the 'Hail Mary,' but that one play just made my career."

—DREW PEARSON

In the uproarious Cowboys locker room after the game, Staubach, a staunch Catholic, admitted he'd muttered a "Hail Mary" as he released the ball. Reporters immediately began referring to the "Hail Mary Pass," which probably remains the most famous play in Cowboys history.

After the miracle in Minnesota, the NFC championship game in Los Angeles against the Rams didn't worry Dallas a bit. The Rams had won their NFC West title with defense; they'd allowed just 135 points all season. It made no difference to the Cowboys as they crushed the heavily favored Rams, 37-7. Dallas was back in the Super Bowl, where they would encounter the defending champion Steelers.

Staubach fades to pass, and Pearson somehow makes the famous "Hail Mary" catch

SUPER BOWL X

Miami had won two Super Bowls in the 1970s; Pittsburgh had won one, as had Dallas. But the Dolphins and Steelers championships had followed that of the Cowboys; Dallas players viewed their meeting with Pittsburgh in Miami's Orange Bowl as a great opportunity to establish their own claim to recognition as the best team of the decade.

Despite Dallas's miracle win against the Vikings and the Cowboys' drubbing of the Rams, the Steelers came to Super Bowl X as prohibitive favorites. They were a powerful, even frightening team. On offense, Terry Bradshaw, Franco Harris, Lynn Swann, and John Stallworth were all household names. The "Steel Curtain" defense, led by Mean Joe Greene, was

Mel Renfro, 20, and Cliff Harris break up a pass to John Stallworth in Super Bowl X

known to consider dirty play a Pittsburgh prerogative. The Steelers beat opponents by intimidating them.

Dallas received the opening kick-off and immediately tried a trick play. Ex-Steeler Preston Pearson took the kick, headed upfield, then handed off to rookie linebacker Thomas Henderson, who was perhaps the best natural athlete among the Cowboys. Henderson raced past the befuddled Steelers for 53 yards before kicker Roy Gerela knocked him out of bounds.

The Cowboys couldn't move the ball on offense and punted. The Steelers offense stalled, too. But on a fourth-down punt, Pittsburgh kicker Bobby Walden dropped the ball. Dallas recovered on the Steelers' 29, and Staubach found Drew Pearson alone in the Pittsburgh end zone. It was 7-0, Dallas.

Ninety seconds later, the Steelers scored on a 7-yard pass from Bradshaw to tight end Randy Grossman. The game stayed tied until the final seconds of the second quarter, when Fritsch kicked a 36-yard field goal to send the Cowboys into the locker room with a 10-7 halftime lead.

Neither team could score during a hard-fought third quarter, but most of the final period belonged to the Steelers. Pittsburgh blocked a punt through the Dallas end zone for a safety; a Staubach interception resulted in a 36-yard Gerela field goal. He kicked another from 18 yards just 2 minutes later.

With 3 minutes left, Bradshaw faded back to pass. Cliff Harris and D.D. Lewis broke through the Steelers line. As Bradshaw heaved the ball, Harris crashed into the Pittsburgh quarterback and knocked him out. Until he was revived in the Steelers dressing room, Bradshaw didn't know that Lynn Swann, his acrobatic wide receiver, had caught the pass 64 yards down-field for a touchdown. Dallas blocked the extra point, but the damage had been done.

Now the Cowboys trailed 21-10, and their Cinderella season apparently was over. Someone forgot to tell Staubach. He drove the Cowboys down the field, finally throwing a 34-yard scoring pass to receiver Percy Howard. With 1:48 left to play, Dallas trailed 21-17.

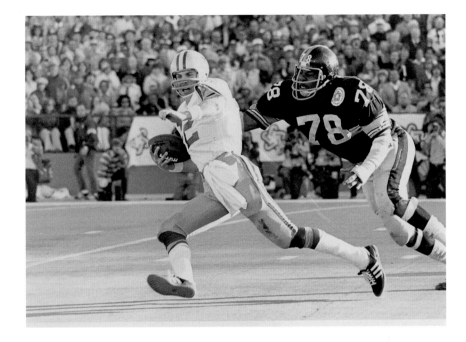

Staubach was always a running threat

Of course, the Cowboys tried an onside kick. Pittsburgh recovered on the Dallas 42. Three straight times the Steelers ran into the middle of the Cowboys line, and the total they gained was 1 yard. On fourth down, Pittsburgh coach Chuck Noll decided not to punt. He sent running back Rocky Bleier up the middle on fourth and 9, and Bleier was stopped after getting 3 yards. Unbelievably, Dallas had the ball on its own 39-yard line with 1:22 left on the clock.

Staubach, Super Bowl X quarterback

The miracle almost happened. Staubach scrambled for 11 yards and hit Preston Pearson for 12 more. The Cowboys had reached the Pittsburgh 38 with 22 seconds to go in the game. But Staubach threw one incomplete pass and had another batted down by the Steelers defensive line. His final pass was another Hail Mary heave into Pittsburgh's end zone. Steeler Glen Edwards intercepted, and Pittsburgh had won its second consecutive Super Bowl.

SUPER BOWL X STATISTICS

SCORING

Pittsburgh	7	0	0	14	**21**
Dallas	7	3	0	7	**17**

FIRST QUARTER:
Dallas, Drew Pearson 29-yard pass from Staubach (Fritsch kick)
Pittsburgh, Grossman 7-yard pass from Bradshaw (Gerela kick)

SECOND QUARTER:
Dallas, Fritsch 36-yard field goal

THIRD QUARTER:
None

FOURTH QUARTER:
Pittsburgh, safety (Harrison blocked Dallas punt out of end zone)
Pittsburgh, Gerela 36-yard field goal
Pittsburgh, Gerela 18-yard field goal
Pittsburgh, Swann 64-yard pass from Bradshaw (kick blocked)
Dallas, Howard 34-yard pass from Staubach (Fritsch kick)

TEAM	PITTSBURGH	DALLAS
First downs	13	14
Net yards	339	270
Fumbles lost	0	0
Interceptions	0	3
Penalty yards	0	20

INDIVIDUAL:

RUSHING
Dallas: Newhouse 56; Staubach 22; Dennison 16; P. Pearson 14
Pittsburgh: F. Harris 82; Bleier 51; Bradshaw 16

PASSING
Dallas: Staubach 15-24, 204 yards, 2 touchdowns
Pittsburgh: Bradshaw 9-19, 209 yards, 1 touchdown

RECEIVING
Dallas: P. Pearson 5-53, Young 3-31, D.Pearson 2-59, Newhouse 2-12, Howard 1-34, Fugett 1-9, Dennison 1-6
Pittsburgh: Swann 4-161, Stallworth 2-8, F. Harris 1-26, L. Brown 1-7, Grossman 1-7

Bob Lilly puts a jacket on Don Meredith, who was inducted into the Ring of Honor

1976 The Cowboys came into training camp as one of the preseason favorites to win the NFC title. The new faces included draftees Aaron Kyle of Wyoming at defensive back, a wide receiver/kick returner from University of California at Riverside named Butch Johnson, offensive lineman Tom Rafferty from Penn State, and defensive back Beasley Reece from North Texas.

For a moment there was an old face. Duane Thomas, fresh from the newly folded WFL, asked Landry for a tryout. Thomas failed to make the team, but he and Landry parted on better terms this time.

Unlike the previous two seasons, Dallas never went through a worrisome losing streak in 1976. The Cowboys roared out of the blocks with five straight wins, and only a 30-27 victory over the Colts was especially close. St. Louis beat Dallas 21-17 in the sixth week. The Cowboys won four more games before succumbing 17-10 to Atlanta. It was the Falcons' first win over the Cowboys; Atlanta wouldn't

beat Dallas again for 10 years. The Cowboys beat the Cardinals and Eagles and lost at home to the Redskins in the final game of the regular schedule. At 11-3, Dallas was back on top of the NFC East, with St. Louis and Washington tied for second at 10-4.

The 296 points Dallas scored during the season were fourth-best in the league; only three teams allowed fewer points than the 194 yielded by the Cowboys defense. Staubach, backed up by WFL returnee Danny White, completed 208 of 369 passes for 2,715 yards, 14 touchdowns, and 11 interceptions. Those were the most passes Landry had called since the early run-for-cover days of LeBaron and Meredith, but in 1976 the Cowboys were passing more for a simple reason: Dallas lacked a breakaway threat at running back.

Dennison led the team in rushing with 542 yards. Newhouse ran for 450 yards, Scott Laidlaw for 424. When the Cowboys ground game was working most effectively, their

The coach and his team, 1976

efforts still resulted in a string of 3-, 3-, and 5-yard gains.

So Staubach threw to move Dallas down the field. His favorite targets were Drew Pearson, who led the NFC with 58 catches for 806 yards and 6 touchdowns; DuPree, who had become a premier tight end with 42 catches good for 680 yards; and backs Laidlaw and Preston Pearson.

That offensive strategy got the Cowboys through the regular season and won them the NFC East, but it wasn't enough in the playoffs. The Rams, still smarting from 1975's 37-7 thrashing by Dallas, eked out a 14-12 win that sent the Cowboys home. Ignoring Dallas running backs, Los Angeles essentially shut down the Cowboys passing game. Staubach finished with only 15 completions in 37 attempts. He had no touchdown passes, but he threw 3 interceptions. Schramm and Landry took note. The Cowboys wouldn't go another season without a running back who could offer opponents cause for serious concern.

1977
The Seattle Seahawks had suffered through a miserable 2-12 season in their first year as an NFL expansion franchise.

Things looked bleak for 1977; stocked with castoffs from established teams, the Seahawks needed help at almost every position.

Tex Schramm understood. He sympathized. Hey, he'd been there in 1960. And he had a great offer for Seattle. Dallas would give the Seahawks the Cowboys' first-round draft pick, the twenty-second overall, and three second-round picks Schramm had acquired through previous wheelings and dealings. Seattle could use those picks to draft four good players. In return, all Dallas wanted was Seattle's first-round pick, the second overall in the draft. Seattle made the trade.

On draft day the Cowboys watched happily as Tampa Bay, a second expansion team that picked first by virtue of an 0-14 inaugural season, made its selection—Heisman Trophy winner Ricky Bell, a running back from Southern California. Then it was the Cowboys' turn, and they got the player they wanted—Pittsburgh running back Tony Dorsett, who lacked Bell's bulk but easily surpassed him in speed and agility.

In later rounds, Dallas added linebacker Guy Brown from Houston,

Preston Pearson and a Bear are separated

Golden Richards scores against the Vikings in NFC title game

Cowboys converge on Walter Payton of the Bears

◆

"We had as good a team as Dallas

has ever had."

—Roger Staubach

offensive lineman Andy Frederick of New Mexico, tackle Jim Cooper of Temple, and a wide receiver from Stanford named Tony Hill. Any other year, those four, especially Hill, would have been enough to label 1977's draft as a benchmark.

But it was Dorsett the Cowboys had to have. The kid arrived at training camp and announced he was changing the pronunciation of his name from DOR-sett to Dor-SETT. Then he settled in as Preston Pearson's backup; when it came to the skill positions, Landry wasn't going to give a free ride to any rookie.

Blaine Nye and Lee Roy Jordan had retired, having been great players for Dallas for a long time. But the 1977 Cowboys had more than enough depth to compensate. On defense, Randy White, Harvey Martin, Too Tall Jones, and Jethro Pugh were a

formidable front four. Brainy Bob Breunig anchored things at middle line-backer. Mel Renfro was still around, and Cliff Harris and Charlie Waters seemed to improve every year.

On offense, Staubach was in his prime. Pat Donovan, Ralph Neely, and Rayfield Wright were among the monsters of the line who protected him. Drew Pearson was the NFC's best wide receiver; Billy Joe DuPree was a terrific tight end; and in the backfield Robert Newhouse and Preston Pearson were now augmented by the break-away speed of Dorsett. Landry felt confident, and with good reason.

All the 1977 Cowboys did was match the franchise's previous best season record of 12-2. Dallas won its first seven games, steamrolling most opponents and finding ways to win in the close ones. Newhouse was having a great season. Time and again, Preston

Pearson picked up big first downs by snaring short Staubach catches and turning upfield for the necessary yards. Staubach himself was nothing short of magnificent. And during those moments in the game that Landry let Dorsett see action, the rookie astounded defenders with his slippery moves.

It was obvious Dorsett had to replace Preston Pearson in the starting lineup. When the Cowboys lost their first game of the year to St. Louis, Landry had his opportunity. Pearson was still a valuable Cowboy; on third downs, he was always back on the field. But Dorsett often made third-down plays unnecessary; one of his touchdown runs, an 83-yarder, was the longest in the league that season.

Pittsburgh hung a 28-13 loss on the Cowboys in the season's tenth week. It served as a good reminder that the other top teams weren't necessarily worse because the Cowboys were so much better. Dallas shrugged off the defeat and won its last four regular season games.

The season statistics spoke for themselves. Though he only started a handful of games, Dorsett still finished fourth among NFC rushers with 1,007 yards. Newhouse finished with 721; his output was aided by the attention defenses had to pay to Dorsett. Drew Pearson led team receivers with 48 catches for 870 yards, good for third place in the league; Preston Pearson wasn't far behind with 46 catches for 535 yards. Staubach led all NFC passers with 210 completions in 361 attempts, finishing with 18 touchdowns and just 9 interceptions.

As a team, Dallas scored 345 points and allowed 212. The former total led the NFC; the latter was sixth-best. The Cowboys entered the playoffs as a heavy favorite to represent the NFC in Super Bowl XII.

They should have been favored. In a first-round game, Dallas brushed aside the Chicago Bears 37-7. The game was so one-sided that Staubach passed only 13 times, completing 8. The NFC championship game matched Dallas with Minnesota, and this time the Cowboys didn't need any Hail Mary passes. They romped, 23-6.

The Cowboys might have hoped Pittsburgh took the AFC title; a chance to avenge the Super Bowl X loss would have been welcome. Failing that, the tough Oakland Raiders were good bets to become the AFC champs. But lightly regarded Denver upset the Steelers in the first round and Oakland in the championship game. It was the Broncos defense, led by Lyle Alzado, Randy Gradishar, and Tom Jackson that made the difference for Denver. Dallas would meet the Broncos in the New Orleans Superdome.

"I sat out most of the preseason and didn't start until the tenth game. Finally, Landry sat me down and talked about my work ethic and what he expected from me, and something got through."

—TONY DORSETT
Dallas Cowboys running back
1977-87

Tony Dorsett runs on the Redskins

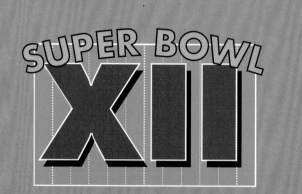

SUPER BOWL XII

Super Bowl XII was the first to be played indoors, and from the beginning of the game, Denver players must have thought the Superdome roof was caving in on them.

The main Broncos defensive strategy was to shut down Dorsett and Drew Pearson. Denver did manage to hold Dorsett to 66 yards rushing and a single touchdown. They did even better with Drew Pearson, limiting him to 1 catch for 13 yards. But the Cowboys had many other offensive weapons, and Landry made good use of them all. Preston Pearson caught 5 passes for 37 yards. Billy Joe DuPree got behind Denver defenders and snagged 4 balls for 66 yards.

Tony Dorsett slips through the tackle of Denver's Bob Swenson in Super Bowl XII

"Against Denver, I remember two plays, two touchdown passes. The first pass was the most important. It's hard to say whether Butch Johnson dropped it or not. I don't think it was a bad call, myself. And the Robert Newhouse pass was incredible. He'd never thrown one before. But we wanted to work on their right corner, and we thought if Roger tossed the ball to Robert, their corner would come up on the play. Golden Richards made a good catch. But the whole thing was funny because when Roger called the play, you could see Robert break out of the huddle and start licking his hands. He had a lot of stickum on them, and he had to try to lick the stuff off so he could throw the ball. I think this was our very best team overall."

—TOM LANDRY

Butch Johnson makes a sensational catch

Dallas got 13 points in the first half, which was plenty since Denver couldn't score at all. The Cowboys front four assaulted the Denver quarterback, whom many from Dallas considered an old friend. Craig Morton was starting in another Super Bowl, but, as in his Super Bowl V experience with Dallas, he wasn't going to win. This time, in fact, he was battered so badly he was forced out of the game early on. Before he left, Morton threw four interceptions.

In the third quarter, Denver finally got on the scoreboard with a 47-yard field goal. Dallas retaliated with a drive that ended with Butch Johnson's spectacular touchdown catch of Staubach's 45-yard pass. For a change, the Cowboys finally got the benefit of a controversial Super Bowl call. Some film angles indicated Johnson might have dropped the ball.

Tex Schramm celebrates the victory

Down 20-3, Denver gamely came back. Rick Upchurch returned the Dallas kickoff 63 yards to the Cowboys 29. Rob Lytle capped a short scoring drive with a 1-yard touchdown plunge. At quarter's end it was 20-10. The Cowboys were dominating, but a few bad breaks could still cost them the game. On the sideline, Landry called "Brown right, X-opposite shift, toss 38, halfback lead fullback pass to Y." Robert Newhouse was supposed to throw a long option pass to Golden Richards. Despite a lot of stickum on his hands, Newhouse completed the pass as instructed. The 29-yard touchdown cinched the game for Dallas. The Cowboys had won Super Bowl XII, 27-10.

Receiver Butch Johnson celebrates touchdown against Broncos

SUPER BOWL XII STATISTICS

SCORING

Dallas	10	3	7	7	**27**
Denver	0	0	10	0	**10**

FIRST QUARTER:
Dallas, Dorsett 3-yard run (Herrera kick)
Dallas, Herrera 35-yard field goal

SECOND QUARTER:
Dallas, Herrera 43-yard field goal

THIRD QUARTER:
Denver, Turner 47-yard field goal
Dallas, Johnson 45-yard pass from Staubach (Herrera kick)
Denver, Lytle 1-yard run (Turner kick)

FOURTH QUARTER:
Dallas, Richards 29-yard pass from Newhouse (Herrera kick)

TEAM	DALLAS	DENVER
First downs	17	11
Net yards	325	156
Fumbles lost	2	4
Interceptions	0	4
Penalty yards	94	60

INDIVIDUAL:
RUSHING
Dallas: Dorsett 66, Newhouse 55, D. White 13, P. Pearson 11, Staubach 6, Laidlaw 1, Johnson 9
Denver: Lytle 35, Armstrong 27, Weese 26, Jensen 16, Keyworth 9, Perrin 8

PASSING
Dallas: Staubach 17-25, 183 yards, 1 touchdown; Danny White 1-2, 5 yards; Newhouse 1-1, 29 yards, 1 touchdown
Denver: Morton 4-15, 39 yards; Weese 4-10, 22 yards

RECEIVING
Dallas: P. Pearson 5-37, DuPree 4-66, Newhouse 3-(-1), Johnson 2-53, Richards 2-38, Dorsett 2-11, D. Pearson 1-13
Denver: Dolbin 2-24, Odoms 2-9, Moses 1-21, Upchurch 1-9, Jensen 1-5, Perrin 1-(-7)

Jim Otis tries to score against the Doomsday Defense—Cowboys vs. St. Louis, 1978

1978 After their Super Bowl victory, the Cowboys were clearly a superior football team. A few NFC clubs might have matched their explosive offense; one or two others, perhaps, were defensively equal. But based on balance and sheer talent, Dallas seemed a notch above any other NFC team and was matched only by Pittsburgh in the AFC.

That remained true even though the 1978 draft didn't yield the usual batch of blue-chippers. Larry Bethea, a defensive lineman from Michigan State, was selected in the first round and spent six undistinguished seasons in Dallas. Of the rest, only eleventh-round choice Dennis Thurman, a safety from Southern California, eventually became a starter.

There were no significant player retirements. Landry prepared to defend the Cowboys' title with essentially the same cast that had won Super Bowl XII.

The new season got off to a rousing start with a 38-0 shutout of Baltimore at Texas Stadium. But a solid win over the Giants was followed by a well-deserved 27-14 loss to the Rams

in Los Angeles. Dallas shrugged, beat St. Louis, and then lost a weird 9-5 game to Washington at RFK Stadium.

With the NFL's new 16-game regular season schedule, Landry had a little more time to tinker with his club and to make any necessary adjustments. The Cowboys responded with three straight wins, but two were close, and one, against the Cardinals, went into overtime.

Then Dallas sputtered again, losing consecutive games to Minnesota and Miami. Ten games into the season, the supposedly elite Cowboys were in the middle of the NFL pack at 6-4.

Talent eventually told. Dallas won its last six games, including a satisfying 42-14 clobbering of the Packers in Green Bay. The Cowboys cruised to a 12-4 finish, with everybody healthy for the playoffs.

Even with its mini-slumps, Dallas still hit statistical heights (with totals increased from 1977, of course, by two additional regular season games).

Dorsett's 1,325 yards rushing placed him second in the NFC, behind Walter Payton. Newhouse had run a

little less, for 584 yards, but only because Scott Laidlaw had developed into a dependable third running back with 312 rushing yards of his own. Preston Pearson continued to do what he did best; he led all Dallas receivers with 47 catches good for 526 yards.

Staubach had another great season, completing 231 of 413 passes for 25 touchdowns and 16 interceptions. Besides Preston Pearson, his favorite targets were second-year receiver Tony Hill (46 catches, 823 yards, 6 touchdowns) and reliable veteran Drew Pearson (44 catches, 714 yards, 3 touchdowns).

As a team, Dallas scored the most points in the NFC, 384, and allowed the fewest, 208. The Cowboys were expected to waltz through the playoffs and meet the eventual AFC champion in Miami's Orange Bowl.

The Atlanta Falcons thought otherwise. A new NFL playoff format gave two wild-card teams the chance to play for the right to advance. The Falcons edged the Eagles 14-13 and advanced to face the Cowboys in Texas Stadium. It took a fourth-quarter touchdown by Laidlaw to hold off Atlanta, 27-20. Dallas actually trailed 20-13 at the half.

The Cowboys moved on to Los Angeles, where they faced the Rams for the NFC crown. Both defenses rose to the occasion; the game was a scoreless tie at halftime. It seemed that the first team to score would probably win the game, and in the third period the Cowboys finally got into the Rams' end zone. Charlie Waters returned an interception all the way to the Los Angeles 10, and Dorsett punched the ball in from there.

The Rams took the ensuing kickoff and forced Dallas deep into its own territory. But the Cowboys defense held on fourth and 1 at the Dallas 13. By the time the game ended, the

Cowboys had tacked on three more touchdowns, with Thomas Henderson's 68-yard interception return capping the 28-0 shutout.

In Super Bowl XII, Dallas had won it all without having to face Pittsburgh. However, the Steelers weren't going to miss Super Bowl XIII. They easily handled the Broncos and Oilers and headed for Miami determined to regain the title they considered rightfully theirs.

Randy White hunts down a quarterback

Drew Pearson pulls in a pass in front of two Eagles

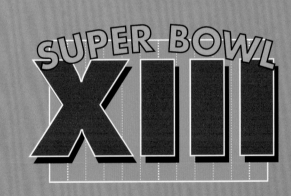

SUPER BOWL XIII

Many Super Bowls pit one great team against an overmatched club that lucked its way to the big game with fluke wins over superior opponents. But Super Bowl XIII had the matchup most football fans wanted—the Cowboys versus the Steelers, the two best teams in professional football facing each other in a showdown that guaranteed thrills.

Seventeen years later, many still consider this Dallas-Pittsburgh clash to be the greatest Super Bowl of all. Both teams played well, at least most of the time; great plays were sometimes followed by inexplicable miscues. One of those would eventually do in Dallas.

The Steelers went into the game irked at Thomas Henderson. The mouthy Cowboy linebacker talked his way into headlines by guaranteeing

"Super Bowl XIII's the one where Hollywood Henderson said that Terry Bradshaw couldn't spell 'cat' if you gave him the 'c' and the 'a.' After Henderson stripped the ball from Bradshaw, we got back into our huddle. Franco Harris, who never said a lot but who could get real emotional, said, 'Give me the football.' And then he broke one off the left side for a score."

—ROCKY BLEIER

Tony Dorsett at work

a Dallas win. He then proceeded to insult the intelligence of Pittsburgh quarterback Terry Bradshaw, calling him "so dumb he couldn't spell 'cat' if you spotted him the c and the a." Henderson's own teammates told him to shut up, but it was too late.

Dallas took the opening kickoff and simply ran the ball down the Steelers' throats. When the drive reached the Pittsburgh 34, Landry tried a trick play. Staubach handed off to Dorsett, who gave the ball to Drew Pearson on an apparent reverse. But Pearson pulled up to pass to a wide-open Billy Joe DuPree. It looked like a sure Cowboys touchdown, but Pearson dropped the ball and Pittsburgh recovered. Bradshaw demonstrated his intelligence by leading a 7 play drive that ended with the maligned quarterback firing a 28-yard touchdown strike to John Stallworth.

Dallas had a pretty smart quarterback, too. The Cowboys took the kickoff and launched a long drive of their

Mike Hegman scores a Super Bowl touchdown

own. Staubach hit Hill from 39 yards out, and the first quarter ended in a 7-7 deadlock.

Thomas Henderson got a measure of revenge early in the second quarter. He and linebacker Mike Hegman tackled Bradshaw behind the line of scrimmage. The officials didn't whistle the play dead; Hegman stole the ball from Bradshaw and raced 37 yards to put the Cowboys ahead.

The experienced Steelers didn't crack. Instead, they stifled the Dallas offense for the rest of the period and scored two touchdowns of their own. Bradshaw hit Stallworth with a 75-yard bomb and running back Rocky Bleier with a 7-yard toss. At halftime the Steelers led 21-14. Bradshaw had already passed for a Super Bowl record 253 yards, and there were still two quarters to play.

Only Dallas scored in the third quarter, on Rafael Septien's 27-yard field goal. The Cowboys, though, didn't take much pleasure from the three points. After dominating play for most of the period, they'd driven close to the Steelers goal line. Staubach dropped back to pass and veteran tight end Jackie Smith, who had been added to the roster to provide a seasoned pair of hands, broke free in the end zone. Staubach threw to the

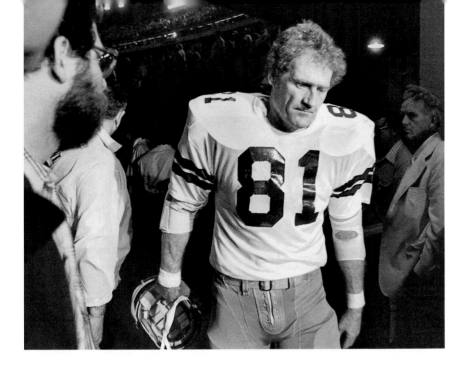

Jackie Smith after dropping a crucial pass

wide-open receiver, and Smith dropped the ball. Smith fell on his back and kicked his legs in absolute frustration and anguish. Instead of having a 21-21 tie, Dallas still trailed 21-17 after making the field goal.

The four lost points would prove fatal. On Pittsburgh's next possession, the Steelers were helped immeasurably by a questionable pass-interference call. Bradshaw threw a long pass in the direction of wideout Lynn Swann, who was closely covered by Dallas's Benny Barnes. Some Cowboys insisted later that Bradshaw was trying to throw the ball away. In any event, the feet of Swann and Barnes tangled up, and Barnes was called for the foul. The

Steelers were too canny not to take advantage of the break; Franco Harris scored on a 22-yard run. It was 28-17.

Things quickly got worse for Dallas. The Cowboys fumbled Pittsburgh's kickoff and the Steelers recovered. Bradshaw threw an 18-yard touchdown pass to Swann; it was now 35-17 and Pittsburgh had scored 14 points in 20 seconds. Less than 7 minutes were left in the game.

Staubach used some of that time to engineer the Cowboys' first long,

"Our second Super Bowl with Pittsburgh was a great game. The turning point was a questionable interference call against Bennie Barnes. It really hurt us. What people remember most is the pass to Jackie Smith in the end zone. Really, Roger tried to throw the ball a little too easily. Jackie was expecting a stronger throw. He tried to grab it, but he didn't catch it. We couldn't say anything to him afterward; everybody felt bad for him. Jackie was a class guy. His son was there with him in the locker room after the game. That play just about broke his heart. All Jackie wanted was to win a Super Bowl."

—TOM LANDRY

An emotional Tom Landry

A triumphant moment for Hollywood Henderson, 56

successful drive since the first quarter. Billy Joe DuPree caught a 7-yard pass from Staubach for a touchdown—35-24, and 2:23 left.

Both teams knew an onside kick was coming; Dallas recovered it, and Staubach moved the Cowboys again. Butch Johnson caught a 4-yard touchdown pass. With 22 seconds left, the score was 35-31. Dallas tried another onside kick, but Pittsburgh got the ball. Bradshaw downed the ball twice, and Super Bowl XIII was over.

The close loss frustrated the Cowboys. They would have been more frustrated if they'd known Dallas wouldn't be back in the Super Bowl for 14 years.

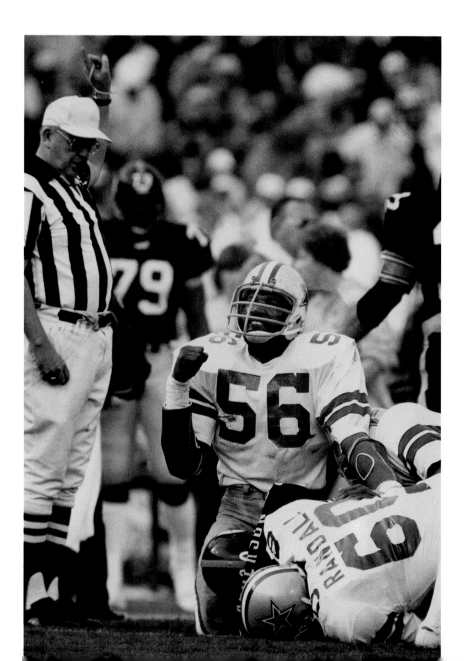

SUPER BOWL XIII STATISTICS

SCORING

Pittsburgh	7	14	0	14	**35**
Dallas	7	7	3	14	**31**

FIRST QUARTER:
Pittsburgh, Stallworth 28-yard pass from Bradshaw (Gerela kick)
Dallas, Hill 39-yard pass from Staubach (Septien kick)

SECOND QUARTER:
Dallas, Hegman 37-yard fumble return (Septien kick)
Pittsburgh, Stallworth 75-yard pass from Bradshaw (Gerela kick)
Pittsburgh, Bleier 7-yard pass from Bradshaw (Gerela kick)

THIRD QUARTER:
Dallas, Septien 27-yard field goal

FOURTH QUARTER:
Pittsburgh, Harris 22-yard run (Gerela kick)
Pittsburgh, Swann 18-yard pass from Bradshaw (Gerela kick)
Dallas, DuPree 7-yard pass from Staubach (Septien kick)
Dallas, Johnson 4-yard pass from Staubach (Septien kick)

TEAM	PITTSBURGH	DALLAS
First downs	19	20
Net yards	357	330
Fumbles lost	2	2
Interceptions	1	1
Penalty yards	35	89

INDIVIDUAL:
RUSHING
Dallas: Dorsett 96, Staubach 37, Laidlaw 12, P. Pearson 6, Newhouse 3
Pittsburgh: Harris 68, Bleier 3, Bradshaw (-5)

PASSING
Dallas: Staubach 17-30, 228 yards, 3 touchdowns
Pittsburgh: Bradshaw 17-30, 318 yards, 4 touchdowns

RECEIVING
Dallas: Dorsett 5-44, D. Pearson 4-73, Hill 2-49, Johnson 2-30, DuPree 2-17, P. Pearson 2-15
Pittsburgh: Swann 7-124, Stallworth 3-115, Grossman 3-29, Bell 2-21, Harris 1-22, Bleier 1-7

1979 In some ways, Dallas felt snakebitten before the season even started. Jethro Pugh retired. Charlie Waters injured a knee in preseason and was out for the year. Too Tall Jones retired to become a boxer, of all things. Center Robert Shaw of Tennessee, running back Ron Springs from Ohio State, and Santa Clara tight end Doug Cosbie arrived via the draft. Still, for once it seemed that off-season additions might not make up for the players who had been lost.

Things initially went well enough, even spectacularly. Dallas won its first three games, lost badly to the Cleveland Browns, then won four straight. At 7-1, they were primed to visit Pittsburgh for a rare regular season meeting with the Steelers. This game didn't reach the same dramatic heights as Super Bowls X and XIII. Pittsburgh won comfortably, 14-3. It was the

Cowboys fan at 1979 playoff game with the Rams

fewest points the Cowboys had scored in a game since 1972.

Dallas edged out the Giants 16-14 in the season's tenth week, and then things really got bad. The Cowboys lost consecutive games against Philadelphia, Washington, and Houston. Landry was perplexed; after the Redskins loss he arbitrarily cut Thomas Henderson, citing the player's poor attitude.

"AMERICA'S TEAM"

★

After each season, personnel at NFL Films put together highlight films of each team's games. After editor Bob Ryan prepared the tape of the Dallas Cowboys following Super Bowl XIII, he had to come up with a title. By 1978, the Cowboys had been on national television far more than any other NFL franchise. Dallas players, from Roger Staubach to Tony Dorsett to Randy White to Too Tall Jones to Harvey Martin, and on and on, were household names regularly featured on billboards and in television, radio, and print advertising. Considering the team's popularity—or notoriety, a term Cowboys haters preferred—Ryan came up with the title of "America's Team." It caught on.

Tom Landry hated the appellation. He thought it would provide extra incentive to opposing teams. Eventually, though, he resigned himself and actually came to like it.

Dallas players, too, had their doubts.

The nickname has stuck with the Cowboys ever since.

After the '78 season, the Cowboys had just lost a crushing Super Bowl to the Steelers. I wanted to come up with a different twist on their team highlight film. I noticed then, and had noticed earlier, that wherever the Cowboys played, you saw people in the stands with Cowboys jerseys and hats and pennants. Plus, they were always the national game on television. If you think back, there has always been one team in each sport that has support from fans nationwide: the Yankees in baseball, Notre Dame in college football, the Boston Celtics in pro basketball. They are all America's teams. So I put that name on the Cowboys' film, and in 1979 the TV announcer for their first game introduced the Cowboys as 'America's Team.' They took a lot of heat for it, but it stuck. Later other clubs like the Atlanta Braves and the U.S. Olympic hockey team have tried to call themselves 'America's Team.' But that name belongs to the Cowboys."

—BOB RYAN
Vice president and editor-in-chief, NFL Films

*"I hated 'America's Team.'
It became bulletin-board material
for every team in the league. PR
people didn't have to go out on the
field and face those other guys."*

—DANNY WHITE
Cowboys quarterback 1976-88

*"The Redskins were ahead 17 to
nothing, then we were ahead 21-17,
then they scored 17 unanswered
points. But we had a team in the
seventies that was never totally out
of a game. Only a few minutes were
left, but everybody believed we
could win. Larry Cole believed he
could make a great tackle, and he
did. I remembered that earlier
when the Redskins beat us at RFK,
they got me in a blitz with the same
situation we were in now. So on the
game's last play I told Tony Hill to
make a good move, 'cause I'd be
throwing him the ball. Sure
enough, they blitzed, and Tony
caught the ball in the end zone."*

—ROGER STAUBACH

Preston Pearson catches a pass against the
Redskins

The message got through. Dallas
won its next two games, which set up
a season finale at home against the
Redskins with the NFC East title at
stake.

The Redskins roared to a 17-0
lead with the help of quarterback Joe
Theismann's hot hand. But Staubach
rallied the Cowboys and, eventually,
they led 21-17. Again, the tide turned
completely. Washington ran off 17
more points to make the score 34-21.
When the Redskins had possession
with 4 minutes left, the Cowboys
seemed done for.

This would be the last regular season game of Roger Staubach's storied
career. Worried about a series of con-
cussions he had suffered, Staubach
decided to put family before football
and retire at the end of the season.
Staubach had yet to announce his
intentions, though, and now against
the Redskins he reached into the
depths of his immeasurable talent one
last time. A miracle was left.

Washington fumbled; Randy
White recovered. Staubach calmly
fired a touchdown pass to Ron
Springs; 34-28.

Washington took the kickoff and
tried to run out the clock. Rugged
Redskins fullback John Riggins had
already gained 150 yards, but on a
third-down play Larry Cole nailed
Riggins for a 2-yard loss. Washington
punted. There was 1:46 left to play.

Staubach kept completing passes.
On the Washington 8-yard line with
45 seconds left, Staubach called a
pass to DuPree but was faced with a
Redskins blitz. Reacting quickly, he
arched the ball to Tony Hill in the
Washington end zone. Septien's extra
point gave Dallas a 35-34 victory.
Staubach's last come-from-behind miracle was another classic.

Staubach's heroics left Dallas with
a season record of 11-5. On offense,
at least, they had performed well—
Dallas's 371 points scored led the
NFC. The crippled defense, though,
had allowed 313 points. To advance
very far in the playoffs, the Cowboys
would have to score early and often.

It seemed as though they should.
Staubach concluded his career by
leading the NFC in passing for a final
time. He completed 267 of 461

ROGER STAUBACH

BY FRANK LUKSA

The short version of quarterback Roger Staubach's career with the Dallas Cowboys goes like this: He helped win almost every game that his team should have won. And he won oh so many games that his team should have lost.

Staubach's defining moments were the times he proved his ability to win when coming from behind. In the trite, but accurate, expression of the time, he became Captain Comeback. Few have led more game-winning rallies then Roger Staubach—23 in the fourth quarter, 14 of them in a game's final 2 minutes or in overtime. No one ever did it better.

"There wasn't a player on the Cowboys, offensive or defensive, who didn't look to Staubach and think, 'As long as we have Roger we have a chance to win this thing,'" said former St. Louis Cardinals coach Jim Hanifan. "That's a real tribute to him. I know this. The opposition thought that way, too."

Staubach made the difference in whether the Cowboys were that year's or next year's champion. He had superb athletic skills. His passing arm was stronger than most suspected. It complemented excellent running ability and an innate sense to improvise and remain poised under stress. As a witness who reported every NFL game he played between 1969-79, I felt there were other assets, too, that helped set Roger Staubach apart.

He was a natural leader whose gift had been refined during four years of active Navy duty as an officer. Teammates saw that he had abundant courage to play under physical duress. Most of all, he had a blowtorch will to win.

Retired Cowboys quarterback Don Meredith was among the first to notice Staubach's intense commitment during a visit by Roger to a Dallas training camp. Yet to be discharged from the military, Staubach spent his Navy leave that year practicing behind Craig Morton, who had inherited the starting position from Don. Meredith saw the future before it arrived.

"I tried to make it a joke," said Meredith. "But I said, 'Craig, I'm glad it's you instead of me against this guy because anybody who takes a vacation and comes to two-a-days has got to be a little weird. He's gonna get your job.'"

Staubach won Morton's job in 1971, his third NFL season, at age 29. A trend soon developed. He could play 58 minutes of pedestrian quarterback, and sometimes did. But the 2-minute warning near game's end would transform him. He would perform brilliantly thereafter.

Staubach is forever linked with 3 title game victories: a 30-28 divisional playoff victory over San Francisco where the Cowboys trailed 28-16 with 4 minutes left; the 50-yard, Hail Mary pass to Drew Pearson to beat Minnesota with 26 seconds remaining in a first-round playoff, 17-14; and his last hurrah in 1979 to beat Washington for the NFC East crown, 35-34, after being down 13 points with 4 minutes to play.

A jubilant Roger Staubach after another touch-down pass

attempts, notching 27 touchdowns and throwing just 11 interceptions.

On the ground, Dorsett's 1,107 yards paced Dallas. Newhouse contributed 449 yards; Springs, 248; Laidlaw, 236. Receivers Tony Hill and Drew Pearson both had exceptional years. Hill grabbed 60 passes for

"When you talk about great quarterbacks, Roger has to stand alongside Otto Graham and Johnny Unitas, of all the ones I can recall," said coach Tom Landry after Staubach retired. "Mainly because he was such a consistent performer and one of the great 2-minute clutch players—like Bobby Layne in his prime. I don't know of any quarterback I played against or watched who I'd rather have than Roger."

The long version of Staubach's career with the Cowboys goes like this. He won regular season games at a remarkable .746 percentage (85-29). He was never shut out. His 11-6 record in playoffs included the Cowboys' first 2 Super Bowl victories (VI and XII). Four of those 6 defeats—among them 21-17 and 35-31 tinglers against Pittsburgh in Super Bowls X and XIII—were by a combined margin of 12 points.

Staubach's eight-year starting tenure reflected near pure championship results. The Cowboys won six divisional titles, became the first wild-card team to qualify for a Super Bowl in 1975, and missed the playoffs once with an 8-6 record in 1974. Dallas was the NFL's winningest team during the 1970s.

HIS GREATEST SEASON?

Landry pointed to the Hail Mary year of 1975 when he dusted off the shotgun formation that meshed so well with Staubach's style. Twelve rookies dotted the Dallas roster, and the Cowboys almost upset the Steelers in Super Bowl X. One player was clearly most responsible for the team's overachieving.

Staubach earned personal honors to a unique degree. He won the Heisman Trophy and Maxwell Trophy at the Naval Academy, plus the Bert Bell Award at the NFL level. Each is emblematic of player-of-the-year status. He also was named MVP of Super Bowl VI, All-NFC 4 times, and he made 5 trips to the Pro Bowl.

Yet Staubach never gained All-Pro credit. Induction into the Pro Football Hall of Fame in his first year of eligibility soothed that glaring omission.

A grandfather now, retired to ownership of a commercial real estate company in Dallas bearing his name, Staubach did more than win games and titles for the Cowboys. His personal and professional conduct influenced a nickname that yet clings to the Cowboys.

"The Cowboys were conceived as America's Team," said teammate Cliff Harris. "We were the clean-cut team. It's because of Roger. They developed his image because that's what he was—Captain America."

1,062 yards and 10 touchdowns. Pearson had 55 catches for 1,026 yards and 8 scores.

But Staubach's playing days came to an abrupt, unhappy end. Dallas's initial playoff opponents were the Rams, who had barely won a weak Western Conference with a 9-7 record, scoring only 14 more points than their defense surrendered. The game was in Texas Stadium, and the Cowboys were heavy favorites. But Los Angeles led 14-5 at the half. Dallas could manage only a field goal and a safety scored when Rams quarterback Vince Ferragamo was tackled in his own end zone.

Dallas came out for the second half like an embarrassed team determined to make up for earlier mistakes. Springs scored a third-quarter touchdown, and Staubach hit Jay Saldi on a short pass for another in the final period. Finally ahead 19-14, the Cowboys soon found themselves eliminated from the playoffs, 21-19, when Ferragamo burned the Dallas sec-

Cliff Harris

ondary for a 50-yard touchdown pass near the end of the game.

Dallas concluded play in the 1970s with a 105-39 regular season record. They didn't have a losing record in any of the 10 seasons, with 1974's 8-6 being their worst finish. Even the Steelers, who lost more games than they won in 1970 and 1971, couldn't match that. The Steelers' regular season record for the 1970s was 99-44-1.

In conference playoffs, Dallas ended the decade with a mark of 12-4. The Cowboys won two of five Super Bowls.

1979 playoff game with the Rams

EIGHTIES

1980 In previous seasons, Danny White had been best-known as the Dallas punter. But outside observers prophesying the imminent fall of the Cowboys juggernaut without Roger Staubach at quarterback didn't appreciate a simple fact: Danny White was a superior athlete. Team insiders had a different concern. How would White's ability as a leader compare to that of the ever-inspirational Staubach?

Not only did the Cowboys have to cope with the loss of their legendary quarterback, they couldn't expect much help from the draft. A year earlier, Dallas had sent its first- and second-round choices in 1980 to the Colts in exchange for massive defensive lineman John Dutton. He had essentially replaced Too Tall Jones, who, after a year on the professional boxing circuit, decided he'd rather play football after all and returned to the Dallas fold.

Somehow, though, the no-help draft turned out well for the Cowboys. They selected Kurt Petersen of Missouri, a defensive lineman who was switched to offensive guard in training camp; running back Timmy Newsome of Winston-Salem State, who would become a useful second-stringer for several seasons; and unknown, rifle-armed Central Michigan quarterback Gary Hogeboom. Petersen helped fill the void created by Rayfield Wright's departure.

The Cowboys wanted badly to prove right from the beginning of the season that they remained a league power. An opening game 17-3 pasting of the Redskins at RFK Stadium seemed to indicate all was well, but a week later the Broncos shellacked Dallas 41-20 at Mile High Stadium. Denver proved to everyone, future Cowboys opponents included, that the Dallas secondary was shaky. Though Staubach's retirement had gotten all the attention, Cliff Harris was gone, too. The defense missed his kamikaze spirit.

White then led the team to three straight victories. If anything, his passing numbers were gaudier than Staubach's, and Dorsett was having a good season, too. When Dallas blasted the 49ers 59-14 to improve its season record to 5-1,

it appeared that the team was back on track to secure another NFC East title and, possibly, a trip to Super Bowl XV.

But the next week, a new rival for division supremacy asserted itself. In 1976, the Philadelphia Eagles had hired head coach Dick Vermeil away from the UCLA Bruins. It had taken Vermeil a few seasons to tear down the existing Eagles roster and replace mediocre players with better ones, but by 1980 he had installed Ron Jaworski at quarterback, Wilbert Montgomery at tailback, and retained towering Harold Carmichael at wide receiver. Even worse for Eagle foes, Vermeil had also instituted a nasty defense that was capable of shutting down almost any opposing offense.

That, apparently, included the Cowboys. When Philadelphia and Dallas met at Veterans Stadium in the season's sixth week, the Eagles won a tense game 17-10. Dallas had over-

whelmed the 49ers a week before, leaving Cowboys fans convinced the team could roll up the score on any-one. Philadelphia proved they were wrong.

While the Eagles went on to win eight straight, the Cowboys barely managed to win two of their next three. Neither victory—42-31 over San Diego and 27-24 over St. Louis—was particularly impressive. Then the New York Giants won a scorefest 38-35, and there was no longer any doubt. In any given game, the Cowboys would probably score a lot of points, but the defense would give up a lot in return.

With a 7-3 record, Dallas pulled itself together and won five of its last six games, including a solid 19-13 victory over the tough Oakland Raiders. That win was followed by a 38-14 beating at the hands of the Los Angeles Rams, but Dallas concluded its regular

Tony Hill hauls in a pass against the Giants

season with a satisfying 35-27 thumping of the Eagles at Texas Stadium.

Dallas's fifteenth consecutive winning season was accomplished with all the offensive glitz imaginable. The 1980 Cowboys scored 454 points, leading the NFC by an almost laughable margin. It was more than any NFC team had scored since the league expanded its season to 16 games. The defense, however, surrendered 311 points. Though that total fell about mid-level in league rankings, it was deceiving. Dallas held several weak opponents to low scores, but when facing any real offensive powers, the Cowboys surrendered points in bunches.

Most of White's numbers for the season were superb. He completed 260 of 436 passes, good for 3,287 yards and 28 touchdowns. That was the good news. On the debit side, he also pitched 25 interceptions.

Dorsett had another fine year, gaining 1,185 yards to finish fifth among NFC rushers. Newhouse and Springs supported him with 451 and 326 yards, respectively.

Tony Hill, gradually supplanting Drew Pearson as Dallas's go-to receiver, caught 60 passes for 1,055 yards. Pearson, though, was far from finished, catching 43 balls himself for 568 yards and 6 touchdowns to Hill's 8.

Having proved to themselves that they could beat the Eagles, Dallas went into the playoffs hoping for an NFC title showdown with Philadelphia. At 12-4, the Cowboys had tied the Eagles for best record in the NFC East, but Philadelphia had been awarded the title on the basis of scoring more points in division play.

Dallas faced the Rams in the first round in a matchup of wild-card teams. The Cowboys remembered their near-blowout loss to Los Angeles during the regular season and got revenge in this second meeting. Dorsett had his best playoff game ever, rambling for 160 yards and 2 touchdowns. White's passing was less impressive; he completed 12 of 25 and threw 3 interceptions. But he also notched 3 touchdown passes, and the interceptions were forgotten in the overall glow of an easy 34-13 win. This was Landry's

Tony Hill scores and spikes the ball in 49ers game

Philly fanatics root for the Eagles in 18-degree weather

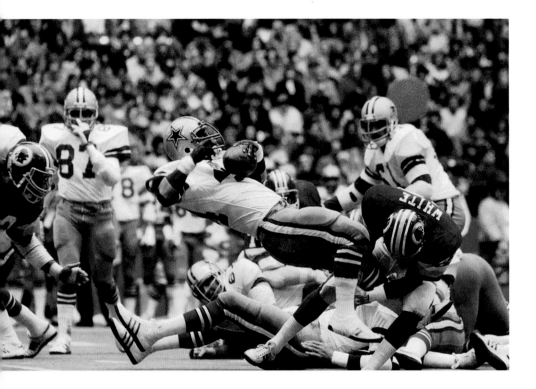

Robert Newhouse, 44, is hit by the Redskins' Jeris White

Gil Brandt in 1983

aging 7.5 yards per carry and finishing with 194 rushing yards.

White didn't have a good passing day. The rugged Eagles defenders held him to 12 completions in 31 attempts. Unlike Philadelphia, though, Dallas couldn't fall back on its running game. Eagles defenders swarmed Dorsett every time he touched the ball; 13 carries netted Dorsett just 41 yards. The Cowboys also lost 3 fumbles.

Other than a short Dorsett scoring run in the second quarter, Dallas's offense was shut down. The Eagles won easily, 20-7.

1981 From training camp until the NFC title game seven months later, it seemed the Cowboys were back and perhaps better than ever.

The draft brought offensive linemen Howard Richards of Missouri and Glen Titensor of Brigham Young. Wide receiver Doug Donley was drafted from Ohio State. Two rookie free agents, Everson Walls and Michael Downs, helped seal the leaky secondary. No significant veterans retired, though Robert Newhouse, after a long and honorable career, began to be phased out of the ground game.

Four straight wins kicked off the season. Then came two losses, the second more worrisome than the first. A narrow 20-17 road loss to St. Louis held little significance, but the next week Dallas went to San Francisco and was destroyed 45-14 by the 49ers. When the teams met during the regular season in 1980, Dallas had romped 59-14. Joe Montana had since become the 49ers' starting quarterback, but could one player make such a huge difference?

The Cowboys pulled themselves together and went 8-2 for the remainder of the season, finishing at 12-4 and reclaiming the Eastern Division

200th victory as coach of the Cowboys.

Playing against Atlanta, Dallas's next playoff foe, was White's first opportunity to shine in a national spotlight. The Cowboys trailed 24-10 after 3 quarters and 27-17 deep into the fourth period. White then led his team to 2 dazzling touchdowns, concluding both with scoring passes to Drew Pearson. Dallas won 30-27. In the interim between the Atlanta victory and the NFC championship game, White was frequently hailed as a "second Staubach."

Dallas met Philadelphia in Veterans Stadium for the right to represent the NFC in Super Bowl XV. The Eagles got off to a fast start; on their second offensive play, Montgomery ran 42 yards for a touchdown. The extra point put Philadelphia ahead 7-0.

The Cowboys' secondary played its best game of the year, virtually shutting down Jaworski. But their attention to pass defense had its price. Montgomery ran almost at will, aver-

The catch that broke the Cowboys' back

crown. White had an exceptional year, completing 223 of 391 passes for 22 touchdowns and just 13 interceptions, a dramatic improvement over his 28-25 ratio in 1980. Dorsett's 1,646 rushing yards were second in the league. Hill had 46 catches for 953 yards. Walls led the league with 11 interceptions. In all, Dallas scored 367 points and surrendered 277. The 90-point difference was a little too small for comfort.

A 38-0 pounding of Tampa Bay in the first playoff game sent Dallas to the NFC finals overflowing with confidence. After a scoreless first quarter, the Cowboys simply pulverized the

Bucs, who had won the NFC Central Division with a 9-7 record. Dallas couldn't wait to take on the 49ers at Candlestick Park and show the upstart youngsters who still was boss in the NFC.

Afterward, Cowboys players and coaches would point to that San Francisco title game as the moment when the Dallas franchise went into a long, downward spiral. There would still be a few playoff visits, even one more game for the NFC title, but the play forever to be known as "The Catch" effectively signaled the beginning of the end for the Schramm-Landry Cowboys.

The Redskins down Dorsett

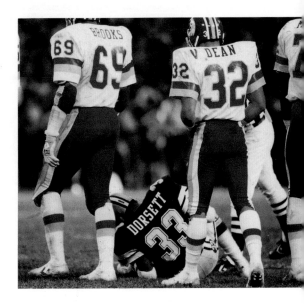

Giants quarterback Phil Simms in the grasp of John Dutton

The title showdown started out positively enough. San Francisco scored first on a short Montana touchdown pass to Freddie Solomon, but Dallas responded with a Rafael Septien field goal and a White-to-Hill scoring strike. After the first quarter, Dallas led 10-7.

In previous years with other opponents, the Cowboys would have dominated the rest of the game. But Montana showed an irritating knack for coming back. He threw a 20-yard touchdown pass to Dwight Clark early in the second period, and the 49ers reclaimed the lead. The Cowboys responded; Dorsett scored from 5 yards out, and Dallas led 17-14 at the half.

White made one mistake in the third quarter, and the Cowboys paid for it. Bobby Leopold intercepted a White pass, and the 49ers quickly followed up the turnover with a touchdown. They had a 21-17 advantage heading into the final period.

The Cowboys quickly asserted themselves, getting a 22-yard field goal from Septien and adding 7 more points on a White touchdown pass to Doug Cosbie and the subsequent extra point. With 5 minutes to play, San Francisco trailed 27-21.

Then Joe Montana launched a long, clock-eating drive. Starting from his own 10, Montana moved his team with a series of short passes. He occasionally mixed in a running play. The Cowboys didn't give up any big gains, but they kept surrendering small ones, which, added together, gave the 49ers too many first downs.

San Francisco eventually reached the Dallas 6-yard line. On third down, Montana dropped back to pass. Larry Bethea of the Cowboys broke through the 49ers line and went for Montana. While his quarterback scrambled, San Francisco wideout Dwight Clark ran along the back of the end zone, tightly covered by Everson Walls. Montana launched a high, floating pass; Clark

Tony Dorsett picks up 175 yards in this 1981 game against the Colts

and Walls leaped together. Somehow, Clark barely clutched the ball by his fingertips and dragged both feet down in the end zone. When Ray Wersching kicked the extra point, San Francisco led 28-27.

They hadn't won the title yet. White completed a long pass to Drew Pearson, who momentarily broke into the clear. It appeared Pearson might score, or, at least, put the Cowboys within field goal range. But a 49ers defender managed to grab Pearson's jersey, bringing him down at midfield. There was still enough time for one or two more plays, but White fumbled the ball on the next snap, and San Francisco recovered.

For the second straight year, Dallas had lost the NFC championship game. The 49ers went on to beat Cincinnati in the Super Bowl, launching San Francisco's bid for eventual recognition as an elite NFL franchise. The frustrated Cowboys had all winter to ponder why they kept coming up just short.

1982 Charlie Waters and D.D. Lewis retired before the 1982 season. With more and more teams emulating the complex Cowboys scouting system, it was tougher than ever for Dallas to replace the skilled veterans lost to retirement. In the draft, the best first-rounder Brandt could come up with was cornerback Rod Hill of Kentucky State. He lasted one season. Linebacker Jeff Rohrer, the second player Dallas ever drafted from Yale, did better, sticking on the roster for five years. So did Notre Dame tackle Phil Pozderac, who unfortunately became best-known for a habit of picking up costly penalties at the worst possible times.

Even before the season began, there were ominous rumblings from the players' union. The latest labor agree-

Danny White looks for a receiver in 49ers game

ment had expired in July, and now players demanded that owners set aside 55 percent of revenues for salaries. Then salaries for individual players would be determined by a formula including years played and recent performance. It became clear the owners weren't going to give in, so the players decided to force the issue.

The season began on schedule. As the darling of television, the Cowboys opened the year playing the Steelers on *Monday Night Football*. White made some questionable plays, and Pittsburgh won 36-28. White became the latest Dallas quarterback booed lustily by the home crowd.

Six days later, the Cowboys whipped the Cardinals 24-7. Then the players went on strike. Eight games were canceled. When the players finally came back after striking for 57 days, their absence had accomplished very little. The owners held firm on the big salary issues and made only a few minor concessions to help the players' union save face.

"Danny threw a perfect pass to me. I was double-covered, but when Lott and Williamson went for the ball they collided. I thought I was gone. Eric Wright got me by my jersey. I thought I'd pull free, but he did a good job, holding on 'til he could get a hand on my shoulder pad. Besides him, there was nothing but football field ahead of me. We almost had another 'Hail Mary' pass, and then Dwight Clark's catch would have been forgotten."

—DREW PEARSON

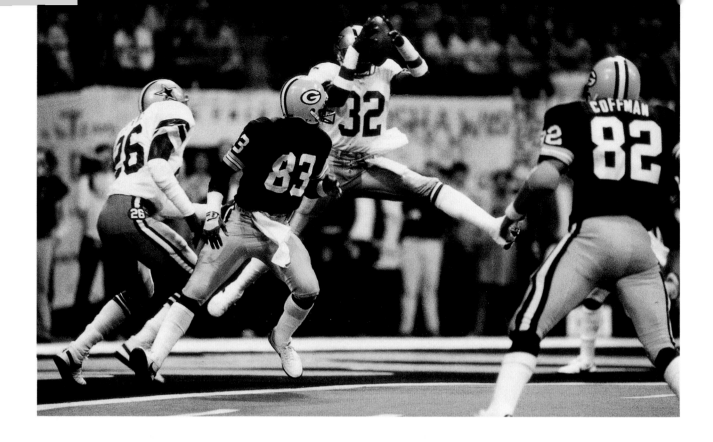

Dennis Thurman pulls in his third interception against the Packers

Dennis Thurman is greeted by Tony Dorsett and Tony Hill after second interception against Green Bay

League officials decided seven of the canceled games would not be made up. The regular season was extended into January 1983, and, to lure back irate fans, the playoff format in each conference would expand so 16 teams could be included. No divisional champions would be crowned. Instead, the top eight teams in each conference would be seeded, with No. 1 playing No. 8 , No. 2 taking on No. 7, and so on.

When play resumed November 21, the Cowboys kicked off a five-game winning streak by beating Tampa Bay 14-9. Dallas then knocked off Cleveland, Washington, Houston, and New Orleans before losing their final two games to Philadelphia and Minnesota. Dorsett supplied a memorable highlight for a bittersweet season when he broke loose on a 99-yard touchdown run against the Vikings.

Regular season statistics were skewed by the strike. White finished second among NFC quarterbacks with 156 completions in 247 attempts, good for 16 touchdowns. His interception rate was up again with 12. Dorsett won his first NFC rushing title with 745 yards, comfortably ahead of Detroit's Billy Sims, who gained 639.

Hill led Dallas receivers with 35 catches for 526 yards. Cosbie edged Drew Pearson 30 catches to 26. Everson Walls again led the league with 7 interceptions.

At 6-3, Dallas finished second in the combined league standings to the Redskins, who were 8-1. As second seeds, Dallas entered the playoffs having scored 226 points during the regular season while giving up 145. No one had scored more; only one team, Washington, had allowed fewer points.

Dallas drew the 5-4 Tampa Bay Bucs in the first game and beat the hapless Floridians 30-17. The score was misleading. The Cowboys had to rally for two fourth-quarter touchdowns to overcome a 17-16 Tampa Bay lead. White had passed for two touchdowns, but he also gave up 2 interceptions.

The Cowboys moved on against Green Bay. The Packers had beaten the Cardinals to advance to the second round. Dallas won 37-26, but in the fourth quarter a 71-yard end-around by James Lofton and an interception from Danny White that the Packers returned for a touchdown let Green Bay make it too close. Dallas

Danny White sits dejectedly on bench during Washington game

tacked on a final touchdown, but the Cowboys hadn't looked especially sharp.

That win set up a game for the conference title between Dallas and Washington. The Redskins were loaded. On offense they blended the passing of Joe Theismann and the straight-ahead running of bull-strong John Riggins. The Washington defense might have been even better; they'd allowed just 128 points during the regular season. Most notorious was a group of shortish Redskins receivers—Charlie Brown, Alvin Garrett, Art Monk, and Virgil Seay had been nicknamed "the Smurfs" after some minuscule cartoon characters popular at the time.

There was nothing comical about what Washington did to Dallas at RFK Stadium. By halftime the Redskins led 14-3, and Danny White was out of the game with a concussion courtesy of Washington's Dexter Manley. Gary Hogeboom was summoned from the Cowboys bench to play the second half. He played well enough to make the game interesting, firing touchdown passes to Drew Pearson and Butch Johnson. The Cowboys entered the fourth quarter behind just 21-17, but Hogeboom's inexperience finally tripped him up. One pass interception by the Redskins led to a field goal. Moments later, another errant Hogeboom toss was picked off by

Washington's Darryl Grant, who ran it in for a touchdown.

Dallas's third straight defeat in an NFC title game didn't sit well with Cowboys fans, most of whom had definite ideas about what was wrong. White drew much of the criticism, but Landry wasn't immune. To complicate matters, word began to spread that longtime Cowboys owner Clint Murchison was in poor health and equally poor financial straits. It seemed almost unthinkable that anyone other than Murchison might own the team.

1983
The annual college draft brought defensive end Jim Jeffcoat of Arizona State in the first round; Oregon linebacker Mike Walter, picked in the second round, lasted just one season. None of the other draftees made any significant impact on the team. In 1983, the

Cowboys' Crazy Ray confronts Redskins' mascot

Monty Hunter returns an interception for a touchdown against Tampa Bay

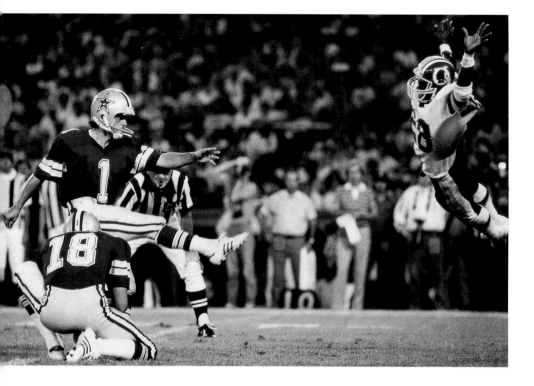

Raphael Septien boots an extra point. Washington's Darrell Green is too late for the block

◆

"*It was a tough situation for Danny. He had the ability to come in and be successful. He took us into three straight NFC championship games, so it's wrong to say he didn't do a good job. But I also have to say that sometimes Danny tried to do a little too much. We were a good team; he didn't have to carry us, he just had to play with us. At times he would try to do things that weren't necessary.*"

—DREW PEARSON

Cowboys would have to play with the same cast they had used in 1982.

On offense, at least, that wasn't a bad thing. Tony Dorsett was still one of the best backs in the NFC, Tony Hill was an excellent wide receiver, and Drew Pearson wasn't finished yet. Many sportswriters and fans urged Landry to replace White at quarterback with Gary Hogeboom, but the head coach stuck with White as he had once stuck with Meredith.

Until the last two weeks of the season, it was possible to think Dallas was still a superior team. After kicking off the season with a dramatic 31-30 win over the Redskins on *Monday Night Football*, the Cowboys rolled through the next 13 games with just two losses, 40-38 to the Raiders and 24-23 to San Diego. With a few breaks in those games, the Cowboys might easily have been undefeated. If the defense was still surrendering too much passing yardage, at least White, Dorsett, and the rest of the offense seemed consistently able to score

more than their defensive teammates gave up.

But the Redskins came into Texas Stadium and blasted the Cowboys, 31-10. The final game of the regular season found Dallas headed back to San Francisco. The Cowboys and 49ers hadn't met since the 1981 NFC title game. That loss, at least, was by 1 point. This time the 49ers gleefully pounded Dallas 42-17 in front of a massive *Monday Night Football* audience.

Still, a 12-4 season record got the Cowboys into the playoffs as a wild card. Washington had won the Eastern Division with a 14-2 mark.

Danny White had thrown 533 passes, completing 334 for 29 touchdowns; 23 interceptions were also part of the mix. Dorsett gained 1,321 yards rushing, with fullback Ron Springs gaining 541 and leading the team with 73 receptions, too. Overall, Dallas had scored 479 points, which sounded impressive unless compared with the 541 amassed by the Redskins. On defense, Dallas surrendered 360 points, by far the most the Cowboys had ever given up. This tendency to let opponents score points in bunches didn't bode well for the playoffs.

In 1983, the Cowboys didn't extend their string of NFC title game

Drew Pearson

108

losses from three to four. Unfortunately, it was because they were knocked out in the opening round. Los Angeles did the 24-17 honors at Texas Stadium. White put the ball in the air 53 times for the Cowboys, completing 32 to teammates and 3 to the Rams.

The game wasn't a blowout; Dallas could have won. But the Cowboys didn't, and they had to watch at home as the Redskins edged San Francisco for the NFC title, then were drubbed by the Raiders in Super Bowl XVIII. Something had to change for Dallas in the off-season, and it did.

Clint Murchison couldn't keep his beloved team any longer. Reluctantly, he instructed Schramm to find a buyer, but only someone who would promise to stay out of the way while Schramm and Landry ran the team. A Dallas businessman named H.R. Bright, more commonly known as "Bum," put together a limited partnership and promised to uphold Murchison's hands-off tradition. Bright bought the Dallas Cowboys for $60 million. As a parting gift, Murchison settled sizable bonuses on Schramm, Brandt, and Landry. An era had ended, and no one could be sure what would happen next.

1984 Harvey Martin, Pat Donovan, Billy Joe DuPree, and Robert Newhouse all retired. Drew Pearson was badly injured in a car crash and never came back.

Even a great draft could never have come close to equaling that erosion of talent. With their No. 1 pick, the Cowboys selected linebacker Billy

Butch Johnson buries his head during final seconds of loss to the Redskins

Raiders' Marc Wilson fumbles, and Mike Hegman flies over the top for the recovery in 1983 game

Mike Renfro

Gary Hogeboom leads the way to a win over the Rams in his first regular season start

Cannon of Texas A&M. Cynics suggested it was a clever ploy by Schramm and Brandt to please their new boss—Bum Bright was an avid Aggie. Though Cannon showed immense potential as a rookie, a neck injury forced him to retire after a single season.

What long-term help the Cowboys found in the draft came in later rounds. Linebacker Steve DeOssie from Boston College was a fixture for several years. Houston linebacker Eugene Lockhart

eventually succeeded Breunig at middle linebacker. Then there was University of Washington quarterback Steve Pelluer, whose future with the Cowboys would be interesting if not rewarding.

Landry wanted desperately to bring some new spark to the team. Just before the season opener against the Rams on *Monday Night Football*, he shocked everyone, especially Danny White, by announcing Gary Hogeboom would be the starting quarterback. This drastic measure produced a good start. Hogeboom threw the ball all over the field, hit his receivers, and Dallas won 20-13. In the next game against the Giants, though, Hogeboom played poorly and the Cowboys lost 28-7.

Landry stayed with Hogeboom as long as he could. But wins against Philadelphia, Green Bay, and Chicago

The Coach

were followed by substantial losses to St. Louis and Washington, both of which played in the same division as the Cowboys. Landry brought White back, but the team stumbled to a 5-4 finish and a record of 9-7 overall. In the final game of the season, with a wild-card slot in the playoffs at stake, Miami beat Dallas 28-21. The Cowboys, Giants, and Cardinals all had 9-7 records, but Dallas had played poorest within the Eastern Division. The Giants got the wild card, but the 49ers dominated everyone in the playoffs. They crushed Miami 38-16 in Super Bowl XIX and stood astride the NFL as the unquestioned superpower.

During the winter, Dallas had plenty of wounds to lick. The team had scored the same number of points it allowed, 308. Hogeboom completed 195 of 367 passes, but had only 7 touchdowns to counter 14 interceptions. White did statistically better at 126-233 with 11 touchdowns and 11 interceptions, but the truth was that neither quarterback had performed adequately. Dorsett rushed for 1,189 yards; Cosbie caught 60 passes to Hill's 58. The numbers didn't really matter. Dallas was in trouble.

1985 One glance at the Cowboys roster could pinpoint the problem. Out of all the players drafted in the last seven years, only defensive lineman Jim

Jeffcoat was a starter. In fact, just 14 players from the last eight drafts were still with the Cowboys.

It wasn't necessarily that Dallas's scouting staff had regressed; the rest of the teams in the NFL had caught up. Besides, Dallas usually drafted at the end of each round, when most of the best prospects had already been taken.

A furious Randy White

Danny White was hurt in 1984 game with the Giants

Bears Coach Mike Ditka in a 1985 game against his old team

The NFL's practice of giving the toughest schedules to the most successful teams didn't help the Cowboys, either. Landry and his players went into 1985 with few expectations. Sportscasters were almost unanimous—it was time to stick a fork in the Cowboys. They were done.

The first players Dallas picked up in the college draft, defensive end Kevin Brooks of Michigan and linebacker Jesse Penn of Virginia Tech, were unexceptional as pros and gone from the Cowboys roster within a few seasons. Florida Gators guard Crawford Ker was better, lasting five years in Dallas after the Cowboys made him their third-round pick.

Dallas's fifth pick was a bonanza. Running back Herschel Walker had left Georgia after a Heisman Trophy-winning sophomore season to sign with the New Jersey Generals of the

new United States Football League. The USFL picked up a TV contract for the novelty of football played in the spring and summer, but fan interest was minimal, and the league didn't last long. With a little fanfare, Schramm drafted Walker while he was still playing in the USFL. It was a shrewd move that would benefit the Cowboys in unexpected ways.

The regular season was a roller coaster for Landry and the Cowboys. White started at quarterback all season, and his erratic performances resulted in surprising wins and equally dismaying losses.

Dallas opened promisingly enough, walloping the Redskins 44-14 on the season's initial *Monday Night Football* telecast. After losing to Detroit, the Cowboys reeled off four straight wins, including a satisfying 27-13 victory over the Steelers.

Then things got confusing. In rapid order Dallas lost to Philadelphia, beat Atlanta, lost to St. Louis, defeated Washington, and got destroyed 44-0 by the Chicago Bears. The latter loss was an embarrassment in front of a huge Texas Stadium crowd. Dallas shouldn't have felt too bad—the Bears ended the season 15-1 and dominated the NFC as no other team had in recent history.

Having seen what Hogeboom had to offer, Texas Stadium crowds began chanting for third-string quarterback Steve Pelluer. Landry kept him on the bench, spelling White with Hogeboom whenever games were out of reach.

White led the Cowboys to wins over the Eagles and Cardinals, but when Dallas visited Cincinnati for its fourteenth game of the year, the lowly Bengals crushed the Cowboys 50-24. Fighting for a division title, or at least a wild-card berth, the Cowboys regrouped to beat the New York

Danny White

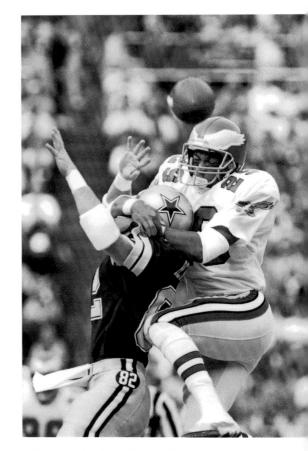

Mike Renfro is interfered with by an Eagle

Dorsett rushed for 1,307 yards in what was to be his last great year. The relatively small halfback took a fearful pounding all through 1985, especially since he made up almost all of the Cowboys' ground attack. Timmy Newsome was second in team rushing with 252 yards.

Tony Hill had a banner year, catching 74 passes for 1,113 yards and 7 touchdowns. Doug Cosbie continued to contribute at tight end, catching 64 throws for 793 yards and 6 touchdowns.

On defense, Everson Walls was a bright spot; he led the NFC in interceptions for the third straight year, a record.

Most considered it a foregone conclusion that the powerful Bears would waltz through the NFC playoffs and annihilate whichever AFC club was unlucky enough to meet them in Super Bowl XX. That's the way it turned out, with the New England Patriots serving as sacrificial lambs. The Cowboys never had a chance to test themselves a second time against former teammate and assistant coach Mike Ditka's club. Dallas drew the

Giants 28-21. Then for the second time in three years, NFC schedule-makers sent the Cowboys to Candlestick Park to conclude their season against the 49ers. Montana & Co. administered a 31-16 thrashing.

Dallas did win the NFC East under a tie-breaking system; the Cowboys, Giants, and Redskins all finished the regular season at 10-6. Once again, the Cowboys had given up almost as many points—333—as they scored—357. White finished fourth among NFC passers, completing 267 of 450 passes. He threw 21 touchdown passes and surrendered 17 interceptions.

Bears fans celebrate big win over Cowboys in 1985

Danny White scores against the Browns

Herschel Walker

In addition, a free agent offensive tackle from Florida A&M made the team. At 320 pounds—or, sometimes, a lot more—Nate Newton was just about the opposite physically of the lean, quick linemen Tom Landry had traditionally favored.

Training camp was memorable. Looking to the future, Landry hired Paul Hackett, a whiz at designing wide-open, pass-oriented offenses, away from Bill Walsh and the 49ers. Landry had begun talking about the time in the indefinite future when he would step down as head coach. Several former Dallas assistant coaches—Dan Reeves, Mike Ditka, John Mackovic— had already found head coaching positions with other NFL teams. Hackett's hiring seemed to indicate Schramm and Landry were at least considering the newcomer as heir to the head coaching position.

It was expected that Danny White, as an intelligent, veteran quarterback, would work well with Hackett. There was other news, too—Herschel Walker had joined the Cowboys.

Subsequent seasons would prove Walker to be a solid, but only infrequently spectacular, running back. He'd electrified college crowds at Georgia; it seemed there wasn't anything he couldn't do on a football field. Most of his new teammates welcomed him, but Tony Dorsett grumbled at the size of Walker's contract, which Dorsett felt unfairly exceeded his own.

Landry's dilemma was simple; both Dorsett and Walker were better suited to play running back. Neither could function at his best as a lead-blocking fullback. Still, Landry tried them together sometimes during the season, or else he went mostly with the back who was playing best in a particular game.

The season got off to a good start. Dallas beat the New York Giants

Los Angeles Rams in the first round, and the Rams made short work of their visitors from Texas. White was intercepted 3 times, and Dorsett was held to 58 yards, while Rams running back Eric Dickerson rolled for 248 yards and 2 long touchdown runs of 55 and 40 yards. The final score was 20-0.

Dallas wouldn't be back in the NFC playoffs until 1991.

1986 The Cowboys used their first pick in the college draft to select wide receiver Mike Sherrard of UCLA. They wanted the speedy youngster badly. With Drew Pearson gone, it was too easy for opposing defenses to zero in on Tony Hill. Besides Sherrard, Dallas also added former Houston Oilers wide receiver Mike Renfro, who, though he wasn't fast, was still a dependable target.

Tony Dorsett

31-28 at Texas Stadium in the Cowboys' first game. The winning touchdown was set up by a well-disguised draw play to Walker. The victory was more significant than Dallas realized at the time; the Giants would lose only one more game during the regular season and then sweep through the NFC playoffs before beating Denver in Super Bowl XXI. Because they were healthy, the Cowboys could beat New York. But Dallas wouldn't stay healthy long.

After an easy 31-7 win over the Lions, Dallas was edged 37-35 by Atlanta. A 31-7 win over St. Louis followed, then a 29-14 loss to Denver. Except for the Denver game, the Cowboys were scoring a lot of points, but their defense remained susceptible to opponents with strong passing attacks.

White, at least, was playing well. Under Hackett, his touchdown/interception rate had improved dramatically. And while Dorsett didn't appreciate Walker's presence, or at least his salary, the duo gave Dallas a balanced ground attack that other NFL teams envied.

Then the defense improved; the Cowboys won three straight, giving up just 6, 14, and 6 points. At 6-2, Dallas hardly looked like a team on the

Dorsett and Walker celebrate during Redskins game

decline. The Giants and Redskins were also 6-2, so the Cowboys were in a dogfight for the NFC East title.

That ended in the season's ninth week, when the Cowboys had a rematch with New York at the Meadowlands. During the game, which Dallas lost 17-14, Danny White broke his wrist. Steve Pelluer, his replacement, fell to the occasion. The Cowboys lost six of their last seven games, finishing 7-9. Dallas's NFL record streak of 20 consecutive winning seasons was snapped. Cowboys fans who had beseeched Landry to play Pelluer instead of White now booed the youngster.

The losing streak wasn't entirely Pelluer's fault. Walker and Dorsett had injuries, too. Both men were tough and

Tom Landry in action

averaged more than 3 yards per carry; he just hadn't run the ball as much. He also caught 25 passes.

Walker's numbers were even better. He had picked up 737 yards with 151 carries to Dorsett's 184. But Walker had also led the club in receptions, catching 76 passes for 837 yards—numbers fit for a wide receiver. In all, he had scored 14 touchdowns.

Tony Hill had a solid final year. His 1986 totals were 49 receptions for 770 yards and 3 touchdowns. Mike Sherrard was, in his rookie season, all Dallas had hoped. He caught 41 balls for 744 yards and 5 touchdowns.

Before his injury Danny White had been enjoying one of the best seasons of his career. He had completed 95 of 153 passes—a 62 percent completion rate—with 12 touchdowns and just 5 interceptions. If his wrist healed over the off-season, maybe he could take Hackett's glitzy offense and get the Cowboys back in the playoffs. Pelluer, on the other hand, didn't seem

Fans can't bear to be seen as the Cowboys lose their fourth straight game

kept playing, but Walker in particular was hampered for several weeks.

At season's end, some Cowboys had the kind of statistics that could generate optimism for 1987. The Dorsett-Walker tandem, when healthy, had been lethal. Dorsett ended the season with 748 yards rushing, his first full NFL season under 1,000. He had still

Herschel Walker goes over Seattle defenders for a touchdown

Tony Dorsett and Walter Payton chat after last game of 1986 season

like playoff material. He had completed 215 of 378 passes, but many were short, safe tosses; when Pelluer tried to throw the ball down the field, things were different. He finished with 8 touchdown passes and 17 interceptions.

There still was juice, then, in the Cowboys offense. The 346 points they had scored, fifth in the NFC, were proof. But the defense had given up 337 points; only three other teams had allowed more.

Cowboys fans dared to hope, but 1987 had more surprises in store. Few of them were good.

1987 Clint Murchison passed away. As long as he owned the Dallas Cowboys, Tom Landry never worried about a contract, particularly after the 10-year extension Murchison had given him, unasked, in 1963. After that contract had expired, Landry simply went on to another, with Schramm telling the head coach what he'd be paid, and Landry never finding any reason to quibble.

But the team was now owned by Bum Bright, who was rumored to be unhappy with a 7-9 season. Landry approached Schramm before the '87 season and asked for a three-year deal. Landry was honest about his reason for wanting a multiyear agreement—the team had declined, and it

would take a few seasons to build it back up. The man widely known as The Only Coach the Cowboys Ever Had didn't want to retire until he could turn over a contending team to his successor.

Schramm agreed; that was that. Landry got on with preparing for the new season.

Schramm and Brandt tried to give their head coach talented new blood to work with. For a change, the Cowboys were drafting twelfth in each

Miami's Mark Clayton is about to take the ball away from Ron Francis of the Cowboys

Tom Landry confers with quarterback Danny White during 1987 game

Kevin Gogan pickets with his dog Lucky

round. Better players were going to be available to them.

Dallas's first-round choice was Nebraska nose tackle Danny Noonan. While he never became a superstar, he was good enough to join Jim Jeffcoat in an otherwise-aging defensive line that still included Randy White, John Dutton, and Too Tall Jones. Second-round pick Ron Francis, a defensive back from Baylor, lasted several seasons on the Cowboys roster, as did third-rounder Jeff Zimmerman, an offensive guard from Florida. Later rounds yielded the draft's two real gems: receiver Kelvin Martin from Boston College would become a top kick returner, and hulking tackle Kevin Gogan from the University of Washington was an instant contributor on the offensive line.

In training camp, it was obvious Danny White's wrist wasn't completely healed. Landry had to choose between a physically hampered White and Steve Pelluer. He hoped one would far outshine the other in exhibition games, but neither played well.

A serious loss to the Cowboys offense came in an August 5 scrimmage game against the Chargers. Trying to make a cut against a San Diego defensive back, Mike Sherrard

fell awkwardly and broke his leg. It was a career-threatening injury; players witnessing the incident said Sherrard's leg was bent almost in half. With Tony Hill gone, Mike Renfro became the only serious Dallas threat at wide receiver. Rival defenses could play accordingly.

By the end of the exhibition season, the Cowboys offense had scored just 36 points with only 3 touchdowns. Since the offense had been expected to carry the team during the regular season, this inability to get into the end zone was of serious concern. Still, the Dallas core was composed of veteran players. Perhaps they would play better in games that counted.

They didn't, at least in the season opener. Against St. Louis, the Cowboys offense scored just 13 points, and the Dallas defense let the Cardinals come from behind with 3 unanswered touchdowns in a 24-13 loss. Dallas beat the New York Giants in their next game, but the 16-14 win was secure only when the Giants' kicker missed an easy field goal late in the game.

Then came another players' strike. Determined to force the owners' hands on free agency and other issues, members of the players' union walked out on Tuesday, September 22. Games

scheduled for that weekend were canceled.

No NFL team came through the
strike unscathed. Management scalded
picketing players in the media; they
threatened the strikers with teams of
players the owners referred to as
"replacements" and the holdout union
members called "scabs."

Tex Schramm became a leader
among hard-line NFL management,
and Dallas's pro-union players resented
Schramm's vociferous opposition. Some
Cowboys didn't want to strike. One,
Randy White, informed his teammates
he wasn't going to strike at all. On
September 23, White and defensive
lineman Don Smerek crossed the union
picket line and reported for practice.

Schramm put on more pressure.
Tony Dorsett, Too Tall Jones, Everson
Walls, and Doug Cosbie were all
signed to long-term contracts that
included annuities. Those players knew
they'd lose their regular paychecks
while on strike. Schramm informed
them they would lose their annuities,
too, unless they came back right away.
Dorsett and Jones gave in.

Meanwhile, Schramm and officials of the other NFL clubs went
ahead and signed rosters of free agent
"replacement players." They
announced the NFL season would
resume on schedule on Sunday,
October 4. One of the first replacement players lined up by Schramm
was Kevin Sweeney, a quarterback
from Fresno State who had set all kinds
of college passing marks. But Sweeney
was shorter than the 6 feet listed in
game programs, and his arm wasn't
strong enough for the pros—as long as
real NFL players were his opponents.
Yet even when Danny White gave up
and reported back to the Cowboys,
Landry played Sweeney.

On October 4, the "Cowboys"
played the "Jets" on the road in front of

about 12,000 paying fans. Randy
White and Smerek started; Dorsett suited out but didn't play. Sweeney had a
big game. The two teams combined
for 9 turnovers, but eventually Dallas
won 38-24. It counted as a regular
season win.

The Cowboys—replacement players and strikebreakers alike—were next
scheduled to play the Eagles at Texas

*Darryl Clack, left, and Jesse Penn leave the
Cowboys training facility*

*Randy White, 54, was a player who chose not
to go on strike*

Fan at Jets game in New York makes his strike statement

Stadium. Remarkably, a crowd of 40,622 showed up. Striking players picketing outside the stadium were brushed aside. Sweeney led a mixed team of replacement players and strikebreakers to a 41-22 win. Now the Cowboys had a 3-1 season record, and Cowboys fans had a new hero at quarterback.

The strike continued, but union support was eroding. Players had missed a paycheck, and many of them didn't want to miss another one.

Before the third game played during the strike, a Monday night matchup against the Redskins, Landry

announced Danny White would start at quarterback. The crowd of 60,415 was the largest at Texas Stadium since Dallas played Oakland in 1986. Everyone expected the Cowboys to win easily since Washington was one of the few teams playing without any strikebreakers. But Dorsett lost two fumbles, a final Cowboys drive stalled on the Washington 12, and the Redskins won 13-7. Dorsett and White were booed throughout the game.

The strike ended before the next game, and once again, the owners had won. Twenty-one Cowboys had crossed the union picket line. Naturally, there were hard feelings afterward in the Dallas locker room.

Emotions ran even higher after the post-strike game with Philadelphia. The Eagles, led by leering head coach Buddy Ryan, whipped Dallas 37-20. Philadelphia had a safe 30-20 lead with just seconds to play. Ryan called for a bomb, the Cowboys were hit with a pass-interference penalty on their 1-yard line, and the Eagles punched the ball in on the last play of the game. The normally stoic Landry was so furious afterward that he wouldn't comment on Ryan's rub-it-in insult.

Danny White had played so poorly that Landry yanked him in favor of Pelluer in the fourth quarter. Pelluer was knocked silly on his first play, so White was sent back in. Predictably, he was booed.

Buddy Ryan, an old nemesis

The Cowboys managed to beat the Giants in their next game—the defending Super Bowl champions were in a horrible slump—and improved their season record to 4-3. Schramm and Landry cautiously began mentioning another winning season and trip to the playoffs. The team responded by losing five of its next six games, several of which were played against some of the weakest teams in the NFL. After a loss to the sad-sack Lions, Schramm made remarks on his Monday radio show that were critical of Landry.

In mid-November, Landry announced Walker would start at half-back and Dorsett would be his back-up. It was a pragmatic decision: Walker was 25, Dorsett was 33.

Against the New England Patriots, Walker celebrated his new status as undisputed starter with a 60-yard run in overtime. In all, Walker gained 173 yards rushing. Dorsett picked up 5 yards. A week later, Steve Pelluer became the Cowboys' starting quarterback. His debut was less distinguished; Miami edged Dallas 20-14. Still, Pelluer expected to start against the Vikings on Thanksgiving Day. Landry played White instead, and he led a late comeback that fell short. Minnesota won 44-38.

The next week, Atlanta beat Dallas 21-10. After the game, owner Bum Bright abandoned any pretense of continuing Clint Murchison's no-criticism policy. Bright told interviewers that "maybe the problem is we can't utilize the talent of certain guys because we don't have anybody to direct how to use them. I don't want to do the coaching, and I don't want to try to run the team, but I'm not satisfied with the results we get. We can't go along like we are."

Picketers march in Philadelphia

Tex Schramm, and Herschel Walker discuss the strike at Valley Ranch

*Herschel Walker takes on the Cardinals in
1988 game*

Dallas lost to the Redskins; the
team's season record was 5-8. Pelluer
started and won the last two games of
the season, which was limited to 15
games because of the strike. The
Cowboys had suffered their second
consecutive losing season.

Except for Herschel Walker, no
Dallas players had numbers worth
bragging about. The offense scored
340 points and the defense gave up
348. It was the first time since 1964
that opponents had outscored the
Cowboys.

Walker gained 891 yards on
291 carries; he also caught 60 passes
for 715 yards. Dorsett, who was sent
to Denver after the season, picked up
456 yards on 131 carries. Pelluer
gained 142 yards, running for self-
preservation rather than first downs.
Mike Renfro, playing well under difficult circumstances, caught 46 balls for
662 yards. Doug Cosbie chipped in
36 catches for 421 yards.

White and Pelluer both had fine
completion rates: White at 59 percent
with 215 connections out of 362 passes, and Pelluer at 54.5 percent with
55 of 101. Those were misleading
statistics because many of the passes
Dallas attempted during the season
were short dump-offs. Even so, White
had 17 interceptions and just 12
touchdowns.

It didn't seem things could get
worse, but they did.

1988 There had been so
many great seasons,
so many glorious moments. But as
training camp began, it seemed hard
to remember them. Fans and sports
columnists had plenty of suggestions
about what was wrong with the
Cowboys.

The criticism made it easy to over-
look the haul Dallas got in the draft. In
their last chance to mine college gold,
Schramm and Brandt hit pay dirt.
Wide receiver Michael Irvin was the
Cowboys' selection with the eleventh
choice in the first round. Irvin came
highly recommended by Jimmy

Ed Jones, Randy White, Jim Jeffcoat, from left, wait for losing game against the Bengals to end

Johnson, his coach at the University of Miami. In the second round, Dallas picked linebacker Ken Norton Jr. from UCLA. The next few rounds didn't bring much, but in the eleventh Dallas resorted to an old strategy. Defensive lineman Chad Hennings of the Air Force Academy was in training to fly fighter jets, not to play football. He wouldn't even be eligible to leave the service and play for the Cowboys until 1992. But the Cowboys brain trust saw something special in Hennings.

Dallas opened the season with Pelluer at quarterback. Recognizing that the youngster didn't have the NFL experience or sophistication to run a complex system, Landry simplified the offense and hoped Walker would compensate.

When the Cowboys kicked off to Pittsburgh in their first game, Landry tied an NFL record long held by Curly Lambeau of the Packers. Like Lambeau,

Landry had now coached the same team for 29 consecutive seasons.

Pittsburgh beat the Cowboys; so did the Giants. Dallas managed to defeat Phoenix and Atlanta, neither one a powerhouse. After four games the Cowboys' record was even at 2-2. Dallas wouldn't be a .500 team again until December 16, 1990.

The Cowboys lost 10 straight games. They lost by huge margins (43-3 to Minnesota) and on last-second

"Those were trying times that season. There was a lot of strain on Coach Landry. He was trying. The players had changed, especially in the way they acted. And the media kept making accusations that he was too old to coach. But the man somehow kept an even keel. I know I wasn't his type of person. I'm a party guy. But I give him credit for giving a big guy like me a chance. You see, when I came to the Cowboys, they didn't even have any extra-large shorts. The biggest size they had was large. I got the first extra-large ones."

—**NATE NEWTON**
*Dallas Cowboys offensive tackle
1988-*

Nate Newton goes through his paces at mini-camp

Danny White, 11, and Steve Pelluer leave the field after losing to Washington

mistakes. (-The Eagles, trailing throughout the game, got a late possession when Pelluer was called for intentional grounding, stalling a Dallas drive. Philadelphia won, 24-23.) Texas Stadium fans booed everyone but Herschel Walker, who continued to rack up big numbers in a losing cause.

Pelluer continued completing a high percentage of short, safe passes, but it seemed that in every game he would make one crucial mistake that would cost Dallas a chance to win. In frustration Landry even tried playing Kevin Sweeney at quarterback, but the smallish Fresno State graduate found it much tougher to play against real NFL players than replacements. His completion rate was a dreadful 33 passes of 78 attempted; he threw 5 interceptions before Landry mercifully sat him back down. White played purely as a backup. This would be his last season with Dallas.

There was an additional distraction for the team. Bum Bright's financial empire was crumbling, and it had become apparent he would sell the Cowboys. No one knew what to expect next.

In their fifteenth game, the Cowboys beat the Redskins in Washington 24-17. Besides breaking the interminable losing streak, the victory was sweet because it eliminated the Cowboys' old rival from the 1988

playoffs. Michael Irvin was the star of the game with 3 touchdown catches. His teammates chose, however, to present the game ball to Tom Landry. It was his last win as the Dallas coach.

The Cowboys ended their season with a 23-7 drubbing by the Eagles. They finished 3-13, which was the worst team record in the entire NFL.

Despite that, Herschel Walker had a great year. He rushed for 1,514 yards on 361 carries. (The rest of the Dallas backs, quarterbacks, and wide receivers who ran occasional end-arounds carried the ball a total of 108 times.) Walker also caught 53 passes for 505 yards. He scored 7 touchdowns.

Though Michael Irvin caught 32 passes for 654 yards and 5 touchdowns, Dallas's leading receiver was journeyman Ray Alexander with 54 catches, 788 yards and 6 scores. Pelluer connected on 245 of 435 passes, but he had 19 interceptions and just 17 touchdowns. He'd spend 1989 as a benchwarmer for the Kansas City Chiefs. Overall season statistics for the team were painful even to read: 265 points scored, 381 points allowed.

Bright put the Cowboys on the market. Schramm and Landry proceeded with planning for 1989. Landry still had a year to go on his three-year contract.

BRIGHT SELLS COWBOYS TO JERRY JONES

★

In February 1989, rumors began circulating that Bum Bright was about to sell the Dallas Cowboys to an Arkansas businessman named Jerry Jones. Jones, who had made a fortune in the oil and gas business, wasn't well known. But that changed quickly.

Just before the sale was officially announced on February 25, Jones was spotted in Mia's, a Dallas restaurant, eating dinner with Jimmy Johnson, who was fresh from guiding the Miami Hurricanes to the national championship in 1987 and to an 11-1 record in 1988. Jones and Johnson had been roommates when they both played college football for the Arkansas Razorbacks. Obviously, Johnson hadn't come all the way to Dallas just to celebrate Jones's pending acquisition of the Cowboys.

When Bum Bright bought the Cowboys from Clint Murchison, Murchison had agreed to the deal only if the new owner would retain Schramm and Landry. Bright had no similar restriction for Jones. Once the team was out of Bright's hands, new owner Jones could do whatever he liked.

Both Landry and Schramm were in the dark about the deal. Landry and his family flew to Austin for a golfing weekend they had planned. The next morning, he received a call from Schramm asking where he could be contacted during the day. Hours later, Schramm and new Cowboys owner Jerry Jones flew to Austin; Landry was told a coaching change would be made.

"My initial interest in the team came five years before I actually bought it. I read in the papers Mr. Bright had bought the Cowboys from Clint Murchison, and my feathers dropped. I said at the time, 'There goes the one team that would have given me the incentive to commit all my time and resources to the National Football League.' Then in 1988 I was on vacation, supposed to be fishing, but I didn't feel well and stayed in my room with a newspaper. Thumbing through the sports section, I saw Bum Bright was going to sell the team. I got to a pay phone, and on a very garbled transmission I told the people who were handling the sale that if I didn't die I'd be in Dallas in twenty hours to talk to them. The negotiations lasted from August 1988 to February 1989. Twice I was ready to walk away from the deal because it didn't make financial sense. But then I lost my father-in-law, one of the people I'd been closest to, and it reminded me of how life is a short journey and how we should do the things we want to do. The deal for the Cowboys was closed on February 26, I believe."

—JERRY JONES
Cowboys team owner 1989-

TOM LANDRY

BY CARLTON STOWERS

He came to the task hesitantly, not at all certain coaching was something he wished to make his life's work. Thomas Wade Landry had, from his hometown high school playing field of little Mission, Texas, to the bright lights of New York, made his athletic mark and was content to let it stand. A fullback and defensive back at the University of Texas, Landry had begun his professional career in 1949 as a punter for the New York Yankees of the soon-to-be-defunct All-American Conference. Then it was on to the fabled NFL Giants, where he developed into an All-Pro defensive back in 1954 and was selected to play in the Pro Bowl the following season. Ultimately, he would become a player-coach, then a full-time assistant during some of the Giants' greatest years.

In time, however, Landry heeded the call of his native state and took leave of New York and the game, looking ahead to new challenges in the business world. It was at that stage of Landry's life that Tex Schramm, newly appointed general manager of the NFL team soon to call Dallas home, found Landry. Schramm urged him to become head coach of the Dallas Cowboys.

Landry, by then a born-again Christian and keenly aware of the dedication required of such a coaching position, made it clear to Schramm, and anyone else who would listen, that his personal priorities did not ideally suit him for the role. The No. 1 thing in his life was his faith; second was his family. Football was, and forever would be, third on the list. Landry could make no promise that he would be along for the Cowboys' long haul.

That was good enough for Schramm. And, for almost three decades, it was good enough for the Dallas Cowboys.

What Landry accomplished during his remarkable career, as he built a ragtag expansion franchise into a club that came to be known as "America's Team," is the kind of stuff Steven Spielberg deals with. Along the way there would be a league-record 20 consecutive winning seasons, 270 victories, 5 Super Bowl trips, 2 world championships, and a love affair with the city of Dallas no single sports personality has been a party to since. Tom Landry, with Coach of the Year honors to his credit and a spot in the Pro Football Hall of Fame, was more than just a winner the community—and the nation— embraced. He was a calming, always-in-control figure who gave strength and comfort to those who devotedly followed his accomplishments.

Even when dismissed by new owner Jerry Jones, Landry's image continued to grow. The icon became a martyr. The city of Dallas quickly forgot the few dismal seasons of the late '80s and focused on the big picture. It remembered the good times and threw him a helluva farewell parade.

Longtime Cowboys defensive lineman Larry Cole was among the former Landry players who stood by cheering—and remembering—that day. "The single thing that most impressed me about Coach Landry," he says, "was the fact he could put so much of himself into a game and still not be consumed by it. When it was over on Sunday, he could walk away and leave it on the field.

Remarkably, Landry was able to do the same thing at the end of his career. No other man I've ever known has shown me that kind of strength and inner peace."

Danny White, who inherited the Cowboys quarterbacking chores at the end of Roger Staubach's brilliant career, is still concerned that the TV-generated image of Landry as the stone-faced, emotionless leader has been taken as fact: "He was never that way. He cared about the players on the team far more than he did wins and losses."

One wonders, then, what milestones such a man will most cherish, what memories will, in years to come, be the sweetest. What are the treasured moments he will carry from a career of such storybook quality as to read like pure fiction?

I'm just guessing, but it could well be that they are not necessarily the things from which the loving headlines were fashioned. Likely, they are more private, more personal.

For instance:

It was 1972, when the afterglow of the Cowboys' first Super Bowl victory still lingered, and fans far and wide were heaping praise and gifts on Landry. Sam Wing, the owner of a Dallas company that specialized in custom-made wooden window shutters, was among those swept up in the celebration.

For some time, he and his employees pondered what they might do to show their appreciation for the accomplishments of Landry and his team. Finally, in the spring following the Cowboys' Super Bowl VI victory over Miami, Wing and a woodcarver named Roy Kelley paid a visit to the coach's office to anxiously outline their proposal.

What they would like to do, they said, was provide Landry with a hand-carved office door, fashioned from the finest mahogany available. They brought with them mock-ups of the proposed design and samples of the different colors of wood for the coach's approval.

The idea fascinated Landry, and he encouraged the Sam Wing Company to proceed.

It was when he returned from training camp in Thousand Oaks that following summer that Landry first saw the new door at the entrance to his North Central Expressway office. Its three panels featured Kelley's detailed carvings of a Cowboys helmet, the Super Bowl trophy, and Texas Stadium.

Landry loved it. When people visiting the Cowboys offices requested a photograph with him, he routinely suggested they pose in front of the door.

And years later, when the coaching staff offices were relocated to the new Valley Ranch facility, the door went along at the coach's request, presenting a problem for construction workers. It was larger than the standard door frame already in place. Workers had to enlarge the entrance to the office that would serve as the coach's new headquarters.

On the Sunday morning following his dismissal, Landry quietly entered his office for the last time to begin the chore of boxing his belongings. All around him was memorabilia—trophies, plaques, and cherished photographs—from his long and storied tenure.

When, finally, his packing was done, Landry sat at his desk for several minutes, surveying the reminders of a 29-year career, then dialed the maintenance department. He asked that someone come and remove his door from its hinges.

He would take it with him.

Bum Bright, left, shakes hands with the new Cowboys owner, Jerry Jones

Soon afterward, Schramm and Brandt would be gone, too.

Jones flew back to Dallas to hold his initial news conference at the Cowboys' headquarters in Valley Ranch. There he told the assembled media horde that it was "like Christmas," and that he would involve himself with every aspect of the team "from socks to jocks." But the news that Landry was being replaced by Johnson preoccupied most of the assembled newspeople, who were glad to report Jones had claimed his new coach would be worth "five No. 1 draft choices." The next day many who'd been openly calling for Landry to step down had completely reversed field and were blasting Jones for callousness.

When Jimmy Johnson held his first news conference as the Dallas

Landry makes his exit

Cowboys' coach, more than 200 media personnel requested credentials. Afterward, most filed negative stories. What many dubbed "the two J.J.'s" era was off to a rocky start.

1989 The resurrection of the Dallas Cowboys began with a kick-start from the same talent pool that originally turned the team into champions—the college draft.

In 1988, Schramm, Landry, and Brandt had already brought Michael Irvin, Ken Norton Jr., and Chad Hennings into the Cowboys fold. Dallas subsequently plummeted to the worst record in the NFL, which meant that, for the first time since 1974, the Cowboys exercised the first pick in the first round of the draft.

Observers predicted disaster. The new Cowboys brain trust had barely been in place for two months, certainly not enough time to evaluate properly the available college talent and use Dallas's draft picks to maximum advantage. They forgot Jimmy Johnson had spent his last 20 years as a college coach. Through recruiting and studying game films supplied by opponent universities, Johnson probably knew more about draft-eligible college players than any other NFL coach.

It showed. Without hesitation, Dallas used the first pick in the entire 1989 draft to select UCLA quarterback Troy Aikman. Aikman had transferred to UCLA after a freshman year spent at

There's a new coach in town

Oklahoma, where he didn't like the run-oriented offense of Sooners coach Barry Switzer.

Of course, everybody in the NFL knew Aikman was a prime prospect, so Dallas didn't show that much ingenuity picking him in the first round. It was in rounds two, three, and four that the new-era Cowboys showed their stuff. First they chose Syracuse fullback Daryl Johnston. Pittsburgh center Mark Stepnoski and Texas-El Paso defensive end Tony Tolbert came in the third and fourth rounds, respectively. Each would play a significant role for the team, and soon.

Johnson followed that epic day by participating in a special supplemental draft; here he shocked everyone by taking Miami quarterback Steve Walsh, who'd run Johnson's offense for the Hurricanes. The possibility of an Aikman/Walsh quarterback controversy titillated the media, but in time Johnson would reveal Walsh's selection as part of a larger overall plan.

The influx of new talent was impressive. Johnson swept out aging veterans to make room for the new-

comers. Defensive lineman Randy White, so long a key player on championship teams, was sent to pasture. Too Tall Jones didn't take the hint, but Johnson's message eventually got through. Jones would retire after the season.

Yet, as good as the newcomers would become, they weren't enough that year. The 1989 Cowboys often made their predecessors from 1988 look downright successful. Any illusions Johnson had about his new team having previously undiscovered ability were dashed in the season's opening game. The New Orleans Saints whipped Dallas 28-0, and worse times were to come. Atlanta beat Dallas, then Washington hung another defeat

Jimmy Johnson and Jerry Jones greet their new quarterback, Troy Aikman

Herschel Walker fumbles in Atlanta game

on the Cowboys. At 0-3, Johnson decided more immediate action was required.

To most of the NFL, and, in fact, to most Dallas Cowboys fans, Herschel Walker was all the once-proud franchise had going for it. Aikman would probably be an eventual star, but in that season he ran for his life and sustained such regular beatings that Walsh ended up playing almost half the time. Another owner, another coach, might have hung onto Walker

just to keep the paying customers happy with something. Jones and Johnson, however, saw Herschel as bait.

The Minnsota Vikings bit. On October 12, after two more losses had the Cowboys reeling at 0-5, Johnson traded his one star player to Minnesota for the Vikings' first-round pick in the 1992 draft, plus veterans Jesse Solomon, David Howard, Alex Stewart, Darrin Nelson, and Issiac Holt or other "conditional" draft choices of

"Today's Cowboys are unbelievable.
That's the obvious answer when
they've got a guy like Emmitt
Smith. But he's not my favorite
back. Daryl Johnston makes
Emmitt Smith go. Johnston's
one of the greatest fullbacks
I've ever seen."

—WALT GARRISON

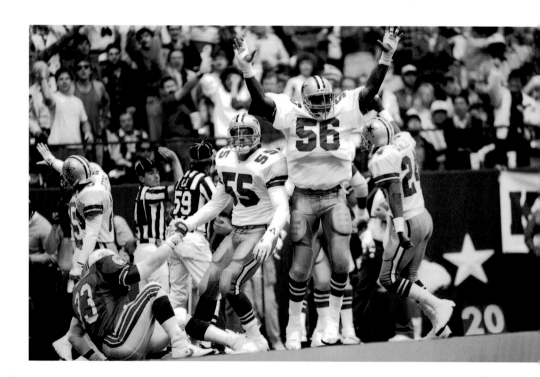

Eugene Lockhart, 56, celebrates against Miami

Jerry Jones celebrates a preseason victory against Houston

Minnesota's which would become Cowboys property if Johnson chose not to keep the players he acquired in the deal. Johnson had no intention of hanging on to them. As they were cut, the conditional draft choices came to Dallas. Walker never got Minnesota to the Super Bowl, but the players Johnson would eventually acquire through those draft picks got Dallas there.

Meanwhile, the Cowboys still were stuck in 1989. Dallas somehow managed to beat the Redskins 13-3 at RFK Stadium, but lost every other game on the schedule. The first year of the Jones/Johnson regime found the Cowboys again on the bottom of the NFL standings at 1-15.

Statistical bright spots were nonexistent. Dallas scored just 204 points, by far the fewest in the NFC, and allowed 393, third-most. Paul Palmer, a journeyman back acquired from the Lions after Walker was traded, led the team in rushing with only 446 yards. Kelvin Martin was the top receiver with 46 catches for 644 yards and 2 touchdowns. In his rookie season,

Aikman completed 155 of 293 passes, throwing for 9 touchdowns but also pitching 18 interceptions. Walsh connected on 110 of 219 passes, with 5 touchdowns and 9 interceptions.

Dallas concluded the 1980s with a 79-73 mark. (Seven games were lost to the players' strike of 1982, and one was cut from the 1987 schedule for the same reason.) The Cowboys were 5-5 in NFC playoff games; they didn't play in the Super Bowl during the decade. Over the final four seasons in the 1980s, the team's record was a dreadful 18-45. Yet Jones and Johnson never wavered. In every interview, they swore they were on track to restore the Cowboys to former glory. And they were.

"Even in a 1-15 year, you knew something was going to happen. Coach Johnson treated each loss like a loss took a year off his life. In time he got better, but that year he sure didn't."

—NATE NEWTON

Jimmy Johnson gives instructions to quarterback Steve Walsh

NINETIES

1990 Jerry Jones and Jimmy Johnson worked their draft magic again in 1990. After finishing 1989 at 1-15, Dallas should have owned the first selection of the entire draft. But that pick had been sacrificed to acquire Steve Walsh. Still, the Cowboys did have a first-round pick, Minnesota's, as part of their complicated haul for Herschel Walker.

They knew exactly how to use it. Minnesota's first-rounder was packaged with a third-rounder Dallas had received in a trade with the 49ers. The package was sent to Pittsburgh in exchange for the Steelers' first-round pick, which was higher than Minnesota's. The Cowboys used that pick to select the running back Jones and Johnson were positive would make Dallas fans finally forget Herschel Walker.

Jimmy Johnson had known about Emmitt Smith for a long time. Johnson wanted Smith to come to Miami, but the youngster chose Florida instead. He'd had three glittering seasons for the Gators, but decided in 1990 to give up his senior year of eligibility and enter the NFL draft instead. Dallas, of course, wasn't the only pro team to know about Smith. But the other NFL clubs had dismissed the 5 feet 9 inch, 208-pound halfback as too small and certainly too slow. But just as Schramm and Landry once had, Jones and Johnson could spot talent where other supposedly expert eyes didn't. Emmitt Smith became a Dallas Cowboy.

So did Auburn wide receiver Alexander Wright, picked in the second round, and Miami defensive tackle Jimmie Jones, selected in the third. A late-round find was Albany State cornerback Kenneth Gant. Dallas had procured a great amount of talent from the draft again.

This year, though, Johnson was convinced he had enough good players to win quite a few NFC games, perhaps enough to put the Cowboys back in the playoffs. He said as much and was mocked by the media. Jones reiterated his faith in Johnson and his belief that Dallas was close to regaining its previous stature as an NFL powerhouse. He became the butt of media jokes, too.

But during the off-season, Dallas veterans and rookies learned that things were going to be very, very different. The Cowboys instituted a new system that paid

Emmitt Smith gets a lift after scoring against the Eagles

Jay Novacek tears away in Jets game

players to work out during the spring and early summer. The team also made attendance mandatory at minicamps and quarterback schools. Johnson wanted his team to be in shape, and he also believed off-season workouts helped new teammates bond with one another. Every time Johnson suggested innovations—which almost always cost

the team owner more money—Jones agreed. While he was already becoming known as an office pinchpenny who wouldn't tolerate unnecessary expenditures by Cowboys employees, Jones was also willing to spend whatever was required to take his team back to the top.

Training camp opened in a new setting. Since 1963, the Cowboys had trained in salubrious Thousand Oaks, California. But Jerry Jones found another site closer to home—the campus of St. Edwards University in Austin. The new location served several purposes. Travel costs for exhibition games in Texas Stadium were drastically decreased. Dallas players got used to working in the same Texas heat they'd have to endure during the early regular season. Best of all, ardent Cowboys fans around the country could visit Austin and enjoy far greater proximity to their heroes. The first St. Edwards' tradition established was "autograph alley"—players walked

James Washington copes with the heat in a summer workout at Valley Ranch

from the locker room to the practice fields down a roped outdoor pathway. Fans were allowed to line the pathway behind the ropes, and players were encouraged, whenever possible, to stop to sign autographs or pose for photos. The new fan-friendly camp has been a continued success; each summer more than one hundred thousand fans have made excursions to St. Edwards.

And when the first Austin training camp opened, there were young veterans in attendance as well as rookies. In 1990 the NFL had adopted a limited program of free agency known as Plan B, and Dallas snapped up several players who would prove useful. In 1990, defensive back Ray Horton was a major contributor. In 1991, linebacker Vinson Smith and safety James Washington were especially valuable acquisitions. So was a tight end the Phoenix Cardinals had discarded; his name was Jay Novacek.

Emmitt Smith was a training camp absentee, though he'd sign in time for the regular season. But the New Orleans Saints had a holdout, too. Their starting quarterback, Bobby Hebert, would eventually sit out the 1990 season. Saints general manager Jim Finks was desperate for a quarterback, any quarterback, with at least the potential to lead the Saints' offense. Jones and Johnson had shrewdly figured some team would find itself in such a predicament; they traded Steve Walsh to New Orleans in

return for first- and third-round picks in 1991 and a second-round pick in 1992.

Yet for all their smart trades, draft picks, Plan B acquisitions, and confidence, after 10 regular season games Dallas was just 3-7. A mid-October, 24-6 loss to the defending Super Bowl champion 49ers showed how far the Cowboys had to go. That loss, though, was followed by the team's first four-game winning streak since 1985. In order, Dallas knocked off the Rams, Redskins, Saints, and Cardinals. At 7-7, the Cowboys fulfilled Johnson's preseason prediction that they'd be in the playoff hunt.

"When we started to win some games, Coach Johnson got on a high you wouldn't believe. I think he was like a manic-depressive. A lot of coaches tell you winning is the only thing, but when it came to winning, well, Coach Johnson was just crazy about it."

—NATE NEWTON

Fan favorite Bill Bates celebrates a fumble recovery against New Orleans

135

Daniel Stubbs pressures Tampa Bay's Vinnie Testaverde

Victory over the Rams leaves Jimmy and Emmitt smiling

But in their next game against the Eagles, Aikman went out early with a shoulder separation. He was lost for the season. Dallas had been clever to trade Walsh for high draft picks, but the Cowboys could have used him against Philadelphia. Babe Laufenberg, who had replaced Walsh as Aikman's backup, couldn't move the team. The

Eagles won easily, 17-3. Dallas still had a faint shot at the playoffs, but a 26-7 loss to Atlanta in the season's final game ended that.

Still, 7-9 was a big improvement over 1-15. Johnson was voted NFL Coach of the Year. Rookie Emmitt Smith, as Johnson and Jones had anticipated, led Dallas with 937 rushing

yards and 11 touchdowns. He had become a firm fan favorite. While Michael Irvin had been hurt much of the year, Kelvin Martin filled in admirably with 64 catches for 732 yards. Plan B acquisition Jay Novacek was a revelation; he caught 59 passes for 657 yards and established himself as a dependable go-to receiver in clutch situations.

Aikman's numbers, though better, still left room for improvement. The second-year pro completed 226 passes in 399 attempts, an admirable 56.6 percentage, but he threw 18 interceptions compared with just 11 touchdowns.

In all, Dallas scored 244 points and allowed 308. But that was deceptive; without Aikman, the offense managed just 10 points in the last 2 games, while the defense yielded 43. Also, none of the losses had been a blowout.

Dallas's goal for 1991 was clear. In 1990, the Cowboys had almost gotten back into the NFC playoffs. In 1991, they expected to participate in them.

1991 Thanks to the Herschel Walker heist, Dallas had yet another first-round pick from the Vikings as well as its own first-round selection. After a complex round of wheeling and dealing, Dallas turned the Minnesota slot, plus a second-round pick, into a package that was traded to the Patriots for the overall first selection of the first round. With that pick, Dallas chose Miami defensive tackle Russell Maryland. Then the Cowboys used their own first-round pick to select Tennessee wide receiver Alvin Harper, whose college records in the high jump surpassed his football exploits.

Daniel Stubbs, 96, and Jim Jeffcoat, 77, sack the Chargers quarterback, Billy Joe Tolliver

Emmitt Smith gets the word during 1991 Giants game

Cowboys try to block a Giants field goal attempt

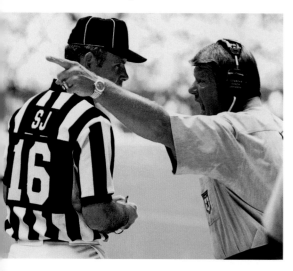

Jimmy Johnson argues with the referee during loss to Eagles

In the second round, Dallas got Michigan State linebacker Dixon Edwards; in the third, Central State (Ohio) tackle Erik Williams. This was one of the draft picks Dallas received from the Saints in exchange for Steve Walsh.

Later rounds yielded running back Curvin Richards, who would make a unique contribution to the Super Bowl drive of 1992; Leon Lett, a defensive end from Emporia State, who would also earn special notoriety; and, in the twelfth and final round, cornerback Larry Brown of Texas Christian University.

Jones then pulled off an unprecedented coup by signing his top three choices before draft day was over. In all, the 1991 draft ranked as one of the very best in Cowboys history.

There wasn't much help to be found among Plan B free agents; only tight end Alfredo Roberts stayed with Dallas very long. And for the first time, but not the last, a key Cowboy who would become a Plan B free agent chose to sign with another team: guard Crawford Ker headed to Denver.

Two trades helped the Cowboys immensely. A second and an eighth-round pick brought defensive lineman Tony Casillas from Atlanta. A fourth-round pick was all Al Davis of the Raiders wanted for quarterback Steve Beuerlein.

For the second consecutive season under Johnson, Dallas opened the season with a victory, this time a 26-14 win over the Browns. Two losses followed, a 33-31 squeaker to the Redskins and a disappointing 24-0 pounding from the Eagles at Texas Stadium.

But then Dallas settled down. Smith began grinding out yardage, and Michael Irvin, enjoying his first injury-free NFL season, displayed a remarkable ability to hang onto the ball against the tightest coverage.

A November win over Washington at RFK Stadium showcased the new-era Cowboys at their finest. The Redskins, who would finish 14-2 and easily win the NFC East, were heavily favored. Johnson told his team before kickoff that he planned to take a lot of chances; any trick play

Dixon Edwards turns his first NFL interception into a touchdown, next page

Michael Irvin makes a great catch against Darrell Green of the Redskins

might be called at any time. Aikman threw an early interception that Washington turned into a 7-0 lead, but Johnson called a draw on third and 15 from the Redskin 32, and Smith ran in virtually untouched to tie the game. Not content with one surprise for Washington, the Cowboys tried an onside kick, and recovered it. They didn't score then, but the Redskins were back on their heels wondering what Dallas was going to try next.

On the last play of the second period, Aikman utilized Alvin Harper's unique leaping ability to complete a lofted pass in the Washington end zone. The Cowboys led 14-7, but Aikman was injured on the play. Beuerlein took over in the second half and guided drives to a touchdown and a field goal. Washington scored late to make the final 24-21 for Dallas. Just two seasons after being the NFC doormat, the Cowboys had knocked off 1991's eventual Super Bowl champions, and on the road at that.

Dallas finished 11-5, ending the season with a five-game winning streak. For the first time since 1986, the Cowboys scored more points—342—than they allowed—310.

Emmitt Smith was almost the entire Dallas running game, but he was all that was needed. Smith's 1,563 rushing yards led the NFC. Many of his longest runs came through gaping holes knocked in the defense by full-back Daryl Johnston, who would become a special favorite, not only of Cowboys fans but of spectators in other NFL cities as well. On those rare occasions Johnston carried the ball,

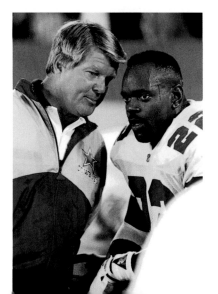

Jimmy Johnson and Emmitt Smith confer during Detroit game

Dallas fans in Texas Stadium or any other NFL park would chant, "Moose! Moose!"—Johnston's nickname.

Irvin, finally getting a chance to show what he could accomplish over a full season, caught 93 passes and led the league with 1,523 receiving yards. Novacek was another favorite Aikman target, pulling in 59 passes for 664 yards.

Aikman's numbers were substantially improved. He completed 237 of 363 passes for an average of 65.3, which also led the league. For the first time, Aikman threw more touchdown passes than interceptions, 11-10.

When Aikman went down with his knee injury, Beuerlein filled in almost too admirably. In the first round of the playoffs, he calmly guided Dallas to a 17-13 win over the Chicago Bears. It was Dallas's first win in the NFC playoffs since 1982.

But Aikman had believed he was well enough to play against the Bears and was unhappy when he didn't. He became even unhappier when Beuerlein was tapped to start against the Detroit Lions in Dallas's second-round game. Aikman eventually got in the game, but it made no difference. Led by quarterback Erik Kramer, the run'n'gun Lions offense shredded the

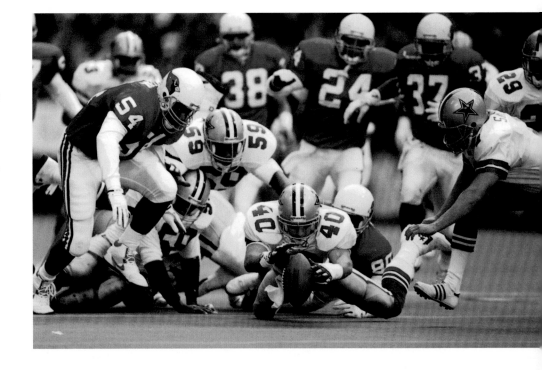

Dallas defense. Detroit won 38-6, and the game was as one-sided as the score indicated.

Jones and Johnson weren't surprised. As proud as they were of the team they had assembled, they realized that any team with a good passing offense stood a good chance of beating Dallas. That defensive weakness was, they concluded, the final flaw. They would correct it in 1992, when simply getting into the playoffs would no longer be good enough.

Bill Bates gets his hands on a loose ball against the Cardinals

Emmitt Smith running hard against the Bears

EMMITT SMITH

BY JIM BROWDER

The day Emmitt Smith first reported to Cowboyland, he was clad in a brown vest splashed with bright yellow polka dots, with matching trousers.

Had the Cowboys drafted Emmitt the Clown in the first round?

Then he skipped training camp, missing all of the 1990 preseason games.

Had the Cowboys hired a troublemaker?

Rumors began drifting around that this 5 feet 9 inch guy who dropped out of college to enter the draft really was too little and too slow to make it in the big, tough NFL.

Maybe the 16 teams that passed up Emmitt in the first round were right. Were the Cowboys wrong?

Well, when Emmitt traded in that polka dot vest for a Cowboys uniform, a magnificent transformation occurred, not unlike Clark Kent stepping into a nearby telephone booth. Once on the playing field, there was no doubt the Cowboys had nabbed a prize.

As they say, the rest is history. And Emmitt Smith continues to make history each season as he rewrites the Cowboys' rushing and scoring records and climbs the ladder toward his rightful place among the NFL all-time elite.

Along the way, Emmitt has established himself as a gentleman, an astute businessman, an able television huckster, a person who devotes himself freely to numerous charitable causes, and, reluctantly, a role model.

"I think everybody is a role model," says Emmitt. "You talk about athletes, yeah, we're all high-profile individuals. But we're all normal people, too. When you talk about the ultimate role models, you talk about the people who were in Oklahoma City (after the federal building bombing) pulling people out of the rubble. You talk about the people who go overseas to fight for our country. You talk about the people in the hospital who are saving lives on a day-to-day basis. You talk about the educational field.

"I get kind of turned off when I hear people saying, 'You are a role model, and you are supposed to do this and do that.' I'm not supposed to be anything but the best person I can possibly be. I try to live my life according to what the laws of the Bible say and the laws of the country say. That's my responsibility to myself, my family, and this country. Whatever else I do is extra."

That's typical Emmitt. After scoring 4 touchdowns in the 1995 season opener against the New York Giants, Emmitt praised everyone but himself: "The line did a great job. They definitely are one of the best lines in the league. If you don't get yards behind these guys, something's wrong. They made my job very easy."

Emmitt was so overjoyed with his opening touchdown run of 60 yards he displayed some uncharacteristic showboating. He raised a hand in the air about the 15-yard line as he looked back at pursuing Giants.

"Oh, man, it was ridiculous, believe me," Emmitt said after the game. "I apologize to the Giants for showboating, or whatever you want to call it. The last thing I want to do is be a showboat player. The emotions just took over.

"My father always said, 'Act like you've been there.' Well, it had been a long time since I'd been there, so it was pretty emotional."

Emmitt normally tucks the football under his arm after a touchdown and walks it to the sideline for safekeeping. Most of his touchdown footballs are on display in a family-operated business back home in Florida. That's a lot of footballs—31 in 1995 alone (25 during the regular season and 6 in the playoffs).

The family business is one of several ventures for Emmitt, who is successfully preparing for his post-football years: "You watch how people spend money on stuff they don't really need, and that's how you learn to put your money in the right place. Because I do that, I don't have to worry about going broke. You have to stay on course. As long as I stay on course, I don't have to worry about doing the wrong thing because I know what will happen if I don't. I don't have to worry about taking drugs because I've seen what drugs do to people."

Late in the 1995 Super Bowl season while he was in hot pursuit of some NFL records, Emmitt said, "I'd give up the rushing title, 2000 yards, the touchdown record—just to win another Super Bowl. Just win. Winning would be significant. Setting records is not significant if the season goes down the tubes."

In 1995, the season didn't go down the tubes. The Cowboys won their third Super Bowl in four years.

During the off-season, Emmitt returned to the University of Florida to finish work on his undergraduate degree. He waved to the audience and flashed a large smile as he received his diploma and saw his mother holding up a sign that read: "Congratulations Emmitt. 'Proud Mary.'" He had promised Mary six years earlier that he would return and get his degree. "I've always been a man of my word," said NFL's rushing champion in four of the past five seasons.

How did it feel?

"This ranks right up there with the Super Bowl, without a doubt. It took a lot of dedication, a lot of determination to come back and get my dream fulfilled."

A nice guy, a man of his word, and a hero, too.

Will Rogers once said, "Heroes are made every little while, but only one in a million conduct themselves afterward so that it makes us proud that we honored them at the time."

Emmitt Smith is one in a million.

Bill Bates, 40, celebrates defensive play against Houston with Dixon Edwards, 58

Jimmy Johnson the motivator

1992 The Cowboys used the draft and a pair of shrewd trades to bulk up their defense. With two first-round picks acquired via deals with other clubs, Dallas drafted cornerback Kevin Smith of Texas A&M and middle linebacker Robert Jones from East Carolina. The second round produced safety Darren Woodson of Arizona State, and cornerback Clayton Holmes from Carson-Newman was snapped up in the third.

The 1992 draft wasn't as glamorous as those the Cowboys had orchestrated in recent years, but it was solid and sensible.

Then, to the amazement of Jones and Johnson, archrival San Francisco came calling. The 49ers wanted to unload defensive lineman Charles Haley, whose strong personality had him at odds with San Francisco team officials and some of his teammates. The 49ers wanted draft choices for Haley, and Dallas found two midlevel picks they could spare. Three weeks later, the Cowboys literally stole defensive back Thomas Everett from the Steelers for a fifth-round choice in 1993.

These ball hawks were badly needed. Having been aided by Plan B free agency in recent years, Dallas had now begun losing players under that system. Linebacker Jack Del Rio, cornerback Manny Hendrix, and kicker Ken Willis all departed via Plan B. Jones shrugged and nabbed Plan B free agents Frank Cornish, an offensive lineman, and kicker Brad Daluiso.

Another 1992 rules change by the NFL would soon affect the Cowboys. After extended negotiations, it was agreed that all veteran players with five years' experience could become free agents when their contracts expired. In return, owners won a team salary cap tied to a percentage of gross revenues. The collegiate draft was also shortened to 8 rounds, which benefited owners instead of players, since individuals who were drafted would receive higher signing bonuses and salaries than those who joined teams as undrafted free agents.

And on May 1, Jerry Jones was appointed by the commissioner to serve on the NFL's Competition Committee. He was the first owner to become a committee member in years. It was tacit recognition by the NFL that

Jones's ingenuity could benefit the league as a whole.

When the season began, very little went wrong for Dallas. The Cowboys opened with a 23-10 trouncing of the Redskins on Monday Night Football. A 34-28 win over the Giants came next; Dallas almost blew a 34-0 lead, and Johnson was able to use the Giants' comeback as a reminder to his players that they should never assume

Helmet-to-helmet against Seattle

Defense rises to the occasion against Cardinals

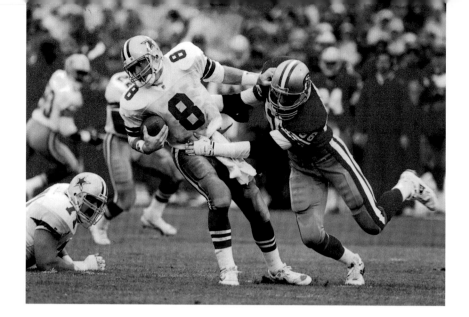

Troy Aikman tries to avoid a sack in NFC title game against the 49ers

"We know certain guys have great talent, but I still see them as members of the team, contributing to winning games and championships. All of us work toward the same goal, to win."

—CHAD HENNINGS
Dallas Cowboys defensive lineman
1992-

Aikman meets the fans after a preseason workout

a game was safely in hand. After blowing out Phoenix to go 3-0, though, Dallas was pummeled 31-7 by the Eagles in Philadelphia. The Eagles, who were also 3-0, had been installed as preseason favorites to win the NFC East. The Cowboys used the loss as impetus; they won their next five in a row. Philadelphia, on the other hand, lost three of its next four. The third loss was to Dallas in Texas Stadium. In the rematch, the Cowboys dominated on offense and defense to win 20-10. A rubber match would take place in the playoffs.

Dallas lost only twice more during the regular season. The Rams edged the Cowboys 27-23 when Dallas accumulated too many costly penalties. The Redskins also claimed a 20-17 victory three weeks later when normally sure-handed Emmitt Smith somehow lost a bizarre fumble in his own end zone late in the game.

Eight days later, the Cowboys walloped Atlanta 41-17 on Monday Night Football. For the first time since 1985, they were champions of the NFC East. With the title wrapped up, Johnson might have been forgiven for dismissing the season's final game against the Bears as meaningless. Instead, he approached it with the same intensity as he would a Super Bowl. By the fourth quarter, Dallas led 27-0. Looking ahead to the playoffs, Johnson pulled Emmitt Smith and put in his backup, Curvin Richards. Richards fumbled, and Chicago came up with the ball. Minutes later, the Bears scored. Dallas took the kickoff and began another offensive drive. Richards fumbled again; a Chicago defender scooped up the loose ball and returned it for a touchdown. The Cowboys still won easily, 27-14, but after the game Jimmy Johnson cut Curvin Richards from his football team. After that, it was a cinch none of the Dallas players would feel complacent going into the playoffs.

The Cowboys' regular season statistics were almost their best ever. Emmitt Smith led the league in rushing with 1,713 yards and 18 touchdowns.

146

Michael Irvin caught 78 passes for 1,396 yards and 7 touchdowns. Kelvin Martin led the league in punt return yardage. Aikman completed a staggering 302 of 473 passes for 23 touchdowns and just 14 interceptions. In all, the offense that was so inept just a few years earlier blitzed opposing defenses for 409 points.

But the defense was Johnson's special pride. They had allowed just 243 points, meaning Dallas won its regular season games by an average score of 26-15, a whopping 11-point margin.

And though Aikman, Smith, Irvin, and Haley got the most headlines, everyone else on the team made contributions that showed up in glittering season records if not league-leading individual statistics.

In their first game of the playoffs, Dallas had the satisfaction of clobbering

Emmitt Smith romps against the Chiefs in 1992 game

A happy Jerry Jones salutes a victory over the Eagles

The Cowboys won the toss against the Lions

comeback, managed just 29 for the Eagles.

Then it was on to Candlestick Park for the NFC championship game. Dallas hadn't beaten San Francisco since 1980. It was against the 49ers in 1982 that Dwight Clark made "The Catch" to send the Cowboys tumbling into a long tailspin. Dallas couldn't have asked for a more appropriate opponent.

But in the week before the game, the skies opened up over San Francisco. It appeared the game would be played underwater, a real disadvantage to a Dallas team that built its whole game plan around a crunching ground attack. The 49ers, though, would benefit from a slick

the Eagles 34-10 at Texas Stadium. Buddy Ryan was long gone; Rich Kotite had replaced him as coach. But Dallas still had no love for the Eagles, and everyone savored the win. Smith raced for 114 yards. Herschel Walker, whose departure in 1989 became the catalyst for the Cowboys team

Michael Irvin scores against the Cardinals

field. Star receivers Jerry Rice, John Taylor, and Brent Jones would find it easier to grab quarterback Steve Young's pinpoint passes if Cowboys defenders slid around while attempting to cover them.

The Candlestick Park grounds crew did yeoman work; by game time, the field's natural turf was fairly firm. The same couldn't be said for the 49ers defense, which had allowed just 236 points during the regular season but hadn't faced Dallas.

The first half was tight, ending in a 10-10 tie. But in the second half, the Cowboys defense asserted itself; the 49ers ended the game with 4 turnovers on 2 interceptions and 2 fumbles. Meanwhile, Troy Aikman got hot. He nailed Emmitt Smith and Kelvin Martin with fourth-quarter touchdown passes. San Francisco's Steve Young played courageously, but his team's

4 turnovers to none for Dallas made the difference. With a 30-20 win, the Dallas Cowboys moved on to Super Bowl XXVII, the team's first Super Bowl trip since its loss to Pittsburgh in Super Bowl XIII.

Emmitt Smith races to a touchdown in NFC title game against the 49ers

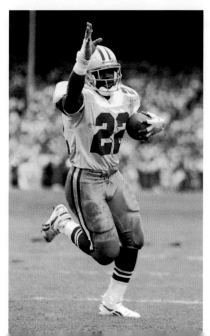

"People thought we got back to the top faster than planned, but if you'll look back at all we said in '89, we never once used a term like 'five-year plan.' We had what Al Davis of the Raiders called 'a sense of urgency.' He came to one of our practices and told me, 'Jerry, there's an urgency about everything done by the Cowboys, by the front office and coaches and individual players. I wish we had that same feeling with the Raiders.' We always planned to rebuild fast. The quickness of it all didn't surprise us. It was all the more exciting to everyone else because they thought, well, here's a once-great franchise that won't ever come back. We NFL newcomers came in and did the job. Success is never as exciting when it's expected. That's why Jimmy Johnson won't be able to duplicate what he did here down in Miami."

—JERRY JONES

SUPER BOWL
XXVII

While the Cowboys hadn't played in a Super Bowl for 13 years, the AFC's Buffalo Bills had a lot of recent experience. The Bills had lost the last two Super Bowls, 20-19 to the New York Giants and 37-24 to the Washington Redskins. Accordingly, prognosticators were split. Some favored Buffalo over Dallas because the majority of the Bills players had Super Bowl experience. Others picked the Cowboys because

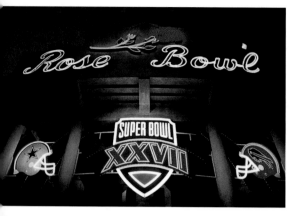

The site of Super Bowl XXVII

That hard-to-get ticket

Buffalo already was linked with the Minnesota Vikings in the pantheon of Super Bowl losers.

On a gorgeous January day at the Rose Bowl in Pasadena, Dallas rained all over the Bills' parade.

The Cowboys spotted Buffalo a brief lead. Buffalo blocked a first-quarter punt by Mike Saxon, and Thurman Thomas scored a few plays later on a 2-yard run. Fans of the Bills' star running back had to make that memory last; Thomas was a non-factor for the rest of the game.

On Buffalo's next possession, James Washington intercepted a pass by Bills quarterback Jim Kelly. It was a harbinger of things to come; by game's end, Dallas would have forced a Super Bowl record 9 turnovers. Troy Aikman made the most of Buffalo's initial miscue. He marched his team down the field and tied the score on a 23-yard touchdown pass to Jay Novacek.

It took Dallas one play after the ensuing kickoff to go ahead for good. Charles Haley sacked Kelly, who fumbled the ball. Jimmie Jones snatched the ball out of the air and rumbled in for a touchdown. It was 14-7 Dallas as the first quarter ended. Buffalo should have waved a white flag.

For a moment, it still seemed like an evenly matched contest. Dallas held Buffalo on fourth down at the

Lineman Jimmie Jones tramples Buffalo's Jim Kelly on the way to a touchdown

Tony Casillas, 75, and Dixon Edwards, 58, stand over a battered Jim Kelly, next page

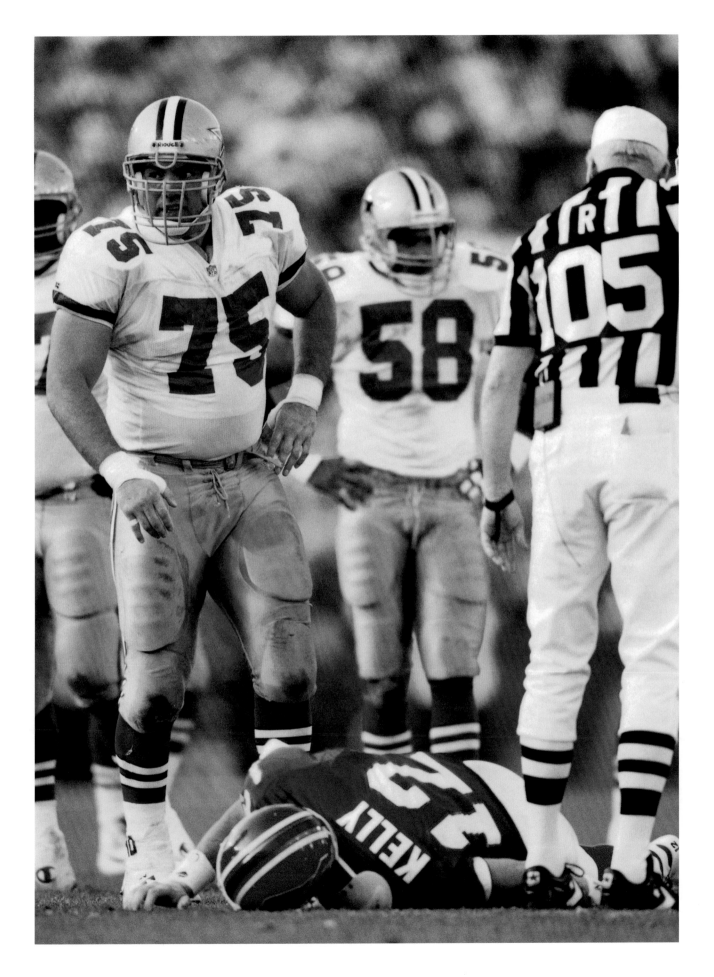

Troy Aikman efficiently picked apart the Buffalo pass defense

Emmitt runs away from the Bills

Cowboys' 1-yard line; on their next possession, the Bills kicked a 21-yard field goal. Then Aikman and Michael Irvin took over. They collaborated on 2 touchdown passes, the first for 19 yards and the second, made possible by a spectacular Irvin catch, an 18-yarder. The score was 28-10 at halftime, and Buffalo fans thought things couldn't get much worse. They did.

Dallas opened the second-half scoring with a 20-yard field goal. To their credit, the Bills didn't quit. Frank Reich, subbing for an injured Kelly, lofted a 40-yard scoring pass to Don Beebe. The play should have been called back; replays clearly showed Reich passing the line of scrimmage before he released the ball. But the pass, which made the score 31-17, was Buffalo's last offensive gasp. In the final period Aikman sailed a 45-yard touchdown pass to Alvin Harper. Emmitt Smith scored his first-ever Super Bowl touchdown on a 10-yard burst. Linebacker Ken Norton returned another Buffalo fumble 9 yards for a score. It was 52-17, and Dallas was closing in on the Super Bowl scoring record of 55 points.

They almost got it. Late in the game, Jim Jeffcoat sacked Reich, who fumbled on the Dallas 31. Leon Lett picked up the ball and set out for the Bills' goal. The mammoth Lett had nothing but open field in front of him and a healthy head start on his Bills pursuers. When he was within 5 yards of a score, Lett celebrated prematurely by hot-dogging, waving his arms out from his sides. Unfortunately, one of those arms ended in a hand that held the football. Beebe, running more out of pride than from hope, caught up with Lett a yard from the goal line and slapped the ball loose. It tumbled out of the end zone, and Buffalo took possession on a touchback. With a blowout lead of 52-17, even Jimmy Johnson could only laugh.

When the final gun sounded to end Super Bowl XXVII, the Dallas Cowboys were champions of the NFL. No other team in the league had ever come back so far, so fast. As Jerry

The game was a blowout, but there was one embarrassing moment. Leon Lett had the ball knocked away just before he could waltz in for a touchdown

Jones accepted the Super Bowl trophy from NFL commissioner Paul Tagliabue, he wore the satisfied smile of a man who had proved he knew what he was doing all along.

The winning coach

SUPER BOWL XXVII STATISTICS

SCORING

Buffalo	7	3	7	0	**17**
Dallas	14	14	3	21	**52**

FIRST QUARTER:
Buffalo, Thomas 2-yard run (Christie kick)
Dallas, Novacek 23-yard pass from Aikman (Elliott kick)
Dallas, Jones 2-yard fumble return (Elliott kick)

SECOND QUARTER:
Buffalo, Christie 21-yard field goal
Dallas, Irvin 19-yard pass from Aikman (Elliott kick)
Dallas, Irvin 18-yard pass from Aikman (Elliott kick)

THIRD QUARTER:
Dallas, Elliott 20-yard field goal
Buffalo, Beebe 40-yard pass from Reich (Christie kick)

FOURTH QUARTER:
Dallas, Harper 45-yard pass from Aikman (Elliott kick)
Dallas, Smith 10-yard run (Elliott kick)
Dallas, Norton 9-yard fumble return (Elliott kick)

TEAM	BUFFALO	DALLAS
First downs	22	20
Net yards	362	408
Fumbles lost	5	0
Interceptions	4	0
Penalty yards	30	53

INDIVIDUAL:
RUSHING:
Buffalo: Davis 86, Thomas 19, Gardner 3, Reich 0
Dallas: Smith 108, Aikman 28, Gainer 1, Johnston 0, Beuerlein 0

PASSING:
Buffalo: Kelly 4-7, 82 yards, 0 TDs; Reich 18-31, 194 yards, 1 touchdown
Dallas: Aikman 22-30, 273 yards, 4 touchdowns

RECEIVING:
Buffalo: Reed 8-152, Thomas 4-10, Davis 3-16, Beebe 2-50, Tasker 2-30, Metzelaars 2-12, McKeller 1-6
Dallas: Novacek 7-72, Irvin 6-114, Smith 6-27, Johnston 2-15, Harper 1-45

Kenneth Gant had a thing for sharks

1993 A week after guiding his team to victory in Super Bowl XXVII, Jimmy Johnson was back in his office planning for the collegiate draft. As NFL champions, Dallas would draft last, or twenty-eighth, in each round. That didn't dismay the Cowboys brain trust. After several years of first-round bonanzas, in fact, Dallas traded away its first-round pick in 1993. The player the Cowboys coveted, Miami wide receiver Kevin Williams, was still available in the second round. In the third, they chose another Miami player, linebacker Darrin Smith. And, in keeping with the longtime Dallas tradition of finding quality players late in the draft, the Cowboys selected Nevada-Reno safety Brock Marion in the seventh round.

This year, there would be no help for Dallas through Plan B free agency. The team made no free agent signings, and it lost backup quarterback Steve Beuerlein and flashy kick returner/wide receiver Kelvin Martin.

The regular season got off to a rocky start. Emmitt Smith and Jerry Jones had trouble agreeing on a new contract for the star running back. Smith held out for Dallas's first two games against the Redskins and Bills, and the Cowboys lost both games. Smith signed before the third game, and Dallas won seven straight. One of the victories was a 26-17 win over the 49ers; obviously, the Cowboys had moved ahead in that rivalry.

But the winning streak was also deceptive. Several key players, including Aikman, Smith, Haley, and Norton, were trying to play through assorted injuries. Too many games against inferior opponents were close. Johnson ranted almost nonstop. And, of course, the rest of the NFL was out to knock off the defending champions.

On October 21, Dallas lost to Atlanta 27-14. Falcons defensive back Deion Sanders, doubling as a wide receiver, gave the Cowboys fits. Four days later in Dallas's traditional Thanksgiving Day game at Texas

Emmitt Smith gets away from Cardinals defenders

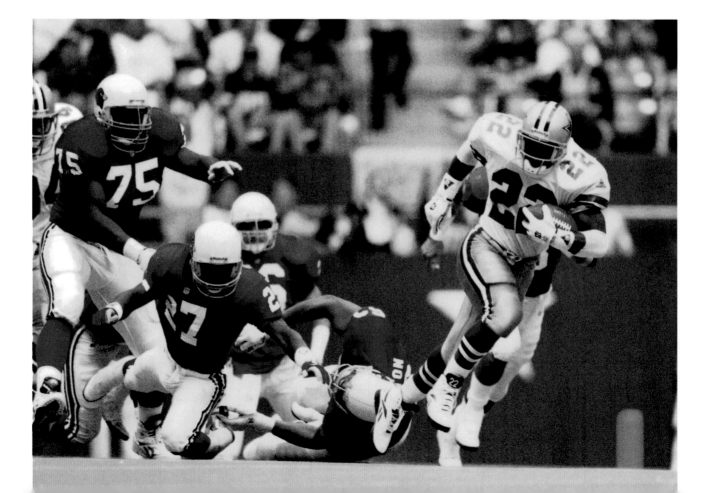

DALLAS COWBOYS IN RING OF HONOR

★

1. Don Perkins, running back, inducted in 1976
2. Don Meredith, quarterback, inducted in 1976
3. Chuck Howley, linebacker, inducted in 1977
4. Bob Lilly, defensive tackle, inducted in 1980
5. Mel Renfro, defensive back, inducted in 1981
6. Roger Staubach, quarterback, inducted in 1985
7. Lee Roy Jordan, linebacker, inducted in 1989
8. Tom Landry, head coach, inducted in 1993
9. Tony Dorsett, running back, inducted in 1994
10. Randy White, defensive tackle, inducted in 1994

Tom Landry is inducted into the Ring of Honor. Behind him are Mel Renfro and Roger Staubach. He shakes hands with Chuck Howley while Bob Lilly, far left, watches

Jimmy Johnson talks to Kenneth Gant

◆

"When I played for other teams, the Cowboys were the team we wanted to hate. They were the team we went after because of their level of success. They were the glittery team, the one with the stars on their helmets."

—WADE WILSON
Former Minnesota Viking, Atlanta Falcon, and New Orleans Saint; Dallas Cowboys quarterback 1995-

Stadium, an ice storm blew through the area. The Cowboys and visiting Dolphins played skidball. Emmitt Smith went out with an injury; his replacement, Lincoln Coleman, performed well. With seconds left to play and the Cowboys nursing a 14-13 lead, Miami attempted a field goal. Jimmie Jones broke through the Dolphins lines and partially blocked the kick. The ball lurched toward the Dallas goal line and spun on the ice a dozen yards

short of it. On the sidelines, Jones threw up his arms in triumph. But Leon Lett, obeying some primal misjudgment, created a disaster of biblical proportions. Unnecessarily, Lett tried to fall on the ball. He bobbled it instead; grateful Miami players grabbed it to regain possession, and the Dolphins kicked the winning field goal. Afterward,

Leon Lett's mistake in the ice against Miami, next page

game. Both teams were 11-4, and the winner would be champion of the NFC East. The Cowboys didn't want to go into the playoffs as a wild-card team. After 4 quarters, it was a 13-13 tie. Emmitt Smith, playing with a painful shoulder injury, refused to come out of the game. His gutty running moved Dallas into a position to win the game in overtime with a field goal. The Cowboys had repeated as champions of their division.

Their regular season statistics were unimpressive only in comparison with what they had accomplished as a healthier club in 1992. Even after missing the first two games of the season, Smith gained 1,486 yards and led the NFC in rushing for the third consecutive year. Irvin snared 88 passes for 1,330 yards and 7 touchdowns; Daryl Johnston, everybody's favorite "Moose," caught 50. Aikman connected on 271 of 392 passes, accumulating 15 touchdown strikes and getting intercepted just 6 times. In all, Dallas

Leon Lett realizes his mistake while Elvis Patterson, 43, questions the referee

though Lett avoided the media, it was unlikely he could avoid Johnson. Unlike Curvin Richards, at least, Lett wasn't cut as an object lesson to the rest of the team.

Dallas won four straight games, then faced the New York Giants in the Meadowlands. It was an important

Loss to Buffalo is upsetting to Mark Stepnoski, left, and Mark Tuinei

Green Bay's Brent Favre is sacked by Jim Jeffcoat, followed by Jimmie Jones, 97, next page

Alvin Harper lands in the end zone during play-off game with Green Bay

Michael Irvin hugs Alvin Harper, 80, who scored on a pass from Troy Aikman against the Giants

scored 376 points, a distant second in the NFC to San Francisco's 473, and allowed 229, second to the 205 allowed by the Giants.

The Cowboys opened the playoffs against the Packers in Texas Stadium. Dallas took a while getting into offensive gear; Green Bay led 3-0 at the end of the first quarter. With Smith still hampered by his ailing shoulder, the Cowboys relied on Aikman's arm to put the Packers away. The five-year veteran threw touchdown passes to

Harper, Novacek, and Irvin, and Dallas won 27-17.

For the second consecutive season, the Cowboys had to beat San Francisco to get to the Super Bowl. This time, the NFC championship showdown between the two was played in Texas Stadium. Because of Smith's injury—he continued to play with a separated shoulder—the game was considered a toss-up. But a 21-point Cowboys explosion in the second half turned a 7-7 tie into a

cakewalk. Aikman threw 3 more touch-down passes and finished the contest with 14 completions in 18 pass attempts. Bernie Kosar, who had been signed as a backup, finished up for Dallas. The Cowboys' 38-21 win sent them to Super Bowl XXVIII, which was to be played in Atlanta. As in the NFC championship game, Dallas would be facing a familiar foe.

Cowboys offense faces 49ers in NFC title game

Jimmy Johnson and Emmitt enjoy the victory over San Francisco

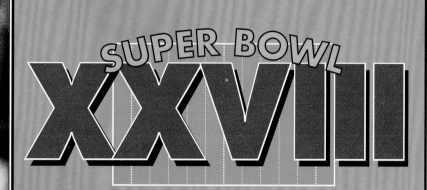

SUPER BOWL XXVIII

Buffalo had won the AFC title for the fourth consecutive year, and comedians across the country unmercifully used the Bills' three straight Super Bowl losses as grist for jokes. The team the Cowboys would face in Atlanta was almost exactly the same as the club they'd blown out in the Rose Bowl. Everyone, Dallas players included, expected Super Bowl XXVIII to be different only in that the break between conference championship games and the Super Bowl had been reduced from two weeks to one.

But it was different. If the Bills didn't own any Super Bowl trophies, they still had their pride. The Cowboys could manage just 2 field goals

against them in the first half. Buffalo matched those with a pair of field goals of their own and upped the scoring ante with a 4-yard touchdown run by Thurman Thomas. At halftime the Bills were ahead 13-6. They compounded Cowboys fans' concern by taking the second half kickoff and marching down the field again. Another Buffalo touchdown would have put the Bills ahead 20-6, and perhaps would have given the perennial Super Bowl losers enough confidence to hold off Dallas.

Thomas took a handoff from Kelly and darted around the line. He was met by Leon Lett, who more than atoned for his Thanksgiving Day turkey imitation by stripping the ball loose. Dallas defensive back James

Emmitt Smith had a big game

Troy Aikman takes off with Jeff Wright, 91, and Cornelius Bennett, 97, in pursuit

166

Washington scooped up the fumble and returned it 46 yards for the tying touchdown. Instead of leading 20-6, Buffalo was stuck in a 13-13 tie. Momentum shifted to the Cowboys.

Emmitt Smith, still hampered by a bad shoulder, took over the game. He scored on a 15-yard run in the third quarter and a 1-yard plunge in the fourth. Dallas kicker Eddie Murray added a late, 20-yard field goal. Despite Buffalo's best efforts, the Cowboys had repeated as NFL champions by winning Super Bowl XXVIII, 30-13.

Thurman Thomas, 34, hangs his head after fumbling to Cowboys, above

Troy Aikman celebrates his second Super Bowl victory

Jimmy Johnson with his signs of victory, next page

SUPER BOWL XXVIII STATISTICS

SCORING

Dallas	6	0	14	10	**30**
Buffalo	3	10	0	0	**13**

FIRST QUARTER:
Dallas, Murray 41-yard field goal
Buffalo, Christie 54-yard field goal
Dallas, Murray 24-yard field goal

SECOND QUARTER:
Buffalo, Thomas 4-yard run (Christie kick)
Buffalo, Christie 28-yard field goal

THIRD QUARTER:
Dallas, J. Washington 46-yard fumble return (Murray kick)
Dallas, Smith 15-yard run (Murray kick)

FOURTH QUARTER:
Dallas, Smith 1-yard run (Murray kick)
Dallas, Murray 20-yard field goal

TEAM	DALLAS	BUFFALO
First downs:	20	22
Net yards:	341	314
Fumbles lost:	0	2
Interceptions:	1	1
Penalty yards:	50	10

INDIVIDUAL:

RUSHING
Dallas: Smith 132, K. Williams 6, Aikman 3, Johnston 0, Kosar -1, Coleman -3
Buffalo: Davis 38, Thomas 37, Kelly 12

PASSING
Dallas: Aikman 19-27, 207 yards
Buffalo: Kelly 31-50, 260 yards

RECEIVING
Dallas: Irvin 5-66, Novacek 5-26, Smith 4-26, Harper 3-75, Johnston 2-14
Buffalo: Brooks 7-63, Thomas 7-52, Reed 6-75, Beebe 6-60, Davis 3-(-5), Metzelaars 1-8, McKeller 1-7

JIMMY JOHNSON

BY GIL LEBRETON

In the beginning, there was the hair.

Long before the Asthma Field, long before the two Super Bowl rings, Jimmy Johnson had the hair.

The hair made for good copy. The hair became the solid symbol of Johnson's unyielding stubbornness. The hair was windproof. Buffalo-proof. Jerry-proof.

Tom Landry had the hat. Coach Jimmy had the hair.

Putting up with hair jokes was Coach Jimmy's trade-off for suckering sportswriters into his weekly web of coaching mind games. He'd say it. We'd print it. It may not have had anything to do with that week's game, but Johnson had a way of furthering his own agenda. He was a psychology major in college, we'd remind readers—and ourselves—week after week.

Dealing with Coach Jimmy for five seasons stands as unofficial proof that jaded media types don't mind being manipulated and patronized, as long as it's done with style and, on occasion, a furnace-red complexion.

Johnson scared Cowboys players silly. Not in a physical sense. But emotionally, he inspired them to fear failure. For whatever reason, they yearned not to disappoint him.

Some stories became part of Johnson's Dallas legend.

When, in Coach Jimmy's early years with the team, a rookie labored through wind sprints and suggested it was due to his ongoing asthma, Johnson—in full view of the TV cameras—raged, "Asthma? Asthma? The Asthma Field is (he pointed in the general direction of North Dakota or the Greyhound bus station) over there!"

The message: Coach Jimmy didn't accept excuses.

When second-string running back Curvin Richards committed the sin of fumbling twice during mop-up time of a December game, Johnson cut him.

The message: Coach Jimmy didn't accept lapses in concentration.

Somewhere in the time vault, too, is that classic Apex One TV commercial, showing Johnson driving through the desert in a convertible filled with Cowboys players. The road signs told us they were on their way to the Super Bowl. But when Johnson encountered a hitchhiking owner Jones, dressed in full business suit by the side of the road, he refused to stop. By the neon glare of what happened months later, the commercial was prophetic. But at the time, it just sent another blunt message: Coach Jimmy doesn't pull over for just anybody. Sometimes life really does imitate art.

Why two men as talented as Jones and Johnson couldn't find peaceful common ground remains a Dallas Cowboys mystery. Maybe each wanted more of the credit. Maybe Jerry Jones accidentally deep-fried one of Coach Jimmy's pet tropical fish. Maybe he just didn't tell enough hair jokes.

Clearly, Johnson made mistakes, even if he never admitted them. Drafting a lump from Florida named Rhondy Weston is something Johnson would like the world to forget. And don't forget His Hairness used a No. 1 draft choice to acquire the rights to quarterback Steve Walsh.

But in the end, Johnson's vagaries and ego never scuttled his part in the sudden, swift resurrection of the Cowboys franchise. His eye for talent—not just players, but for the assistant coaches he surrounded himself with—just about lived up to Jerry Jones's memorable 1989 claim that Coach Jimmy was worth "five Heisman Trophy winners and five No. 1 draft picks."

In print, Johnson was fun to tease. He made for great theater, whether he was dodging barbs and snowballs at Buddy Ryan's place or questioning the manhood of George Seifert on the eve of the NFC title game.

One of the last visions we have is from Super Bowl XXVIII in Atlanta. The victory is certain, and Johnson has been doused with Gatorade. Emmitt Smith turns to Johnson and, in the ultimate show of confidence, runs his hands around and through Coach Jimmy's prized coiffure.

It was the last hair joke. Two months later, Johnson was gone. The Asthma Field hasn't seemed the same since.

★ ★ ★

1994 The collegiate draft brought Dallas defensive end Shante Carver from Arizona State, offensive lineman Larry Allen of Sonoma State, and defensive back Darren Studstill of West Virginia. The new blood was needed. During the off-season, other NFL teams snapped up Cowboys free agents. Tony Casillas, Frank Cornish, John Gesek, Kevin Gogan, Jimmie Jones, Bernie Kosar, Eddie Murray, and Ken Norton Jr. all moved on. Salary cap constraints limited Dallas's free agent signings to guard Derek Kennard and quarterback Rodney Peete. The Super Bowl champions would try to three-peat with a vastly different lineup.

They also would play with a new head coach. In five years, Jimmy Johnson and Jerry Jones had rebuilt the Cowboys, but after Super Bowl XXVIII they came to a parting of the ways.

Johnson took a two-year hiatus from the sidelines as a broadcaster for the Fox Network, then in 1996 he was hired as head coach of the Miami Dolphins.

Taking Johnson's place with the Cowboys was former Oklahoma coach Barry Switzer. He had been out of football since 1988, tending to

Barry Switzer takes over

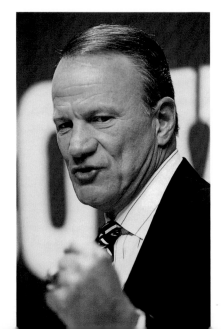

business interests but still keeping in touch with Jones, whom he'd coached at the University of Arkansas.

Switzer's laid-back ways were the antithesis of Johnson's aggressive personality. No one except Jones seemed quite certain the new coach could equal the winning ways of the old one.

Dallas opened the regular season with a solid 26-9 win over the Steelers

Emmitt Smith dives for yardage against the Lions in 1994 game

Barry Switzer, the new coach

in Pittsburgh. Emmitt Smith rushed for 171 yards, and the Pittsburgh offense was unable to move the ball. The Cowboys next edged Houston 20-17, but they lost to Detroit by the same score a week later. The team regrouped and won six in a row; then came a road trip to Candlestick Park in San Francisco. The 49ers had used all sorts of salary cap maneuvers to strengthen their team, and it showed.

"Without being critical of Jimmy, if you look at his history you could say it's one of five-year tenures. By his nature he's not a long-term man for an organization, as opposed, for instance, to Coach Landry. It became apparent to me during the '93 season that Jimmy was not going to be long-term with the Cowboys. I made the coaching change because I'm just not comfortable working with someone who isn't thinking more than a few years ahead. But it's also true that Jimmy and I had five great years together. On balance, our differences were minimal. We had a lot of energy, and we had success beyond most people's wildest dreams."

—**JERRY JONES**

"It was inconceivable to me Barry Switzer would not take the job. Presumptuous, maybe, but still inconceivable. I felt our team would flourish with his skills and the way he appreciates players as people. Barry is recognized as a motivator and he's loyal to his players to a fault. Those were the traits I wanted in my head coach."

—**JERRY JONES**

Michael Irvin pulls in a touchdown pass against the Cardinals

Chad Hennings has become a force on the defensive line

They beat Dallas 21-14. Troy Aikman had a rare bad day, throwing 3 interceptions. The following week Aikman was injured during a 31-7 win over the Redskins. It was particularly bad timing because Dallas had just four days until its annual Thanksgiving Day game at Texas Stadium; Aikman's leg wasn't seriously injured, but it needed time to heal. The Cowboys had signed Rodney Peete for just such an emergency, but Peete was injured, too. That left untested third-string quarterback Jason Garrett as the Dallas starter against the Green Bay Packers.

The youngster played brilliantly, passing for 311 yards and a pair of touchdowns. The Cowboys won a slugfest, 42-31. Peete took over the team for its next game against Philadelphia and led Dallas to a 31-19 win.

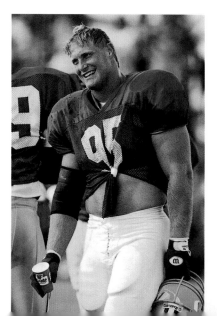

Aikman returned, but Dallas lost two of its last three regular season games. Emmitt Smith was too battered to play in the final contest, a 15-10 loss to the Giants. The Cowboys finished the season at 12-4.

It had been another good year statistically. Smith, hampered by various aches and pains, still rushed for 1,484 yards and scored 22 touchdowns. Michael Irvin led the team with 79 receptions good for 1,241 yards and 6 touchdowns. Aikman completed 233 of 361 passes for 2,676 yards and 13 touchdowns. In all, Dallas scored 414 points while giving up just 248.

The Green Bay Packers returned to Dallas for the first round of the playoffs. The Cowboys clobbered the visitors 35-9. Smith, playing only part of the game, still managed to rush for 44 yards and a touchdown. The Dallas victory sent the Cowboys to their third consecutive NFC championship game against San Francisco.

The first five minutes of the contest were gruesome. Aikman was intercepted on Dallas's third play from scrimmage; Eric Davis returned the ball 44 yards for a touchdown. Three plays after that, Michael Irvin had the ball

Emmitt Smith has just scored another touchdown, this time against archrival 49ers, next page

> *"I met the Shipmans, and they invited me to see the farm. My wife Mary and I had been looking to become part of the community because we felt we had that responsibility. Somewhere along the way Mary's mother suggested a cookbook. A number of Cowboys would go out and visit the farm. It's good to help a little in something so miraculous."*
>
> —BOB BREUNIG
> *Dallas Cowboys linebacker 1975-84*

THE COWBOYS AND CHARITY

Happy Hill Farm Academy in Glen Rose is a residential treatment facility and school for children who, for various reasons, have problems functioning in society. The program is funded solely through private gifts and contributions, and for almost 15 years the Cowboys have been helping farm founder Ed Shipman publicize his operation.

"It's so amazing how the Cowboys, as an organization made up of some very wonderful people, are always willing to help us and so many other community groups, too," Shipman says. "These days, it's always negative stuff about professional athletes that makes the headlines. I wish the good things the Cowboys do would get more attention."

In 1995 the Cowboys' commitment to charitable works was recognized by the NFL Alumni Association, which honors one NFL franchise each year for exemplifying sportsmanship on and off the field with the Ed Block Courage Award. The team being honored is allowed to select a program offering treatment to abused children; the program then receives a substantial donation from the association.

The Cowboys chose Happy Hill Farm Academy. The dedication of the Ed Block Courage House was a gala event attended by Jerry Jones, Tom Landry, and a host of active and retired Cowboys players.

"And this was only the latest in a long line of Dallas Cowboys efforts on our behalf," Shipman said. "Originally, they helped us in 1979 with *The Dallas Cowboys Wives Cookbook*, which was organized by Bob and Mary Breunig."

"The team has always been very kind about helping our kids attend games," Shipman added, "and often players have come to spend time at the farm with our kids. The youngsters we have living here badly need heroes, and I can't imagine any professional sports team having more good, decent people associated with it than the Cowboys. Jerry Jones does so many things for so many people, and yet when he's with you he gives you his total, complete attention."

Happy Hill Farm is just one of many organizations that has benefited from the Dallas Cowboys' commitment to serving their community. Innumerable schools, hospitals, nursing homes, telethons, fund-raising dinners, children's clubs, and church organizations have been helped out with player appearances, donations of autographed memorabilia for auctions, and other team contributions.

It's impossible, of course, to grant every request. Each week finds the Cowboys receiving 50 or more calls for help. As many as possible are honored. As far as the Cowboys are concerned, their responsibilities stretch far beyond the parking lots of Texas Stadium or the practice facilities at Valley Ranch.

Young fans support favorite quarterback, favorite team

1995 As usual, other NFL clubs were glad to sign free agent Cowboys. The team lost wide receiver Alvin Harper, safety Kenneth Gant, defensive end Jim Jeffcoat, center Mark Stepnoski, and safety James Washington. Dallas signed free agent center Ray Donaldson and quarterback Wade Wilson. The draft yielded running back Sherman Williams and tight end Eric Bjornson.

The Cowboys' return to excellence had been accomplished so quickly that many fans and sportscasters considered 1994 a disaster because Dallas hadn't won its third consecutive Super Bowl. At least Switzer felt he had convinced the players they could win with him at the helm.

Shortly after the first game of the regular season—in which Dallas

stripped, and the 49ers recovered. Steve Young hit Ricky Watters with a touchdown pass. Then Kevin Williams fumbled the ensuing kickoff; San Francisco scored again. It was 21-0.

The Cowboys fought back, but the 3 touchdown lead they had given the 49ers was too much to overcome. The final score was 38-28. The 49ers, not the Cowboys, would go on to Super Bowl XXIX.

◆

"Coach Switzer looks for leadership from the veterans, the big guys— Emmitt, Michael, Troy, Deion, Charles Haley. Sure, sometimes he gets angry, sometimes he gets tough, but mostly he's just checking to see that everyone's in line. His way puts some extra pressure on the older guys. That was different for us."

—NATE NEWTON

Emmitt Smith dives for a touchdown against Houston in 1994

BARRY SWITZER

BY JIM REEVES

For all intents and purposes, the relationship was over. Only the infighting remained.

In the blue corner, brash and still hungry, Jerry Jones, owner of the Dallas Cowboys.

In the silver corner, fresh from consecutive Super Bowl championships in 1992 and 1993, Jimmy Johnson, the coach Jones once claimed was worth five No.1 draft picks.

Together, in just five years, they had conquered the world of professional football. In the space of 12 months the Cowboys had twice massacred the AFC champion Buffalo Bills in the world's single biggest sporting event, first at Pasadena and then again a year later in Atlanta.

Now, as the world looked on at the NFL meetings in Orlando in March of 1994, they were headed for a bitter divorce. The insults, lobbed back and forth like incoming mortar rounds, were explosive.

Johnson snubbed Jones at a gala NFL party in front of current and former Cowboys assistant coaches and employees, refusing to acknowledge the owner's toast to Dallas's success. Back at the hotel bar a few hours later, the Cowboys owner intentionally returned fire in front of a room full of league executives and a handful of national newspaper reporters. He suggested that any of a thousand coaches could have coached the Cowboys to the Super Bowl and hinted he might just fire Johnson.

And if he did, he knew exactly whom he would hire.

Barry Switzer.

Consider the long shot a direct hit.

There was no name that would irritate Johnson more than that of his former fellow assistant coach at Arkansas and, later, Big Eight rival. Switzer had been entrenched at Oklahoma during a wildly successful 16-year run when Johnson was getting his first chance as a major college head coach at Oklahoma State.

At first, the concept of Switzer as Cowboys coach was meant as a needle to get under Johnson's skin. The idea, however, grew on Jones. The more he thought about it, the more he realized that Switzer, who had been out of coaching for five years after being forced to resign at Oklahoma in 1989, would be the perfect fit for the Cowboys.

By the end of March, the "Bootlegger's Boy" was on his way back to football in Cowboys' style.

"When you go back and analyze everything, it was a smart thing for Jerry to do," Switzer would say of Jones's decision to bring him in to replace Johnson. "First of all, Jerry went back and did his homework. He felt like he knew what kind of person I was. He did his research with due diligence and got the right answers from the people he asked. I wasn't even aware he was doing it.

"I fit in [with the Cowboys] because I'm not the type of personality that would want to come in and bring in my staff, my playbooks and try to challenge the system that was in place. It goes back to the old adage: You don't fix something that ain't broke."

That had definite appeal for Jones, who was facing a media firestorm over his breakup with the coach who had just won two Super Bowls. Two months earlier, popular offensive coordinator Norv Turner had taken over as head coach of the Washington Redskins. A year before, it had been defensive coordinator Dave Wannstedt who had departed, taking over the Chicago Bears.

Still, the Cowboys coaching staff remained one of the most respected groups in the league. Jones needed someone to oversee that talented collection of men, someone who didn't feel a mandate to bring in his own assistants and entourage. Someone who wouldn't feel a need to tinker with the most successful franchise in the NFL.

Someone like Switzer, the son of an Arkansas bootlegger who died in a violent car accident on the way to the hospital after being shot by his mistress.

Switzer, who won three national collegiate championships (1974, 1975, 1985), a dozen Big Eight titles, and whose .837 (157-29-4) winning percentage ranked as the fourth best in college history behind legends such as Notre Dame's Knute Rockne and Frank Leahy and Carlisle's George Woodruff.

It was, Jones didn't mind telling anyone who stopped by Valley Ranch, a stroke of genius. As Switzer pointed out, the Cowboys' offensive and defensive philosophies are virtually the same as the ones he lived by at Oklahoma. Run the football on offense. Attack the ball on defense.

"I believe in that," Switzer said before his first Cowboys training camp in Austin. "That fits my personality. It's what I can sell and believe in. I don't have to adjust anything. That's me, and that's my philosophy."

He would not, in any way, be another Jimmy Johnson.

"I'm not a barker," he said. "I'm not an actor. I don't try to create situations. When things occur that need to be handled I can usually handle them. (Jimmy) and I are two different people. We do it different ways. I think that would be the case no matter who was brought in here."

In many ways, Switzer stepped into a no-win situation. He couldn't change a thing. Yet if he didn't win a third straight Super Bowl, something no team had ever done, he would be branded a failure.

Switzer understood that when he took the job. Sure enough, going 12-4 in his first season as the Cowboys' head coach only whetted Dallas fans' appetite for a third Super Bowl appearance. That chance died on the soggy Candlestick Park turf when the Cowboys lost to the San Francisco 49ers 38-28 in the NFC championship game.

Switzer bumped an official and got flagged for a critical 15-yard penalty in the fourth quarter. Ironically, the same media and fans who had spent much of the season begging Switzer to do something—anything!—were livid now that he had.

The following season, 1995, brought more of the same. Switzer was ridiculed across the country for a failed fourth-and-one call deep in Dallas territory that helped the Cowboys lose a key game in

Philadelphia during a December slump. Local columnists called for Switzer's immediate dismissal. He was the butt of jokes by Leno and Letterman.

Jones and Switzer bowed their heads in the midst of the media storm and plowed ahead. Vindication came when the Cowboys rolled through the playoffs and beat Green Bay in the NFC championship game at Texas Stadium, stamping Dallas's ticket to the biggest show of all for the third time in four years.

Then Switzer and the Cowboys, pulling together despite Super Bowl week revelations detailing the frosty relationship between the head coach and quarterback Troy Aikman, held off the Pittsburgh Steelers to win Super Bowl XXX, 27-17.

Clutching the Lombardi Trophy with a death grip, Switzer knew exactly what to say.

"I'm going to stand on the curb when we have our parade," Switzer promised, "and I'm going to applaud as the players go by."

"The fact we were within sixty minutes of going to three straight Super Bowls and didn't get the job done was a tremendous letdown. We knew we weren't physically the same team without a healthy Emmitt Smith, without Erik Williams [who had been injured in a car crash]. But with all that, I still don't think I've ever seen a Cowboys team that was more prepared to play hard. I use 1994 to this day as a constant reminder to do whatever we can every day to get better as a football team."

—JERRY JONES

pounded the Giants 35-0—Jerry Jones engineered the headline-making signing of free agent Deion Sanders. The flashy defensive back had spent 1994 with the 49ers, determined to own a Super Bowl ring after years with the hapless Atlanta Falcons. He got it. While his major league baseball career still kept him busy during the

summer months, Sanders's attention turned to Dallas and the $35 million contract Jones offered him.

Because of an injury, Sanders wasn't able to play until late October. The Cowboys managed without him, sweeping their first four games. Then, in a game against the Redskins at RFK Stadium, Aikman was injured early.

Fan support as Cowboys take on the Eagles

Michael Irvin is always a threat after making a catch

Wade Wilson filled in adequately, but Washington held off a late Dallas rally to win 27-23. It was further proof of something the Cowboys, their fans, and almost everyone else following the NFL knew to be true: Troy Aikman had become the finest quarterback in the league. With him, Dallas would be the favorite against any opponent. Without him, the Cowboys could lose to anyone.

Aikman was back the next week, and Dallas won four straight games, including a 28-13 pounding of Atlanta that saw Sanders make his Dallas debut. Besides contributing on defense, Sanders played a few downs at wide receiver, catching one pass for 6 yards.

Things took a nasty turn in the Cowboys' tenth game. The 49ers

rolled in to Texas Stadium and blasted Dallas for 17 points in the first quarter. The final score was 38-20. Now the Cowboys had lost to San Francisco three times in a row. Dallas fans were unhappy, and Switzer came in for scathing criticism from broadcasters and sportswriters.

Deion Sanders, a new Cowboy

Troy Aikman has earned his reputation for toughness

Dallas won its next two games, beating Oakland and Kansas City. The Cowboys then inexplicably lost to Washington again in what was supposed to be a rebuilding season for the once-proud Redskins franchise. The 24-17 defeat was a discouraging one. Dallas dominated statistically, but Washington won on the scoreboard.

Still, that game was a picnic compared with what followed. Dallas had already defeated Philadelphia earlier in the season. Now, on the road at Veterans Stadium, Dallas frittered away a 17-3 lead and allowed the Eagles to pull even at 17-17 with little time left in the fourth quarter. On fourth and a foot on the Dallas 29, Switzer opted to go for the first down instead of punting. Emmitt Smith, whose fumble had set up the Eagles' tying field goal, was stopped for no gain. As the Eagles celebrated, officials waved off the play, saying the two-minute warning had been called before Smith took the handoff. Faced with a second chance,

Switzer called for the same play, and Smith was stopped for no gain again. The jubilant Eagles took over on offense and kicked the game-winning field goal as time ran out. Switzer was maligned in headlines all over the country, and again late-night television hosts worked his name into their monologues.

A young fan totes a full-sized cutout of his favorite quarterback

Troy Aikman signals a touchdown against Green Bay, previous page

"The key to continued success is an organizational thing. The Cowboys are very strong that way. If you're going to get on a coach and complain about him or assign blame to him, then give the guy credit if he wins. The Cowboys themselves, because of their personalities, are not a smooth ride for a coach. Switzer kept the transition as smooth as the thing could be done. Also, Jerry Jones is gonna do whatever you as a coach might need."

—JOHN MADDEN

"We're a family here. Adversity makes us stick together. When I made that call I was telling them I believed in them. If it had been fourth and a yard, I would have punted like anybody else. But it was fourth and a foot. We'd been successful ten consecutive times going for that, so I was playing percentages. When we weren't successful, I knew where the blame was going to fall. I also know this to be true—coaches get too much credit when we win and far too much damn criticism when we lose."

—BARRY SWITZER

But Switzer's critics didn't include most of his players, who vigorously defended him. Switzer himself shrugged off all the insults. He had, he said, been around too long to take sportswriters' gibes seriously.

The Cowboys won their last two regular season games, finishing with a 12-4 record for the third year in a row. Smith regained the NFC rushing title with 1,773 yards. He also set a new NFL record with 25 touchdowns. Michael Irvin nabbed a career-high 111 passes, good for 1,603 yards and 10 touchdowns. Aikman's passing numbers were, as usual, solid: 280

THE COWBOYS ARE OFFICIALLY AMERICA'S FAVORITE TEAM

The ESPN Chilton Sports Poll, conducted over 12 months in 1995-96, made it official: The Dallas Cowboys really *are* America's favorite team.

Sports enthusiasts around the country were each asked to name their favorite professional sports franchise. Teams in any pro sport were eligible. Only one team scored in double digits.

The top 10:

TEAM	PCT. of VOTE
Dallas Cowboys	10.7
San Francisco 49ers	6.8
Chicago Bulls	5.6
Atlanta Braves	3.4
Pittsburgh Steelers	3.0
Miami Dolphins	2.5
Washington Redskins	2.2
Green Bay Packers	2.0
Chicago Bears	2.0
Oakland Raiders	1.8
Orlando Magic	1.8

Then there's the matter of most popular licensed team merchandise. Last year, Dallas dominated all NFL teams. Almost one-fourth of all team jerseys, helmets, lamps, wallets, dolls, and other NFL-related items—24.2 percent—bear the logo of the Dallas Cowboys. Except for a dip in 1985-91, and a second-place finish in 1980, the Cowboys have ranked first every season since 1979.

Cowboys popularity extends to individual players. The top-selling replica jerseys among NFL heroes belong to Troy Aikman, Deion Sanders, and Emmitt Smith. (Others in the top echelon include Drew Bledsoe, John Elway, Brett Favre, Dan Marino, Jerry Rice, and Steve Young.)

Irvin, Aikman, and Harper, from left, take the field against Detroit

completions in 432 attempts for 3,304 yards, 16 touchdowns and just 7 interceptions. He also paced the NFL in an intangible category—leadership on the field.

For the season, Dallas scored 435 points, the team's highest total since 1983, and allowed 291.

Yet the Cowboys entered the NFC playoffs as the butt of too many jokes. It was widely prophesied they would get blown out by San Francisco in the championship game if they didn't lose to the Eagles in the first round. Besides the negative attention given to Switzer, all during the regular season there had been stories about Dallas players in various types of trouble. America's Team, it appeared, had to prove itself all over again.

Philadelphia came to Texas Stadium, and the Cowboys weren't in a hospitable mood. Chris Boniol kicked 3 field goals, Deion Sanders scored his first Dallas touchdown on a reverse, and the Cowboys romped 30-11. Some of Switzer's toughest

media critics now began to concede that the former Oklahoma coach knew something about the pro game, too.

It would have been fitting for Dallas to face the 49ers for the NFC

Darrin Woodson, Larry Brown, Deion Sanders, from left, kneel prior to Atlanta game

JERRY JONES

BY JEFF GUINN

The three men to own the Dallas Cowboys might be best described this way:

Clint Murchison was the Invisible Man.

Bum Bright was a hiccup who didn't have time to turn into indigestion.

Jerry Jones is Frank Sinatra.

Like Sinatra, Jones elicits extreme reactions. People love him or hate him; there's very little in-between. That's because he approaches professional football the same way Sinatra did music: Just because nobody else has done something before doesn't mean it can't be done that way now. Modesty may not be a Jones character trait, but decisiveness is. Vision, too.

That's why Jerry Jones had the nerve, once he'd bought the most famous franchise in professional sports, to shake things up. Trusting his own judgment, Jones brought in a highly successful college coach and promised everybody that his man would get things turned around. In the process, Jones stepped on toes, hurt feelings, said things that could have been phrased more tactfully.

But Jones is one of those people who wants things to happen *now*. Taking a losing season or two to ease out the old Cowboys regime would have been more painful to the new owner than the torrent of criticism he got for swinging his new broom from the get-go. And the results, of course, speak for themselves. No team ever won three Super Bowls in four years before Jones's Cowboys did it. The old saying that you can't argue with success may not be true, but even Jones's most vociferous critics can't *deny* it.

Most Dallas Cowboys fans who disliked Jerry Jones initially have long since forgiven him whatever transgressions they thought he'd committed. How can you not like someone who rebuilt the team you love, who made them champions again quicker than some NFL club owners can spell "Super Bowl"? In fact, those people who own other NFL franchises sometimes seem to be the most ardent Jones-haters, which is natural. It's hard to be friends with a competitor who's always finding new ways to beat you.

And competition is what Jones is all about. He didn't get rich enough to buy the Cowboys by sitting back and letting good business deals pass on by. So today, if he thinks it's best for the Cowboys to affiliate with Nike, or for Pepsi to be the official soft drink, and American Express the official credit card of Texas Stadium because they're elite companies, he's going to make those deals and not beg the NFL's permission first. The NFL indicated its admiration for his aggressiveness by suing him for $300 million, since everybody else had always followed along with league deals before. Pick a fight with Jerry Jones, and he raises the stakes. Now he's suing the NFL for $750 million. By the time all that gets settled, the league will undoubtedly be mad at Jones for something else. (It's interesting that most people didn't notice or else forgot that, a few months after the Jones-Nike deal, the NFL signed a deal making Nike its official shoe, too.)

The man does have a heart, a big one that's usually in the right place. The receptionist at the Valley Ranch main office is thrilled to have her own Super Bowl ring. If the charities benefiting from Jerry Jones's personal time and attention were listed here, this book would be one hundred pages longer. So why can't everyone, not just Cowboys fans, let bygones be bygones?

For many, the problem is that Jones keeps on being right. He was right about Jimmy Johnson, and, when the two couldn't get along despite unparalleled success, he was right about Barry Switzer. Deion Sanders cost $35 million, but Jones got a lot of that back when he starred with Sanders in a TV commercial for a pizza company. The man who once promised to get involved with jocks and socks might someday make one brand of athletic supporter the official jockstrap of the Dallas Cowboys and turn a tidy profit by doing it. Don't be surprised.

Jerry Jones may sometimes be infuriating, but he's never dull. There's no telling what he'll do next, except for one thing. Though occasional bumps are inevitable, Jerry Jones has never failed at anything he set out to do. If you have to be unpopular with some people for something, it might as well be for success.

★ ★ ★

title, but Green Bay had upset San Francisco in the first playoff round.

The Packers arrived in Texas determined to make it to their third Super Bowl. Aikman staked the Cowboys to an early lead with 2 touchdown passes, but Brett Favre, who would later be voted the NFC's Most Valuable Player, came back with 3 of his own. Green Bay led 27-24 entering the fourth quarter. Then Emmitt Smith broke loose on two touchdown runs, and the Cowboys were NFC champions for the third time in four years with their 38-27 victory. When Switzer said he was having a good time and didn't expect to give up coaching any time soon, there was no doubt he meant it.

There was still one more game to go, Super Bowl XXX, where Dallas would beat archenemy Pittsburgh and enable Barry Switzer to tell Jerry Jones, "We did it our way, baby!"

Barry Switzer, a study in concentration

"I don't think anyone has ever accomplished anything like [Jerry Jones]. Dallas has been the dominant team over the last several years. This is great as far as getting rid of old ghosts, especially beating the Steelers in a Super Bowl. It's great to be part of a team history with so much success. And there's still more to come. This team has proven it can win Super Bowls with consistency. In a historical context, what the Dallas Cowboys have done in the nineties has been fantastic."

—ROGER STAUBACH

◆

"I own cars and homes. I don't really feel like I own the Dallas Cowboys. Nobody can, any more than you can own Notre Dame or the Texas Longhorns. The way I look at it, this is just my chance to carry the ball for a while. I hope someday when people look back, what they'll say is that I gave 100 percent for as long as I had that special opportunity."

—JERRY JONES

◆

"The NFL is pretty close to parity already. The Cowboys and 49ers, and to a lesser extent Green Bay— Jerry Jones was way ahead of everyone else except the 49ers in that key players are under long-term contracts. As long as the Cowboys' nucleus stays together, the team can dominate. When this team or any team can no longer keep its stars, when they retire or get too expensive, then there won't be dominant teams. That's what free agency is going to do."

—PAT SUMMERALL

THE FUTURE

The Cowboys enter 1996 with a 67-29 regular season record in the 1990s. They're 8-2 in playoff games, and 3-0 in Super Bowls.

The challenge, of course, is to maintain a level of excellence. With free agency and the salary cap, it won't be easy. Since Super Bowl XXX, the Cowboys have lost Russell Maryland, Robert Jones, Larry Brown, and Dixon Edwards. Jerry Jones has proved ingenious in acquiring new players to fill team needs; it's a tradition he'll have to continue.

Barry Switzer, who says he doesn't see how his relationship with Jones could be any better, insists he's having fun as the Cowboys' coach. That

THE ALL-TIME DALLAS COWBOYS TEAM

★

As Selected by

John Madden and Pat Summerall

Players were selected from those the top Fox NFL broadcast team have personally seen in action.

Offense

Quarterback:	Roger Staubach, Troy Aikman
Running back:	Tony Dorsett, Walt Garrison, Robert Newhouse, Emmitt Smith
Wide receiver:	Bob Hayes, Drew Pearson, Michael Irvin
Tight end:	Billy Joe DuPree, Jay Novacek
Center:	Tom Rafferty, Mark Stepnoski
Guard:	Nate Newton, John Niland, Blaine Nye
Tackle:	Ralph Neely, Mark Tuinei, Erik Williams, Rayfield Wright

Defense

Defensive tackle:	Bob Lilly, Randy White
Defensive end:	Jim Jeffcoat, Ed Jones, Harvey Martin, Charles Haley
Middle linebacker:	Lee Roy Jordan
Outside linebacker:	Dave Edwards, Mike Hegman, Chuck Howley, D.D. Lewis
Cornerback:	Mel Renfro, Everson Walls, Charlie Waters
Safety:	Cliff Harris, Darren Woodson

Special Teams

Special teams player:	Bill Bates
Punter:	Danny White
Kicker:	Rafael Septien

enjoyment is underscored by the three Super Bowl trophies that adorn Valley Ranch, and Switzer will only continue to have fun if his team continues to add to that already impressive collection.

Veterans who have been with the team through all its recent successes aren't worried about staying on top. New players are informed in no uncertain terms that they have to take their turns furthering the Dallas championship traditions.

High expectations have never intimidated the Dallas Cowboys.

Owner Jerry Jones, executive vice president Stephen Jones, and vice president of marketing George Hays swear they'll use every minute of every working day keeping the team financially competitive. Barry Switzer and the Cowboys staff and players won't forget their responsibility to the team's fans and the Dallas tradition of on-the-field excellence. As Barry Switzer says, "This organization is about one thing, and has always been about one thing only—winning Super Bowls. We'll never be happy with anything less."

George Hays, above left, vice president of marketing for the Cowboys, with Jerry Jones

Stephen Jones, left, plays a major role in the Cowboys organization as executive vice president

"If you're a head coach you're going to get a lot of pressure. I enjoy it. When it isn't fun, I'll get out. There's no time frame; I'm healthy enough, and Jerry talks in the long term. Jerry and I have a tremendous working relationship. I don't know how it could be better."

—Barry Switzer

"We're not trying to bring peace to Bosnia or rework the minimum wage. What we're doing is trying to offer a respite to the fans from their hard work on their jobs or whatever personal troubles they might have. We want them to have fun with the Cowboys, and the way to do that is to give them a winning team. All of us with the Cowboys realize the fans are the people who count the most, and we try not to let them down."

—Jerry Jones

"Remember this— there's the Cowboys, and then there's the rest."

—Nate Newton

STATISTICS

★

WINS, LOSSES, AND TIES THROUGH 1996
For NFL Teams Active in 1960

COWBOYS

wins	losses	ties	winning %
318	206	06	60.000%

49ERS					PACKERS			
wins	losses	ties	winning %		wins	losses	ties	winning %
293	227	10	55.233%		266	251	13	50.189%

BROWNS					COLTS			
wins	losses	ties	winning %		wins	losses	ties	winning %
286	236	08	53.962%		257	267	06	48.490%

STEELERS					GIANTS			
wins	losses	ties	winning %		wins	losses	ties	winning %
281	241	08	53.019%		252	270	08	47.547%

REDSKINS					EAGLES (tie)			
wins	losses	ties	winning %		wins	losses	ties	winning %
280	234	11	52.830%		245	274	11	46.226%

RAMS					LIONS (tie)			
wins	losses	ties	winning %		wins	losses	ties	winning %
277	242	11	52.264%		245	270	15	46.226%

BEARS					CARDINALS			
wins	losses	ties	winning %		wins	losses	ties	winning %
271	252	07	51.132%		230	286	14	43.396%

ALL-TIME
CAREER PASSING LEADERS

★

ATTEMPTS

	Player	Years	Attempts
1.	Dan Marino	1983-	6,531
2.	Fran Tarkenton	1961-78	6,049
3.	John Elway	1983-	5,926
4.	Warren Moon	1984-	5,753
5.	Dan Fouts	1973-87	5,604
6.	Joe Montana	1979-94	5,391
7.	Johnny Unitas	1956-73	5,186
8.	Jim Hart	1966-84	5,076
9.	Steve DeBerg	1977-93	4,965
10.	Dave Krieg	1980-	4,911
54.	Roger Staubach	1969-79	2,958

COMPLETIONS

	Player	Years	Completions
1.	Dan Marino	1983-	3,913
2.	Fran Tarkenton	1961-78	3,686
3.	Joe Montana	1979-94	3,409
4.	Warren Moon	1984-	3,380
5.	John Elway	1983-	3,346
6.	Dan Fouts	1973-87	3,297
7.	Dave Krieg	1980	2,866
8.	Steve DeBerg	1978-93	2,844
9.	Johnny Unitas	1956-73	2,830
10.	Boomer Esiason	1984-	2,661
45.	Danny White	1976-88	1,761

COMPLETION PERCENTAGE (minimum 1,925 attempts)

	Player	Attempts	Completions	Percentage
1.	Steve Young	2,876	1,845	64.15
2.	Joe Montana	5,391	3,409	63.24
3.	Troy Aikman	2,713	1,704	62.81
4.	Jim Kelly	4,400	2,652	60.27
5.	Dan Marino	6,531	3,913	59.91
6.	Ken Stabler	3,793	2,270	59.85
7.	Danny White	2,950	1,761	59.70
8.	Ken Anderson	4,475	2,654	59.31
9.	Jim Harbaugh	2,275	1,348	59.25
10.	Bernie Kosar	3,333	1,970	59.11
21.	Wade Wilson	2,301	1,319	57.32

YARDS PER ATTEMPT

	Player	Yards	Attempts	Yards/ Attempt
1.	Otto Graham	23,584	2,626	8.98
2.	Norm Van Brocklin	23,611	2,895	8.16
3.	Steve Young	23,069	2,876	8.02
4.	Ed Brown	15,600	1,987	7.85
	Bart Starr	24,718	3,149	7.85
6.	Johnny Unitas	40,239	5,186	7.76
7.	Earl Morrall	20,809	2,689	7.74
8.	Len Dawson	28,711	3,741	7.68
	Dan Fouts	43,040	5,604	7.68
10.	Roger Staubach	22,700	2,958	7.67
19.	Danny White	21,959	2,950	7.44

TOUCHDOWNS

	Player	Years	TDs
1.	Dan Marino	1983-	352
2.	Fran Tarkenton	1961-78	342
3.	Johnny Unitas	1956-73	290
4.	Joe Montana	1979-94	273
5.	Sonny Jurgensen	1957-74	255
6.	Dan Fouts	1973-87	254
7.	Warren Moon	1984-	247
	Dave Krieg	1980-	247
9.	John Hadl	1962-77	244
10.	Y.A. Title	1948-64	242
46.	Danny White	1976-88	155
48.	Roger Staubach	1969-79	153

PERCENT INTERCEPTED (minimum 1,925 attempts)

	Player	Attempts	Interceptions	Percentage
1.	Joe Montana	5,391	139	2.58
2.	Bernie Kosar	3,333	87	2.61
3.	Ken O'Brien	3,602	98	2.72
4.	Steve Young	2,876	79	2.75
5.	Neil Lomax	3,153	90	2.85
6.	Jeff George	2,613	75	2.87
7.	Jim Harbaugh	2,275	67	2.95
8.	Dan Marino	6,531	200	3.06
9.	Randall Cunningham	3,362	105	3.12
10.	Troy Aikman	2,713	85	3.13
23.	Roger Staubach	2,958	109	3.68
36.	Wade Wilson	2,301	97	4.22
43.	Danny White	2,950	132	4.47

RUSHING

★

ATTEMPTS

	Player	Years	Attempts
1.	Walter Payton	1975-87	3,838
2.	Eric Dickerson	1983-93	2,996
3.	Franco Harris	1972-84	2,949
4.	**Tony Dorsett**	**1977-88**	**2,936**
5.	John Riggins	1971-85	2,740
6.	Marcus Allen	1982-	2,692
7.	Ottis Anderson	1979-92	2,562
8.	O.J. Simpson	1969-79	2,404
9.	Jim Brown	1957-65	2,359
10.	Thurman Thomas	1989-	2,285
12.	**Emmitt Smith**	**1990-**	**2,007**
15.	**Herschel Walker**	**1986-**	**1,938**

YARDS

	Player	Years	Yards
1.	Walter Payton	1975-87	16,726
2.	Eric Dickerson	1983-93	13,259
3.	**Tony Dorsett**	**1977-88**	**12,739**
4.	Jim Brown	1957-65	12,312
5.	Franco Harris	1972-84	12,120
6.	John Riggins	1974-85	11,352
7.	O.J. Simpson	1969-79	11,236
8.	Marcus Allen	1982-	10,908
9.	Ottis Anderson	1979-92	10,273
10.	Barry Sanders	1989-	10,172
12.	**Emmitt Smith**	**1990-**	**8,956**
17.	**Herschel Walker**	**1986-**	**8,122**

AVERAGE YARDS (MINIMUM 700 ATTEMPTS)

	Player	Attempts	Yards	Avg.
1.	Marion Motley	828	4,720	5.70
2.	Jim Brown	2,359	12,312	5.22
3.	Mercury Morris	804	4,133	5.14
4.	Joe Perry	1,929	804	5.04
5.	Gale Sayers	991	4,956	5.00
6.	Barry Sanders	2,077	10,172	4.90
7.	Paul Lowe	1,026	4,995	4.87
8.	Lenny Moore	1,069	5,174	4.84
9.	Tony Nathan	732	3,543	4.84
10.	Marv Hubbard	951	4,544	4.78
30.	**Emmitt Smith**	**2,007**	**8,956**	**4.46**

RUSHING TOUCHDOWNS

	Player	Years	TDs
1.	Walter Payton	1975-87	110
2.	Jim Brown	1957-65	106
3.	John Riggins	191-85	104
4.	Marcus Allen	1982-	103
5.	**Emmitt Smith**	**1990-**	**96**
6.	Franco Harris	1972-84	91
7.	Eric Dickerson	1983-93	90
8.	Jim Taylor	1958-67	83
9.	**Tony Dorsett**	**1977-88**	**· 77**
10.	Pete Johnson	1977-84	76

RECEIVING

★

RECEPTIONS

	Player	Years	Receptions
1.	Jerry Rice	1985-	942
2.	Art Monk	1980-	940
3.	Steve Largent	1976-89	819
4.	James Lofton	1978-93	764
5.	Charlie Joiner	1969-86	750
6.	Henry Ellard	1983-	723
7.	Andre Reed	1985-	700
8.	Gary Clark	1985-	699
9.	Ozzie Newsome	1978-90	662
10.	Charley Taylor	1964-77	649
30.	**Lance Alworth**	**1962-72**	**542**
35.	**Michael Irvin**	**1988-**	**527**
52.	**Drew Pearson**	**1973-83**	**489**
61.	**Tony Hill**	**1977-86**	**479**

YARDS

	Player	Years	Yards
1.	Jerry Rice	1985-	15,123
2.	James Lofton	1978-93	14,004
3.	Steve Largent	1976-89	13,089
4.	Art Monk	1980-	12,721
5.	Henry Ellard	1983-	12,163
6.	Charlie Joiner	1969-86	12,146
7.	Don Maynard	1958-73	11,834
8.	Gary Clark	1985-	10,856
9.	Stanley Morgan	1977-90	10,716

Player	Years	Yards
10. Harold Jackson	1968-83	10,372
11. Lance Alworth	1962-72	10,266
26. Michael Irvin	1988-	8,538
35. Tony Hill	1977-86	7,988
39. Drew Pearson	1973-83	7,822

RECEIVING TOUCHDOWNS

Player	Years	TDs
1. Jerry Rice	1985-	146
2. Don Hutson	1935-45	100
Steve Largent	1976-89	100
4. Don Maynard	1958-73	88
5. Lance Alworth	1962-72	85
Paul Warfield	1964-77	85
7. Tommy McDonald	1957-68	84
Mark Clayton	1983-93	84
9. Art Powell	1959-68	81
10. Charley Taylor	1964-77	79
Harold Carmichael	1971-84	79
56. Tony Hill	1977-86	51
60. Michael Irvin	1988-	50

SUPER BOWL SCORES
★

I.	Green Bay 35, Kansas City 10
II.	Green Bay 33, Oakland 14
III.	New York Jets 16, Baltimore 7
IV.	Kansas City 23, Minnesota 7
V.	**Baltimore 16, Dallas 13**
VI.	**Dallas 24, Miami 3**
VII.	Miami 14, Washington 7
VIII.	Miami 24, Minnesota 7
IX.	Pittsburgh 16, Minnesota 6
X.	**Pittsburgh 21, Dallas 17**
XI.	Oakland 32, Minnesota 14
XII.	**Dallas 27, Denver 10**
XIII.	**Pittsburgh 35, Dallas 31**
XIV.	Pittsburgh 31, Los Angeles Rams 19
XV.	Oakland 27, Philadelphia 13
XVI.	San Francisco 26, Cincinnati 21
XVII.	Washington 27, Miami 17
XVIII.	Los Angeles Raiders 38, Washington 6
XIX.	San Francisco 38, Miami 16
XX.	Chicago 46, New England 10

XXI.	New York Giants 39, Denver 20
XXII.	Washington 42, Denver 10
XXIII.	San Francisco 20, Cincinnati 16
XXIV.	San Francisco 55, Denver 10
XXV.	New York Giants 20, Buffalo 19
XXVI.	Washington 37, Buffalo 24
XXVII.	**Dallas 52, Buffalo 17**
XXVIII.	**Dallas 30, Buffalo 13**
XXIX.	San Francisco 49, San Diego 26
XXX.	**Dallas 27, Pittsburgh 17**

SUPER BOWL RECORDS
★

Dallas	5-3
San Francisco	5-0
Pittsburgh	4-1
Oakland/Los Angeles Raiders	3-1
Washington	3-2
New York Giants	2-0
Green Bay	2-0
Miami	2-3
New York Jets	1-0
Chicago	1-0
Kansas City	1-1
Baltimore	1-1
Minnesota	0-4
Denver	0-4
Buffalo	0-4
Cincinnati	0-2
Los Angeles Rams	0-1
Philadelphia	0-1
New England	0-1
San Diego	0-1

DALLAS COWBOYS IN NFL HALL OF FAME
★

1. Bob Lilly, defensive tackle, inducted in 1980
2. Roger Staubach, quarterback, inducted in 1985
3. Tom Landry, head coach, inducted in 1990
4. Tex Schramm, president, inducted in 1991
5. Tony Dorsett, running back, inducted in 1994
6. Randy White, defensive tackle, inducted in 1994
7. Mel Renfro, defensive back, inducted in 1995

SEASON -BY-SEASON RESULTS

★

1962 continued

Philadelphia	W	41-19
at Pittsburgh	W	42-27
St. Louis	L	24-28
at Washington	W	38-10
New York	L	10-41
Chicago	L	33-34
at Philadelphia	L	14-28
Cleveland	W	45-21
at St. Louis	L	20-52
at New York	L	31-41
Total		**393-402**

1960 (0-11-1)

Tom Landry, head coach
Seventh Place, Western Conference

Pittsburgh	L	28-35
Philadelphia	L	25-27
at Washington	L	14-26
Cleveland	L	7-48
at St. Louis	L	10-12
Baltimore	L	7-45
Los Angeles	L	13-38
at Green Bay	L	7-41
San Francisco	L	14-26
at Chicago	L	7-17
at New York	T	31-31
at Detroit	L	14-23
Total		**177-369**

1963 (4-10)

Tom Landry, head coach
Fifth Place, Eastern Conference

St. Louis	L	7-34
Cleveland	L	24-41
at Washington	L	17-21
at Philadelphia	L	21-24
Detroit	W	17-14
at New York	L	21-37
at Pittsburgh	L	21-27
Washington	W	35-20
at San Francisco	L	24-31
Philadelphia	W	27-20
at Cleveland	L	17-27
New York	L	27-34
Pittsburgh	L	19-24
at St. Louis	W	28-24
Total		**305-378**

1961 (4-9-1)

Tom Landry, head coach
Sixth Place, Eastern Conference

Pittsburgh	W	27-24
Minnesota	W	21-7
at Cleveland	L	7-25
at Minnesota	W	28-0
New York	L	10-31
Philadelphia	L	7-43
at New York	W	17-16
St. Louis	L	17-31
at Pittsburgh	L	7-37
Washington	T	28-28
at Philadelphia	L	13-35
at Cleveland	L	17-38
at St. Louis	L	13-31
at Washington	L	24-34
Total		**236-380**

1964 (5-8-1)

Tom Landry, head coach
Fifth Place, Eastern Conference

St. Louis	L	6-16
Washington	W	24-18
at Pittsburgh	L	17-23
at Cleveland	L	6-27
New York	T	13-13
Cleveland	L	16-20
at St. Louis	W	31-13
at Chicago	W	24-10
at New York	W	31-21
Philadelphia	L	14-17
at Washington	L	16-28

1962 (5-8-1)

Tom Landry, head coach
Fifth Place, Eastern Conference

Washington	T	35-35
Pittsburgh	L	28-30
at Los Angeles	W	27-17
at Cleveland	L	10-19

Green Bay	L	21-45
at Philadelphia	L	14-24
Pittsburgh	W	17-14
Total		**250-280**

1965 (7-7)

Tom Landry, head coach
Second Place, Eastern Conference

New York	W	31-2
Washington	W	27-7
at St. Louis	L	13-20
Philadelphia	L	24-35
at Cleveland	L	17-23
at Green Bay	L	3-13
at Pittsburgh	L	13-22
San Francisco	W	39-31
Pittsburgh	W	24-17
Cleveland	L	17-24
at Washington	L	31-34
at Philadelphia	W	21-19
St. Louis	W	27-13
at New York	W	38-20
Total		**325-280**

Playoff Bowl Game (at Miami)

Baltimore	L	3-35

1966 (10-3-1)

Tom Landry, head coach
First Place, Eastern Conference

New York	W	52-7
Minnesota	W	28-17
at Atlanta	W	47-14
Philadelphia	W	56-7
at St. Louis	T	10-10
at Cleveland	L	21-30
Pittsburgh	W	52-21
at Philadelphia	L	23-24
at Washington	W	31-30
at Pittsburgh	W	20-7
Cleveland	W	26-14
St. Louis	W	31-17
Washington	L	31-34
at New York	W	17-7
Total		**445-239**

1966 Championship Game (at Dallas)

Green Bay	L	27-34

1967 (9-5)

Tom Landry, head coach
First Place, Capitol Division

at Cleveland	W	21-14
New York	W	38-24
Los Angeles	L	13-35
at Washington	W	17-14
New Orleans	W	14-10
at Pittsburgh	W	24-21
at Philadelphia	L	14-21
Atlanta	W	37-7
at New Orleans	W	27-10
Washington	L	20-27
St. Louis	W	46-21
at Baltimore	L	17-23
Philadelphia	W	38-17
at San Francisco	L	16-24
Total		**342-268**

1967 Eastern Championship Game (at Dallas)

Cleveland	W	52-14

1967 Championship Game (at Green Bay)

Green Bay	L	17-21

1968 (12-2)

Tom Landry, head coach
First Place, Capitol Division

Detroit	W	59-13
Cleveland	W	28-7
at Philadelphia	W	45-13
at St. Louis	W	27-10
Philadelphia	W	34-14
at Minnesota	W	20-7
Green Bay	L	17-26
at New Orleans	W	17-3
New York	L	21-27
at Washington	W	44-24
at Chicago	W	34-3
Washington	W	29-20
Pittsburgh	W	28-7
at New York	W	28-10
Total		**431-186**

1968 Eastern Championship Game (at Cleveland)

Cleveland	L	20-31

Playoff Bowl Game (at Miami)

Minnesota	W	17-13

Tom Landry, head coach
First Place, Capitol Division

St. Louis	W	24-3
at New Orleans	W	21-17
at Philadelphia	W	38-7
at Atlanta	W	24-17
Philadelphia	W	49-14
New York	W	25-3
at Cleveland	L	10-42
New Orleans	W	33-17
at Washington	W	41-28
at Los Angeles	L	23-24
San Francisco	T	24-24
at Pittsburgh	W.	10-7
Baltimore	W	27-10
Washington	W	20-10
Total		369-233

1969 Eastern Championship Game (at Dallas)

Cleveland	L	14-38

Playoff Bowl Game (at Miami)

Los Angeles	L	0-31

Tom Landry, head coach
First Place, NFC East

at Philadelphia	W	17-7
NY Giants	W	28-10
at St. Louis	L	7-20
Atlanta	W	13-0
at Minnesota	L	13-54
at Kansas City	W	27-16
Philadelphia	W	21-17
at NY Giants	L	20-23
St. Louis	L	0-38
at Washington	W	45-21
Green Bay	W	16-3
Washington	W	34-3
at Cleveland	W	6-2
Houston	W	52-10
Total		299-221

1970 Divisional Playoff (at Dallas)

Detroit	W	5-0

1970 NFC Championship Game (at San Francisco)

San Francisco	W	17-10

Super Bowl V (at Miami)

Baltimore	L	13-16

Tom Landry, head coach
First Place, NFC East

at Buffalo	W	49-37
at Philadelphia	W	42-7
Washington	L	16-20
NY Giants	W	20-13
at New Orleans	L	14-24
New England	W	44-21
at Chicago	L	19-23
at St. Louis	W	16-13
Philadelphia	W	20-7
at Washington	W	13-0
Los Angeles	W	28-21
NY Jets	W	52-10
at NY Giants	W	42-14
St. Louis	W	31-12
Total		406-222

1971 Divisional Playoff (at Minnesota)

Minnesota	W	20-12

1971 NFC Championship Game (at Dallas)

San Francisco	W	14-3

Super Bowl VI (at New Orleans)

Miami	W	24-3

Tom Landry, head coach
Second Place, NFC East

Philadelphia	W	28-6
at NY Giants	W	23-14
at Green Bay	L	13-16
Pittsburgh	W	17-13
at Baltimore	W	21-0
at Washington	L	20-24
Detroit	W	28-24
at San Diego	W	34-28
St. Louis	W	33-24
at Philadelphia	W	28-7
San Francisco	L	10-31
at St. Louis	W	27-6
Washington	W	34-24
NY Giants	L	3-23
Total		319-240

1972 Divisional Playoff (at San Francisco)

San Francisco	W	30-28

1972 NFC Championship Game (at Washington)

Washington	L	3-26

Tom Landry, head coach
First Place, NFC East

at Chicago	W	20-17
New Orleans	W	40-3
St. Louis	W	45-10
at Washington	L	7-14
at Los Angeles	L	31-37
NY Giants	W	45-28
at Philadelphia	L	16-30
Cincinnati	W	38-10
at NY Giants	W	23-10
Philadelphia	W	31-10
Miami	L	7-14
at Denver	W	22-10
Washington	W	27-7
at St. Louis	W	30-3
Total		**382-203**

1973 Divisional Playoff (at Dallas)

Los Angeles	W	27-16

1973 NFC Championship Game (at Dallas)

Minnesota	L	10-27

Tom Landry, head coach
Third Place, NFC East

at Atlanta	W	24-0
at Philadelphia	L	10-13
NY Giants	L	6-14
Minnesota	L	21-23
at St. Louis	L	28-31
Philadelphia	W	31-24
at NY Giants	W	21-7
St. Louis	W	17-14
San Francisco	W	20-14
at Washington	L	21-28
at Houston	W	10-0
Washington	W	24-23
at Oakland	L	23-27
Total		**297-235**

Tom Landry, head coach
Second Place, NFC East

Los Angeles	W	18-7
St. Louis	W	37-31 (OT)
at Detroit	W	36-10
at NY Giants	W	13-7
Green Bay	L	17-19
at Philadelphia	W	20-17
at Washington	L	24-30 (OT)
Kansas City	L	31-34
at New England	W	34-31
Philadelphia	W	27-17
NY Giants	W	14-3
at St. Louis	L	17-31
Washington	W	31-10
at NY Jets	W	31-21
Total		**350-268**

1975 Divisional Playoff (at Minnesota)

Minnesota	W	17-14

1975 NFC Championship Game (at Los Angeles)

Los Angeles	W	37-7

Super Bowl X (at Miami)

Pittsburgh	L	17-21

Tom Landry, head coach
First Place, NFC East

Philadelphia	W	27-7
at New Orleans	W	24-6
Baltimore	W	30-27
at Seattle	W	26-13
at NY Giants	W	28-14
at St. Louis	L	17-21
Chicago	W	31-21
at Washington	W	20-7
NY Giants	W	9-3
Buffalo	W	17-10
at Atlanta	L	10-17
St. Louis	W	19-14
at Philadelphia	W	26-7
Washington	L	14-27
Total		**296-194**

1976 Divisional Playoff (at Dallas)

Los Angeles	L	12-14

Tom Landry, head coach
First Place, NFC East

at Minnesota	W	16-10 (OT)
NY Giants	W	41-21
Tampa Bay	W	23-7
at St. Louis	W	30-24
Washington	W	34-16
at Philadelphia	W	16-10
Detroit	W	37-0
at NY Giants	W	24-10
St. Louis	L	17-24
at Pittsburgh	L	13-28
at Washington	W	14-7
Philadelphia	W	24-14
at San Francisco	W	42-35
Denver	W	14-6
Total		345-212

1977 Divisional Playoff (at Dallas)

Chicago	W	37-7

1977 NFC Championship Game (at Dallas)

Minnesota	W	23-6

Super Bowl XII (at New Orleans)

Denver	W	27-10

Tom Landry, head coach
First place, NFC East

Baltimore	W	38-0
at NY Giants	W	34-24
at Los Angeles	L	14-27
St. Louis	W	21-12
at Washington	L	5-9
NY Giants	W	24-3
at St. Louis	W	24-21 (OT)
Philadelphia	W	14-7
Minnesota	L	10-21
at Miami	L	16-23
at Green Bay	W	42-14
New Orleans	W	27-7
Washington	W	37-10
New England	W	17-10
at Philadelphia	W	31-13
at NY Jets	W	30-7
Total		384-208

1978 Divisional Playoff (at Dallas)

Atlanta	W	27-20

1978 NFC Championship Game (at Los Angeles)

Los Angeles	W	28-0

Super Bowl XIII (at Miami)

Pittsburgh	L	31-35

Tom Landry, head coach
First Place, NFC East

at St. Louis	W	22-21
at San Francisco	W	21-13
Chicago	W	24-20
at Cleveland	L	7-26
Cincinnati	W	38-13
at Minnesota	W	36-20
Los Angeles	W	30-6
St. Louis	W	22-13
at Pittsburgh	L	3-14
at NY Giants	W	16-14
Philadelphia	L	21-31
at Washington	L	20-34
Houston	L	24-30
NY Giants	W	28-7
at Philadelphia	W	24-17
Washington	W	35-34
Total		371-313

1979 Divisional Playoff (at Dallas)

Los Angeles	L	19-21

Tom Landry, head coach
Second Place, NFC East

at Washington	W	17-3
at Denver	L	20-41
Tampa Bay	W	28-17
at Green Bay	W	28-7
NY Giants	W	24-3
San Francisco	W	59-14
at Philadelphia	L	10-17
San Diego	W	42-31
at St. Louis	W	27-24
at NY Giants	L	35-38
St. Louis	W	31-21
Washington	W	14-10
Seattle	W	51-7
at Oakland	W	19-13

at Los Angeles	L	14-38
Philadelphia	W	35-27
Total		454-311

1980 Wild Card Game (at Dallas)

Los Angeles	W	34-13

1980 Divisional Playoff (at Atlanta)

Atlanta	W	30-27

1980 NFC Championship (at Philadelphia)

Philadelphia	L	7-20

1981 (12-4)

Tom Landry, head coach
First Place, NFC East

at Washington	W	26-10
St. Louis	W	30-17
at New England	W	35-21
NY Giants	W	18-10
at St. Louis	L	17-20
at San Francisco	L	14-45
Los Angeles	W	29-17
Miami	W	28-27
at Philadelphia	W	17-14
Buffalo	W	27-14
at Detroit	L	24-27
Washington	W	24-10
Chicago	W	10-9
at Baltimore	W	37-13
Philadelphia	W	21-10
at NY Giants	L	10-13 (OT)
Total		367-277

1981 Divisional Playoff (at Dallas)

Tampa Bay	W	38-0

1981 NFC Championship Game (at San Francisco)

San Francisco	L	27-28

1982 (6-3)

Tom Landry, head coach
Second Place, NFC East

Pittsburgh	L	28-36
St. Louis	W	24-7
at Minnesota	canceled	
NY Giants	canceled	
at Philadelphia	canceled	
at Cincinnati	canceled	
at NY Giants	canceled	
St. Louis	canceled	

at San Francisco	canceled	
Tampa Bay	W	14-9
Cleveland	W	`31-14
at Washington	W	24-10
at Houston	W	37-7
New Orleans	W	21-7
Philadelphia	L	20-24
at Minnesota	L	27-31
Total		226-145

1982 Super Bowl Tournament (at Dallas)

Tampa Bay	W	30-17

1982 Super Bowl Tournament (at Dallas)

Green Bay	W	37-26

1982 NFC Championship Game (at Washington)

Washington	L	17-31

1983 (12-4)

Tom Landry, head coach
Second Place, NFC East

at Washington	W	31-30
at St. Louis	W	34-17
NY Giants	W	28-13
New Orleans	W	21-20
at Miinesota	W	37-24
Tampa Bay	W	27-24 (OT)
Philadelphia	W	37-7
LA Raiders	L	38-40
at NY Giants	W	38-20
at Philadelphia	W	27-20
at San Diego	L	23-24
Kansas City	W	41-21
St. Louis	W	35-17
at Seattle	W	35-10
Washington	L	10-31
at San Francisco	L	17-42
Total		479-360

1983 NFC Wild Card Game (at Dallas)

LA Rams	L	17-24

1984 (9-7)

Tom Landry, head coach
Fourth Place, NFC East

at LA Rams	W	20-13
at NY Giants	L	7-28
Philadelphia	W	23-17
Green Bay	W	20-6

at Chicago	W	23-14
St. Louis	L	20-31
at Washington	L	14-34
New Orleans	W	30-27 (OT)
Indianapolis	W	22-3
NY Giants	L	7-19
at St. Louis	W	24-17
at Buffalo	L	3-14
New England	W	20-17
at Philadelphia	W	26-10
Washington	L	28-30
at Miami	L	21-28
Total		**308-308**

Tom Landry, head coach
First Place, NFC East

Washington	W	44-14
at Detroit	L	21-26
Cleveland	W	20-7
at Houston	W	17-10
at NY Giants	W	30-29
Pittsburgh	W	27-13
at Philadelphia	L	14-16
Atlanta	W	24-10
at St. Louis	L	10-21
at Washington	W	13-7
Chicago	L	0-44
Philadelphia	W	34-17
St. Louis	W	35-17
at Cincinnati	L	24-50
NY Giants	W	28-21
at San Francisco	L	16-31
Total		**357-333**

1985 Divisional Playoff (at Los Angeles)

LA Rams	L	0-20

Tom Landry, head coach
Third Place, NFC East

NY Giants	W	31-28
at Detroit	W	31-7
Atlanta	L	35-37
at St. Louis	W	31-7
at Denver	L	14-29

Washington	W	30-6
at Philadelphia	W	17-14
St. Louis	W	37-6
at NY Giants	L	14-17
LA Raiders	L	13-17
at San Diego	W	24-21
at Washington	L	14-41
Seattle	L	14-31
at LA Rams	L	10-29
Philadelphia	L	21-23
Chicago	L	10-24
Total		**346-337**

Tom Landry, head coach
Second Place, NFC East

at St. Louis	L	13-24
at NY Giants	W	16-14
Buffalo	canceled	
at NY Jets	W	38-24
Philadelphia	W	41-22
Washington	L	7-13
at Philadelphia	L	20-37
NY Giants	W	33-24
at Detroit	L	17-27
at New England	W	23-17 (OT)
Miami	L	14-20
Minnesota	L	38-44 (OT)
Atlanta	L	10-21
at Washington	L	20-24
at LA Rams	W	29-21
St. Louis	W	21-16
Total		**340-348**

Tom Landry, head coach
Fifth Place, NFC East

at Pittsburgh	L	21-24
at Phoenix	W	17-14
NY Giants	L	10-12
Atlanta	W	26-20
at New Orleans	L	17-20
Washington	L	17-35
at Chicago	L	7-17
at Philadelphia	L	23-24

Phoenix	L	10-16
at NY Giants	L	21-29
Minnesota	L	3-43
Cincinnati	L	24-38
Houston	L	17-25
at Cleveland	L	21-24
at Washington	W	24-17
Philadelphia	L	7-23
Total		**265-381**

1989 (1-15)

Jimmy Johnson, head coach
Fifth Place, NFC East

at New Orleans	L	0-28
at Atlanta	L	21-27
Washington	L	7-30
NY Giants	L	13-30
at Green Bay	L	13-31
San Francisco	L	14-31
at Kansas City	L	28-36
Phoenix	L	10-19
at Washington	W	13-3
at Phoenix	L	20-24
Miami	L	14-17
Philadelphia	L	0-27
LA Rams	L	31-35
at Philadelphia	L	10-20
at NY Giants	L	0-15
Green Bay	L	10-20
Total		**204-393**

1990 (7-9)

Jimmy Johnson, head coach
Fourth Place, NFC East

San Diego	W	17-14
NY Giants	L	7-28
at Washington	L	15-19
at NY Giants	L	17-31
Tampa Bay	W	14-10
at Phoenix	L	3-20
at Tampa Bay	W	17-13
Philadelphia	L	20-21
at NY Jets	L	9-24
San Francisco	L	6-24
at LA Rams	W	24-21

Washington	W	27-17
New Orleans	W	17-13
Bye		
Phoenix	W	41-10
at Philadelphia	L	3-17
at Atlanta	L	7-26
Total		**244-308**

1991 (11-5)

Jimmy Johnson, head coach
Second Place, NFC East

at Cleveland	W	26-14
Washington	L	31-33
Philadelphia	L	0-24
at Phoenix	W	17-9
NY Giants	W	21-16
at Green Bay	W	20-17
Cincinnati	W	35-23
Bye		
at Detroit	L	10-34
Phoenix	W	27-7
at Houston	L	23-26 (OT)
at NY Giants	L	9-22
at Washington	L	24-21
Pittsburgh	W	20-10
New Orleans	W	23-14
at Philadelphia	W	25-13
Atlanta	W	31-27
Total		**342-310**

1991 First Round Playoffs (at Chicago)

| Chicago | W | 17-13 |

1991 Divisional Playoffs (at Detroit)

| Detroit | L | 6-38 |

1992 (13-3)

Jimmy Johnson, head coach
First Place, NFC East

Washington	W	23-10
at NY Giants	W	34-28
Phoenix	W	31-20
Bye		
at Philadelphia	L	7-31
Seattle	W	27-0
Kansas City	W	17-10
at LA Raiders	W	28-13

Philadelphia	W	20-10
at Detroit	W	37-3
LA Rams	L	23-27
at Phoenix	W	16-10
NY Giants	W	30-3
at Denver	W	31-27
at Washington	L	17-20
at Atlanta	L	41-14
Chicago	W	27-14
Total		**409-243**

1992 Divisional Playoffs (at Dallas)

Philadelphia	W	34-10

1992 NFC Championship Game (at San Francisco)

San Francisco	W	30-20

Super Bowl XXVII (at Pasadena)

Buffalo	W	52-17

Jimmy Johnson, head coach
First Place, NFC East

at Washington	L	16-35
Buffalo	L	10-13
at Phoenix	W	17-10
Bye		
Green Bay	W	36-14
Indianapolis	W	27-3
San Francisco	W	26-17
Bye		
at Philadelphia	W	23-10
NY Giants	W	31-9
Phoenix	W	20-15
at Atlanta	L	14-27
Miami	L	14-17
Philadelphia	W	23-17
at Minnesota	W	37-20
at NY Jets	W	28-7
Washington	W	38-3
at NY Giants	W	16-13 (OT)
Total		**376-229**

1993 Divisional Playoff (at Dallas)

Green Bay	W	27-17

1993 NFC Championship Game (at Dallas)

San Francisco	W	38-21

Super Bowl XXVIII (at Atlanta)

Buffalo	W	30-13

Barry Switzer, head coach
First Place, NFC East

at Pittsburgh	W	26-9
Houston	W	20-17
Detroit	L	17-20 (OT)
Bye		
at Washington	W	34-7
Arizona	W	38-3
Philadelphia	W	24-13
at Arizona	W	28-21
at Cincinnati	W	23-20
NY Giants	W	38-10
at San Francisco	L	14-21
Washington	W	31-7
Green Bay	W	42-31
at Philadelphia	W	31-19
Cleveland	L	14-19
at New Orleans	W	24-16
at NY Giants	L	10-15
Total		**414-248**

1994 Divisional Playoffs (at Dallas)

Green Bay	W	35-9

1994 NFC Championship Game (at San Francisco)

San Francisco	L	28-38

Barry Switzer, head coach
First Place, NFC East

at NY Giants	W	35-0
Denver	W	31-21
at Minnesota	W	23-17 (OT)
Arizona	W	34-20
at Washington	L	23-27
Green Bay	W	34-24
at San Diego	W	23-9
Bye		
at Atlanta	W	28-13
Philadelphia	W	34-12
San Francisco	L	20-38
at Oakland	W	34-21
Washington	L	17-24
at Philadelphia	L	17-20
NY Giants	W	21-20
at Arizona	W	37-13
Total		**435-291**

1995 Divisional Playoffs (at Dallas)

Philadelphia	W	30-11

1995 NFC Championship (at Dallas)

Green Bay	W	38-27

Super Bowl XXX (at Tempe)

Pittsburgh	W	27-17

NFL NO. 1 DRAFT PICKS

★

(1960-1996)

1960 NFL: Billy Cannon, HB, LSU (LA Rams)
AFL: None

1961 NFL: Tommy Mason, HB, Tulane (Minn. Vikings)
AFL: Ken Rice, G, Auburn (Buffalo Bills)

1962 NFL: Ernie Davis, HB, Syracuse (Wash. Redskins)
AFL: Roman Gabriel, QB, N.C. State (Oakland Raiders)

1963 NFL: Terry Baker, QB, Oregon St. (LA Rams)
AFL: Buck Buchanan, DT, Grambling (KC Chiefs)

1964 NFL: Dave Parks, E, Texas Tech (San Fran. 49ers)
AFL: Jack Concannon, QB, Boston College (Boston Patriots)

1965 NFL: Tucker Frederickson, HB, Auburn (NY Giants)
AFL: Lawrence Elkins, E, Baylor (Houston Oilers)

1966 NFL: Tommy Nobis, LB, Texas (Atlanta Falcons)
AFL: Jim Grabowski, FB, Illinois (Miami Dolphins)

1967 Bubba Smith, DT, Michigan St. (Baltimore Colts)

1968 Ron Yary, T, USC (Minn. Vikings)

1969 O.J. Simpson, RB, USC (Buffalo Bills)

1970 Terry Bradshaw, QB, Louisiana Tech (Pitt. Steelers)

1971 Jim Plunkett, QB, Stanford (New England Patriots)

1972 Walt Patulski, DE, Notre Dame (Buffalo Bills)

1973 John Matuszak, DE, Tampa (Houston Oilers)

1974 Ed Jones, DE, Tenn. State (Dallas Cowboys)

1975 Steve Bartkowski, QB, Calif. (Atlanta Falcons)

1976 Lee Roy Selmon, DE, Oklahoma (Tampa Bay Buccaneers)

1977 Ricky Bell, RB, USC (Tampa Bay Buccaneers)

1978 Earl Campbell, RB, Texas (Houston Oilers)

1979 Tom Cousineau, LB, Ohio St. (Buffalo Bills)

1980 Billy Sims, RB, Oklahoma (Detroit Lions)

1981 George Rogers, RB, S. Carolina (New Orleans Saints)

1982 Kenneth Sims, DT, Texas (New England Patriots)

1983 John Elway, QB, Stanford (Baltimore Colts)

1984 Irving Fryar, WR, Nebraska (New England Patriots)

1985 Bruce Smith, DE, Virginia Tech (Buffalo Bills)

1986 Bo Jackson, RB, Auburn (Tampa Bay Buccaneers)

1987 Vinny Testaverde, QB, Miami (Tampa Bay Buccaneers)

1988 Aundray Brice, LB, Auburn (Atlanta Falcons)

1989 Troy Aikman, QB, UCLA (Dallas Cowboys)

1990 Jeff George, QB, Illinois (Indianapolis Colts)

1991 Russell Maryland, DL, Miami (Dallas Cowboys)

1992 Steve Emtman, DL, Washington (Indianapolis Colts)

1993 Drew Bledsoe, QB, Washington St. (New England Patriots)

1994 Dan Wilkinson, DT, Ohio St. (Cincinnati Bengals)

1995 Ki-Jana Carter, RB, Penn St. (Cincinnati Bengals)

1996 Keyshawn Johnson, WR, USC (New York Jets)

COWBOYS ALL-TIME REGULAR SEASON W-L RECORD
vs. other NFL franchises (1960-1995)

★

Arizona Cardinals,	44-22-1
Atlanta Falcons,	12-6
Buffalo Bills,	5-2
Chicago Bears,	10-6
Cincinnati Bengals,	4-2
Cleveland Browns,	10-17
Denver Broncos,	5-2
Detroit Lions,	8-7
Green Bay Packers,	11-10
Houston Oilers,	5-3
Indianapolis Colts,	7-3
Kansas City Chiefs,	3-2
Miami Dolphins,	2-6
Minnesota Vikings,	12-7
New England Patriots,	6-0
New Orleans Saints,	14-3
New York Giants,	43-22-2
New York Jets,	5-1
Oakland Raiders,	3-3
Philadelphia Eagles,	44-28
Pittsburgh Steelers,	13-13

St. Louis Rams,	12-13
San Diego Chargers,	5-1
San Francisco 49ers,	12-12-1
Seattle Seahawks,	4-1
Tampa Bay Buccaneers,	8-0
Washington Redskins,	39-31-2

COWBOYS ALL-TIME LEADERS

★

SCORING (REGULAR SEASON)

		TD	PAT	FG	Total points
1.	Rafael Septien	—	388	162	874
2.	Emmitt Smith	100	—	—	600
3.	Tony Dorsett	86	—	—	516
4.	Bob Hayes	76	—	—	456

PASSING (REGULAR SEASON)

		Att.	Comp.	%	Yds.	TD	Int.
1.	Staubach	2,958	1,685	57.0	22,700	153	109
2.	White	2,950	1,761	59.7	21,959	55	132
3.	Aikman	2,713	1,704	62.8	19,607	98	85
4.	Meredith	2,308	1 170	50.7	17,199	135	111

RUSHING (REGULAR SEASON)

		Att.	Yds.	Average	TD
1.	Tony Dorsett	2,755	12,036	4.4	72
2.	Emmitt Smith	2,007	8,956	4.5	96
3.	Herschel Walker	1,938	8,122	4.2	60
4.	Don Perkins	1,500	6,217	4.2	42
5.	Calvin Hill	1,166	5,009	4.3	39

RECEIVING (REGULAR SEASON)

		Catches	Yds.	Average	TD
1.	Michael Irvin	527	8,538	16.2	50
2.	Drew Pearson	489	7,822	16.0	48
3.	Tony Hill	479	7,988	16.7	51
4.	Tony Dorsett	382	3,432	9.0	13

COWBOYS POSTSEASON RESULTS (1960-1996)

★

Date	Opponent	Result	Score
Jan. 9, 1966	Baltimore Colts (Playoff Bowl)	L	35-3
Jan. 1, 1967	Green Bay Packers (1966 champ. game)	L	34-27
Dec. 24, 1967	Cleveland Browns (Eastern champ. game)	W	52-14
Dec. 31, 1967	Green Bay Packers (1967 champ. game)	L	21-17
Dec. 21, 1968	Cleveland Browns (Eastern champ. game)	L	31-20
Jan. 5, 1969	Minn. Vikings (Playoff Bowl)	W	17-13
Dec. 28, 1969	Cleveland Browns (Eastern champ. game)	L	38-14
Jan. 3, 1970	Los Angeles Rams (Playoff Bowl)	L	31-0
Dec. 26, 1970	Detroit Lions (Div. playoff)	W	5-0
Jan. 3, 1971	San Francisco 49ers (NFC champ. game)	W	17-10
Jan. 17, 1971	Baltimore Colts (Super Bowl V)	L	16-13
Dec. 25, 1971	Minn. Vikings (Div. playoff)	W	20-12
Jan. 2, 1972	San Francisco 49ers (NFC champ. game)	W	14-3
Jan. 16, 1972	Miami Dolphins (Super Bowl VI)	W	24-3
Dec. 23, 1972	San Francisco 49ers (Div. playoff)	W	30-28
Dec. 31, 1972	Washington Redskins (NFC champ. game)	L	26-3
Dec. 23, 1973	Los Angeles Rams (Div. playoff)	W	27-16
Dec. 30, 1973	Minn. Vikings (NFC champ. game)	L	27-10
Dec. 28, 1975	Minn. Vikings (Div. playoff)	W	17-14
Jan. 4, 1976	Los Angeles Rams (NFC champ. game)	W	37-7
Jan. 18, 1976	Pitt. Steelers (Super Bowl X)	L	21-17
Dec. 19, 1976	Los Angeles Rams (Div. playoff)	L	14-12

Dec. 26, 1977	Chicago Bears (Div. playoff)	W	37-7
Jan. 1, 1978	Minn. Vikings (NFC champ. game)	W	23-6
Jan. 15, 1978	Denver Broncos (Super Bowl XII)	W	27-10
Dec. 30, 1978	Atlanta Falcons (Div. playoff)	W	27-20
Jan. 7, 1979	Los Angeles Rams (NFC champ. game)	W	28-0
Jan. 21, 1979	Pitt. Steelers (Super Bowl XIII)	L	35-31
Dec. 30, 1979	Los Angeles Rams (Div. playoff)	L	21-19
Dec. 28, 1980	Los Angeles Rams (Wild Card game)	W	34-13
Jan. 4, 1981	Atlanta Falcons (Div. playoff)	W	30-27
Jan. 11, 1981	Phil. Eagles (NFC champ. game)	L	20-7
Jan. 2, 1982	Tampa Bay Bucc. (Div. playoff)	W	38-0
Jan. 10, 1982	San Francisco 49ers (NFC champ. game)	L	28-27
Jan. 9, 1983	Tampa Bay Bucc. (SB Tournament)	W	30-17
Jan. 16, 1983	Green Bay Packers (SB Tournament)	W	37-26
Jan. 22, 1983	Washington Redskins (NFC champ. game)	L	31-17
Dec. 26, 1983	Los Angeles Rams (Wild Card)	L	24-17
Jan. 4, 1986	Los Angeles Rams (Div. playoff)	L	20-0
Dec. 29, 1991	Chicago Bears (First round playoff)	W	17-13
Jan. 5, 1992	Detroit Lions (Div. playoff)	L	38-6
Jan. 10, 1993	Phil. Eagles (Div. playoff)	W	34-10
Jan. 17, 1993	San Francisco 49ers (NFC champ. game)	W	30-20
Jan. 31, 1993	Buffalo Bills (Super Bowl XXVII)	W	52-17
Jan. 16, 1994	Green Bay Packers (Div. playoff)	W	27-17
Jan. 23, 1994	San Francisco 49ers (NFC champ. game)	W	38-21
Jan. 30, 1994	Buffalo Bills (Super Bowl XXVIII)	W	30-13

Jan. 8, 1995	Green Bay Packers (Div. playoff)	W	35-9
Jan. 15, 1995	San Francisco 49ers (NFC champ. game)	L	38-28
Jan. 7, 1996	Phil. Eagles (Div. playoff)	W	30-11
Jan. 14, 1996	Green Bay Packers (NFC champ. game)	W	38-27
Jan. 28, 1996	Pitt. Steelers (Super Bowl XXX)	W	27-17

COWBOYS NFL MOST VALUABLE PLAYERS

★

1966	Don Meredith, QB
1971	Roger Staubach, QB
1993	Emmitt Smith, RB

COWBOYS NFC PLAYER OF THE YEAR AWARD WINNERS

★

1981	Tony Dorsett, RB
1993	Emmitt Smith, RB
1994	Charles Haley, DE

COWBOYS ROOKIES OF THE YEAR

★

1969	Calvin Hill, RB
1977	Tony Dorsett, RB
1992	Robert Jones, LB

COWBOYS COACHES OF THE YEAR

★

1966	Tom Landry
1975	Tom Landry
1990	Jimmy Johnson

COWBOYS ROSTERS 1960-1996

1960

NAME	POSITION
Byron Bradfute	OT
Paul Dickson	OT
Bob Fry	OT
Dick Klein	OT
Mike Falls	OG
Buzz Guy	OG
Duane Putnam	OG
Mike Connelly	C
John Houser	C
Nate Borden	DE
Gene Cronin	DE
John Gonzaga	DE
Don Healy	DT
Bill Herchman	DT
Ed Husmann	DT
Tom Braatz	LB
Wayne Hansen	LB
Jack Patera	LB
Jerry Tubbs	LB
Bob Bercich	DB
Don Bishop	DB
Bill Butler	DB
Fred Doelling	DB
Tom Franckhauser	DB
Jim Mooty	DB
Gary Wisener	OE-DB
Don Heinrich	QB
Eddie LeBaron	QB
Don Meredith	QB
L.G. Dupre	HB
Don McIlhenny	HB
Gene Babb	FB
Mike Dowdle	FB
Walt Kowalczyk	FB
Ray Mathews	FL
Dick Bielski	OE
Frank Clarke	OE
Jim Doran	OE
Fred Dugan	OE
Billy Howton	OE
Woodley Lewis	OE
Dave Sherer	OE
Fred Cone	K
Ray Fisher	injury
Chuck Howley	injury

1961

NAME	POSITION
Byron Bradfute	OT
Bob Fry	OT
Bob McCreary	OT
Andy Cvercko	OG
Mike Falls	OG
Bob Grottkau	OG
John Houser	OG
Mike Connelly	C
Nate Borden	DE
Bob Lilly	DE
Ken Frost	DT
Don Healy	DT
Bill Herchman	DT
Sonny Davis	LB
Mike Dowdle	LB
Chuck Howley	LB
Jack Patera	LB
Jerry Tubbs	LB
Gene Babb	FB-LB
Bob Bercich	DB
Don Bishop	DB
Tom Franckhauser	DB
Jimmy Harris	DB
Warren Livingston	DB
Dick Moegle	DB
Buddy Humphrey	QB
Eddie LeBaron	QB
Don Meredith	QB
L.G. Dupre	HB
Don Perkins	HB
J.W. Lockett	FB
Amos Marsh	FB
Merrill Douglas	HB-FB
Dick Bielski	OE
Frank Clarke	OE
Jim Doran	OE
Bill Howton	OE
Lee Murchison	OE
Glynn Gregory	DB-OE
Allen Green	K

1962

NAME	POSITION
Jerry Cornelison	OT
Charley Diamond	OT

NAME	POSITION
Jim Tyrer	OT
Carl Larpenter	OG-OT
Sonny Bishop	OG
Curt Merz	OG
Al Reynolds	OG
Marvin Terrell	OG
Jon Gilliam	C
Mel Branch	DE
Dick Davis	DE
Bill Hull	DE
Paul Rochester	DT
Jerry Mays	DE-DT
Walt Corey	LB
Ted Greene	LB
Sherrill Headrick	LB
Smokey Stover	LB
E.J. Holub	C-LB
Dave Grayson	DB
Bobby Hunt	DB
Ed Kelley	DB
Bobby Ply	DB
Duane Wood	DB
Johnny Robinson	HB-DB
Len Dawson	QB
Eddie Willson	QB
Abner Haynes	HB
Frank Jackson	HB
Jimmy Saxton	HB
Curtis McClinton	FB
Jack Spikes	FB
Fred Arbanas	OE
Tommy Brooker	OE
Chris Furford	OE
Bill Miller	OE
Tom Pennington	K
Dave Webster	injury

1963

NAME	POSITION
Bob Fry	OT
Tony Lescio	OT
Ed Nutting	OT
Ray Schoenke	OT
Joe Bob Isbell	OG
Dale Memmelaar	OG
Lance Poimbeouf	OG
Jim Ray Smith	OT-OG
Mike Connelly	C

NAME	POSITION
Lynn Hoyem	OG-C
George Andrie	DE
Larry Stephens	DE
Bob Lilly	DT-DE
John Meyers	DT
Guy Reese	DT
Dave Edwards	LB
Harold Hays	LB
Chuck Howley	LB
Lee Roy Jordan	LB
Jerry Tubbs	LB
Don Bishop	DB
Mike Gaechter	DB
Cornell Green	DB
Warren Livingston	DB
Jerry Overton	DB
Jimmy Ridlon	DB
Eddie LeBaron	QB
Don Meredith	QB
Amos Bullocks	HB
Wendell Hays	HB
Amos Marsh	HB
Jim Stiger	HB
Don Perkins	FB
Frank Clarke	FL
Gary Barnes	OE
Lee Folkins	OE
Billy Howton	OE
Pettis Norman	OE
Sam Baker	K
Maury Youmans	injury
Dan Talbert	military service

1964

NAME	POSITION
Jim Boeke	OT
Bill Frank	OT
Bob Fry	OT
Tony Liscio	OT
Ray Schoenke	OT
Jim Ray Smith	OG-OT
Jo Bob Isbell	OG
Jake Cupp	OG
Mike Connelly	C
Dave Manders	C
George Andrie	DE
Larry Stephens	DE
Maury Youmans	DE

Name	Position
Jim Colvin	DT
Bob Lilly	DT
Dave Edwards	LB
Harold Hays	LB
Chuck Howley	LB
Lee Roy Jordan	LB
Jerry Tubbs	LB
Don Bishop	DB
Mike Gaechter	DB
Cornell Green	DB
Warren Livingston	DB
Mel Renfro	DB
Jimmy Ridlon	DB
Billy Lothridge	QB
Don Meredith	QB
John Roach	QB
Amos Bullocks	HB
Perry Lee Dunn	HB
Amos Marsh	HB
Jim Stiger	FB-HB
Don Perkins	FB
Frank Clarke	FL
Buddy Dial	FL
Tommy McDonald	FL
Lee Folkins	OE
Pete Gent	OE
Pettis Norman	OE
Dick Van Raaphorst	K
Jerry Overton	off season accident
Don Talbert	military service

1965

NAME	POSITION
Jim Boeke	OT
Ralph Neely	OT
Don Talbert	OT
Mike Connelly	OG
Leon Donahue	OG
Mitch Johnson	OG
Jake Kupp	OG
Dave Manders	C
George Andrie	DE
Gary Porterfield	DE
Jethro Pugh	DE
Maury Umans	DE
Larry Stephens	DT-DE
Jim Colvin	DT
John Diehl	DT
Bob Lilly	DT
Dave Edwards	LB
Harold Hays	LB
Chuck Howley	LB
Lee Roy Jordan	LB
Jerry Tubbs	LB
Russell Wayt	LB
Don Bishop	DB
Mike Gaechter	DB
Cornell Green	DB
Warren Livingston	DB
Obert Logan	DB
Mel Renfro	HB-DB
Don Meredith	QB
Craig Morton	QB
Jerry Rhome	QB
Perry Lee Dunn	HB
Dan Reeves	HB
Don Perkins	FB
J.D. Smith	FB
A.D. Whitfield	FB
Buddy Dial	FL
Pete Gent	FL
Pettis Norman	TE
Frank Clarke	OE
Bob Hayes	OE
Colin Ridgway	K
Danny Villanueva	K
Joe Bob Isbell	injury
Tony Liscio	injury

1966

NAME	POSITION
Jim Boeke	OT
Ralph Neely	OT
Tony Liscio	OG-OT
Leon Donahue	OG
John Niland	OG
Mike Connelly	OT-OG
Dave Manders	C
Malcolm Walker	OT-C
George Andrie	DE
Larry Stephens	DE
Jethro Pugh	DT-DE
John Wilbur	DT-DE
Jim Colvin	DT
Bob Lilly	DT
Bill Sandeman	DT
Willie Townes	DE-DT
Dave Edwards	LB
Harold Hays	LB
Chuck Howley	LB
Lee Roy Jordan	LB
Jerry Tubbs	LB
Dick Daniels	DB
Mike Gaechter	DB
Cornell Green	DB
Mike Johnson	DB
Warren Livingston	DB
Obert Logan	DB
Mel Renfro	HB-DB
Don Meredith	QB
Craig Morton	QB
Jerry Rome	QB
Dan Reeves	HB
Les Shy	HB
Walt Garrison	FB-HB
Don Perkins	FB
J.D. Smith	FB
Buddy Dial	FL
Pete Gent	FL
Frank Clarke	TE
Bob Hayes	OE
Danny Villanueva	K
Jim Steffen	injury

1967

NAME	POSITION
Jim Boeke	OT
Ralph Neely	OT
Tony Liscio	OT
Leon Donahue	OG
John Niland	OG
John Wilbur	OG
Mike Connelly	C
Malcolm Walker	OT-C
George Andrie	DE
Larry Stephens	DE
Willie Townes	DE
Ron East	DT
Bob Lilly	DT
Jethro Pugh	DT
Dave Edwards	LB
Harold Hays	LB
Chuck Howley	LB
Lee Roy Jordan	LB
Phil Clark	DB
Dick Daniels	DB
Mike Gachter	DB
Cornell Green	DB
Mike Johnson	DB
Mel Renfro	DB
Don Meredith	QB
Craig Morton	QB

1968

NAME	POSITION
Tony Liscio	OT
Ralph Neely	OT
Rayfield Wright	TE-OT
John Niland	OG
Blaine Nye	OG
John Wilbur	OG
Dave Manders	C
Malcolm Walker	OT-C
George Andrie	DE
Larry Cole	DE
Willie Townes	DE
Andy Stynchula	DT-DE
Ron East	DT
Bob Lilly	DT
Jethro Pugh	DT
Jackie Burkett	LB
Dave Edwards	LB
Chuck Howley	LB
Lee Roy Jordan	LB
D.D. Lewis	LB
Dave Simmons	LB
Phil Clark	DB
Dick Daniels	DB
Mike Gaechter	DB
Cornell Green	DB
Mike Johnson	DB
Mel Renfro	DB
Don Meredith	QB
Craig Morton	QB
Craig Baynham	HB
Dan Reeves	HB

Additional roster entries (right column):

Name	Position
Jerry Rome	QB
Craig Baynham	HB
Dan Reeves	HB
Les Shy	HB
Don Perkins	FB
Walt Garrison	HB-FB
Pete Gent	FL
Lance Rentzel	OE-FL
Frank Clarke	TE
Pettis Norman	TE
Ray Field	Right-TE
Bob Hayes	OE
Sims Stokes	OE
Harold Deters	K
Danny Villanueva	K
Buddy Dial	injury
Dave Manders	injury

Name	Position
Les Shy	HB
Walt Garrison	FB
Don Perkins	FB
Bob Hayes	WR
Dennis Homan	WR
Dave McDaniels	WR
Sonny Randle	WR
Lance Rentzel	WR
Pete Gent	TE
Pettis Norman	TE
Mike Clark	K
Ron Widby	K
Buddy Dial	injury
Leon Donahue	injury

1969

NAME	POSITION
Tom Liscio	OT
Ralph Neely	OT
Rayfield Wright	TE-OT
John Niland	OG
Blaine Nye	OG
John Wilbur	OG
Dave Manders	C
Malcolm Walker	C
George Andrie	DE
Larry Cole	DE
Halvor Hagen	OT-DE
Ron East	DT
Bob Lilly	DT
Jethro Pugh	DT
Jackie Burkett	LB
Dave Edwards	LB
Chuck Howley	LB
Lee Roy Jordan	LB
Tom Stincic	LB
Fred Whittingham	LB
Otto Brown	DB
Phil Clark	DB
Mike Gaechter	DB
Cornell Green	DB
Mike Johnson	DB
Mel Renfro	DB
Bob Belden	QB
Craig Morton	QB
Roger Staubach	QB
Craig Baynham	HB
Calvin Hill	HB
Les Shy	HB
Dan Reeves	FB-HB
Walt Garrison	FB

Name	Position
Claxton Welch	FB-HB
Bobby Joe Conrad	WR
Richmond Flowers	WR
Bob Hayes	WR
Dennis Homan	WR
Lance Rentzel	WR
Mike Ditka	TE
Pettis Norman	TE
Mike Clark	K
Ron Widby	K
D. D. Lewis	Military service
Willie Townes	injury

1970

NAME	POSITION
Bob Asher	OT
Tony Liscio	OT
Ralph Neely	OT
Rayfield Wright	OT
John Niland	OG
Blaine Nye	OG
Halbor Hagen	C-OG
Dave Manders	C
George Andrie	DE
Larry Coles	DE
Pat Toomay	DE
Ron East	DT
Bob Lilly	DT
Jethro Pugh	DT
Dave Edwards	LB
Chuck Howley	LB
Lee Roy Jordan	LB
Steve Kiner	LB
D. D. Lewis	LB
Tom Stincic	LB
Herb Adderley	DB
Richmond Flowers	DB
Cornell Green	DB
Cliff Harris	DB
Mel Renfro	DB
Mark Washington	DB
Charlie Waters	DB
Bob Welden	QB
Craig Morton	QB
Roger Staubach	QB
Dan Reeves	HB
Claxton Welch	HB
Calvin Hill	FB-HB
Duane Tomas	FB-HB
Walt Garrison	FB
Margene Atkins	WR

Name	Position
Bob Hayes	WR
Dennis Homan	WR
Lance Rentzel	WR
Reggie Rucker	WR
Mike Ditka	TE
Pettis Norman	TE
Mike Clark	K
Ron Widby	K

1971

NAME	POSITION
Forrest Gregg	OT
Tony Liscio	OT
Ralph Neely	OT
Don Talbert	OT
Rayfield Wright	OT
John Niland	OG
Blaine Nye	OG
Rodney Wallace	OG
John Fitzgerald	C
Dave Manders	C
George Andrie	DE
Larry Cole	DE
Tody Smith	DE
Pat Toomay	DE
Bill Gregory	DT
Bob Lilly	DT
Jethro Pugh	DT
Lee Roy Caffey	LB
Dan Edwards	LB
Chuck Howley	LB
Lee Roy Jordan	LB
D.D. Lewis	LB
Tom Stincic	LB
Herb Adderley	DB
Cornell Green	DB
Cliff Harris	DB
Mel Renfro	DB
Ike Thomas	DB
Mark Washington	DB
Charlie Waters	DB
Craig Morton	QB
Roger Staubach	QB
Dan Reeves	HB
Claxton Welch	HB
Joe Williams	HB
Calvin Hill	FB-HB
Duane Thomas	FB-HB
Walt Garrison	FB
Margene Adkins	WR
Lance Alworth	WR

Name	Position
Bob Hayes	WR
Gloster Richardson	WR
Mike Ditka	TE
Billy Truax	TE
Mike Clark	K
Toni Fritsch	K
Ron Widby	K
Bob Asher	injury

1972

NAME	POSITION
Ralph Neely	OT
Rayfield Wright	OT
Rodney Wallace	OG-OT
John Niland	OG
Blaine Nye	OG
John Fitzgerald	C-OG
Dave Manders	C
George Andrie	DE
Larry Cole	DE
Tody Smith	DE
Pat Toomay	DE
Billy Gregory	DT
Bob Lilly	DT
Jethro Pugh	DT
John Babinecz	LB
Ralph Coleman	LB
Dave Edwards	LB
Chuck Howley	LB
Lee Roy Jordan	LB
Mike Keller	LB
D.D. Lewis	LB
Herb Adderly	DB
Benny Barnes	DB
Cornell Green	DB
Cliff Harris	DB
Mel Renfro	DB
Mark Washington	DB
Charlie Waters	DB
Craig Morton	QB
Roger Staubach	QB
Mike Montgomery	HB
Dan Reeves	HB
Calvin Hill	FB-HB
Robert Newhouse	FB-HB
Walt Garrison	FB
Bill Thomas	FB
Lance Alworth	WR
Bob Hayes	WR
Billy Parks	WR
Ron Sellers	WR

Name	Position
Mike Ditka	TE
Jean Fugett	TE
Billy Truax	TE
Marv Bateman	K
Toni Fritsch	K

1973

NAME	POSITION
Ralph Neely	OT
Rayfield Wright	OT
Rodney Wallace	OG-OT
John Niland	OG
Blaine Nye	OG
Jim Arneson	C-OG
Bruce Walton	C-OG
John Fitzgerald	C
Dave Manders	C
Larry Cole	DE
Harvey Martin	DE
Pat Toomay	DE
Billy Gregory	DT
Bob Lilly	DT
Jethro Pugh	DT
John Babinecz	LB
Rodrigo Barnes	LB
Dave Edwards	LB
Chuck Howley	LB
Lee Roy Jordan	LB
Mike Keller	LB
D.D. Lewis	LB
Benny Barnes	DB
Cornell Green	DB
Cliff Harris	DB
Mel Renfro	DB
Mark Washington	DB
Charlie Waters	DB
Craig Morton	QB
Roger Staubach	QB
Cyril Pinder	HB
Les Strayhorn	HB
Calvin Hill	FB-HB
Robert Newhouse	FB-HB
Walt Garrison	FB
Larry Robinson	FB-HB
Bob Hayes	WR
Mike Montgomery	WR
Drew Pearson	WR
Golden Richards	WR
Otto Stowe	WR
Billy Joe DuPree	TE
Jean Fugett	TE

Name	Position
Billy Truax	TE
Marv Bateman	K
Toni Fritsch	K
Mike Clark	K

1974

NAME	POSITION
Ralph Neely	OT
Bruce Walton	OT
Rayfield Wright	OT
Gene Killian	OG
John Niland	OG
Blaine Nye	OG
Jim Arneson	C-OG
John Fitzgerald	C
Dave Manders	C
Larry Cole	DE
Too Tall Jones	DE
Harvey Martin	DE
Pat Toomay	DE
Bill Gregory	DT
Bob Lilly	DT
Jethro Pugh	DT
Dave Edwards	LB
Ken Hutcherson	LB
Lee Roy Jordan	LB
D.D. Lewis	LB
Cal Peterson	LB
Louie Walker	LB
Benny Barnes	DB
Cornell Green	DB
Cliff Harris	DB
Mel Renfro	DB
Mark Washington	DB
Charlie Waters	DB
Clint Longley	QB
Roger Staubach	QB
Doug Dennison	HB
Dennis Morgan	HB
Les Strayhorn	HB
Charles Young	HB
Calvin Hill	FB-HB
Walt Garrison	FB
Robert Newhouse	FB-HB
Bob Hayes	WR
Bill Houston	WR
Drew Pearson	WR
Golden Richards	WR
Billy Joe DuPree	TE
Jean Fugett	TE
Ron Howard	TE

Name	Position
Duane Carrell	K
Efren Herrera	K
Mac Percival	K
Tony Fritsch	knee injury
Rodney Wallace	injury
John Babinecz	injury

1975

NAME	POSITION
Pat Donovan	OT
Ralph Neely	OT
Bruce Walton	OT
Rayfield Wright	OT
Burton Lawless	OG
Blaine Nye	OG
Herbert Scott	OG
Kyle Davis	C
John Fitzgerald	C
Too Tall Jones	DE
Harvey Martin	DE
Randy White	LB-DT-DE
Larry Cole	DT
Bill Gregory	DT
Jethro Pugh	DT
Bob Breunig	LB
Warren Capone	LB
Dave Edwards	LB
Thomas Henderson	LB
Lee Roy Jordan	LB
D.D. Lewis	LB
Cal Peterson	LB
Benny Barnes	DB
Cliff Harris	DB
Randy Hughes	DB
Mel Renfro	DB
Mark Washington	DB
Charlie Waters	DB
Roland Woolsey	DB
Clint Longley	QB
Roger Staubach	QB
Preston Pearson	HB
Charley Young	HB
Doug Dennison	FB-HB
Scott Laidlaw	FB
Robert Newhouse	FB
Percy Howard	WR
Drew Pearson	WR
Golden Richards	WR
Billy Joe DuPree	TE
Ron Howard	TE
Jean Fugett	WR-TE

Name	Position
Tony Fritsch	K
Mitch Hoopes	K
Efren Herrera	injury

1976

NAME	POSITION
Pat Donovan	OT
Ralph Neely	OT
Rayfield Wright	OT
Jim Eidson	OG-C
Burton Lawless	OG
Blaine Nye	OG
Tom Rafferty	OG-C
Herbert Scott	OG
John Fitzgerald	C
Too Tall Jones	DE
Harvey Martin	DE
Greg Schaum	DE
Larry Cole	DT
Bill Gregory	DT
Jethro Pugh	DT
Bob Breunig	LB
Mike Hegman	LB
Thomas Henderson	LB
Lee Roy Jordan	LB
D.D. Lewis	LB
Randy White	LB
Benny Barnes	DB
Cliff Harris	DB
Randy Hughes	DB
Aaron Kyle	DB
Beasley Reece	DB
Mel Renfro	DB
Mark Washington	DB
Charlie Waters	DB
Roger Staubach	QB
Danny White	QB
Doug Dennison	HB-FB
Preston Pearson	HB
Charley Young	HB
Jim Jensen	FB
Scott Laidlaw	FB
Robert Newhouse	FB-HB
Butch Johnson	WR
Drew Pearson	WR
Golden Richards	WR
Billy Joe DuPree	TE
Jay Saldi	TE
Efren Herrera	K
Percy Howard	injury
Kyle Davis	injury

1977

NAME	POSITION
Pat Donovan	OT
Andy Fredrick	OT
Ralph Neely	OT
Rayfield Wright	OT
Jim Cooper	OG-C
Burton Lawless	OG
Tom Rafferty	OG-C
Herbert Scott	OG
John Fitzgerald	C
Too Tall Jones	DE
Harvey Martin	DE
David Stalls	DE
Larry Cole	DT-DE
Bill Gregory	DT
Jethro Pugh	DT
Randy White	DT
Bob Breunig	LB
Guy Brown	LB
Mike Hegman	LB
Thomas Henderson	LB
Bruce Huther	LB
D.D. Lewis	LB
Benny Barnes	DB
Cliff Harris	DB
Randy Hughes	DB
Aaron Kyle	DB
Mel Renfro	DB
Mark Washington	DB
Charlie Waters	DB
Glen Corano	QB
Roger Staubach	QB
Danny White	QB
Doug Dennison	HB
Tony Dorsett	HB
Larry Brinson	FB
Scott Laidlaw	FB
Robert Newhouse	FB
Tony Hill	WR
Butch Johnson	WR
Drew Pearson	WR
Golden Richards	WR
Billy Joe DuPree	TE
Jay Saldi	TE
Efern Herrera	K
Jim Eidson	injury
Greg Schaum	knee injury
Charley Young	knee injury
Percy Howard	injury

1978

NAME	POSITION
Pat Donovan	OT
Andy Fredrick	OT
Rayfield Wright	OT
Burton Lawless	OG
Tom Rafferty	OG
Tom Randall	OG
Herbert Scott	OG
Jim Cooper	C-OG
John Fitzgerald	C
Too Tall Jones	DE
Harvey Martin	DE
Larry Bethea	DT
Larry Cole	DT-DE
Jethro Pugh	DT
David Stalls	DT-DE
Randy White	DT
Bob Breunig	LB
Guy Brown	LB
Mike Hegman	LB
Thomas Henderson	LB
Bruce Huther	LB
D.D. Lewis	LB
Benny Barnes	DB
Cliff Harris	DB
Randy Hughes	DB
Aaron Kyle	DB
Dennis Thurman	DB
Mark Washington	DB
Charlie Waters	DB
Glen Corano	QB
Roger Staubach	QB
Danny White	QB
Alois Blackwell	HB
Doug Dennison	HB
Tony Dorsett	HB
Preston Pearson	HB
Larry Brinson	FB
Scott Laidlaw	FB
Robert Newhouse	FB
Tony Hill	WR
Butch Johnson	WR
Drew Pearson	WR
Robert Steele	WR
Billy Joe DuPree	TE
Jay Saldi	TE
Jackie Smith	TE
Rafael Septien	K

1979

NAME	POSITION
Jim Cooper	OT
Pat Donovan	OT
Andy Fredrick	OT
Rayfield Wright	OT
Burton Lawless	OG
Tom Rafferty	OG
Herbert Scott	OG
John Fitzgerald	C
Robert Shaw	C-OG
Larry Cole	DE-DT
John Dutton	DE
Harvey Martin	DE
Bruce Thornton	DE-DT
Larry Bethea	DT
David Stalls	DT
Randy White	DT
Bob Breunig	LB
Guy Brown	LB
Mike Hegman	LB
Thomas Henderson	LB
Bruce Huther	LB
D.D. Lewis	LB
Benny Barnes	DB
Cliff Harris	DB
Randy Hughes	DB
Aaron Kyle	DB
Wade Manning	DB
Aaron Mitchell	DB
Dennis Thurman	DB
Glen Corano	QB
Roger Staubach	QB
Danny White	QB
Alois Blackwell	HB
Tony Dorsett	HB
Preston Pearson	HB
Ron Springs	HB
Larry Brinson	FB
Scott Laidlaw	FB
Robert Newhouse	FB
Tony Hill	WR
Butch Johnson	WR
Drew Pearson	WR
Steve Wilson	WR
Doug Cosbie	TE
Billy Joe DuPree	TE
Jay Saldi	TE
Rafael Septien	K
Too Tall Jones	voluntarily retired
Charlie Waters	knee injury

1980

NAME	POSITION
Jim Cooper	OT
Pat Donovan	OT
Andy Fredrick	OT
Kurt Petersen	OG
Tom Rafferty	OG
Herbert Scott	OG
Norm Wells	OG
John Fitzgerald	C
Robert Shaw	C
Too Tall Jones	DE
Harvey Martin	DE
Bruce Thornton	DE-DT
Larry Bethea	DT
Larry Cole	DT
John Dutton	DT
Randy White	DT
Bob Breunig	LB
Guy Brown	LB
Anthony Dickerson	LB
Mike Hegman	LB
Bruce Huther	LB
D.D. Lewis	LB
Bill Roe	LB
Benny Barnes	DB
Dextor Clinkscale	DB
Randy Hughes	DB
Eric Hurt	DB
Wade Manning	DB
Aaron Mitchell	DB
Roland Solomon	DB
Dennis Thurman	DB
Charlie Waters	DB
Steve Wilson	DB
Glen Corano	QB
Gary Hogeboom	QB
Danny White	QB
Tony Dorsett	HB
James Jones	HB-FB
Preston Pearson	HB
Robert Newhouse	FB
Timmy Newsome	FB
Ron Springs	FB
Tony Hill	WR
Butch Johnson	WR
Drew Pearson	WR
Doug Cosbie	TE
Billy Joe DuPree	TE
Jay Saldi	TE
Rafael Septien	K

1981

NAME	POSITION
Jim Cooper	OT
Pat Donovan	OT
Andy Fredrick	OT
Steve Wright	OT
Kurt Petersen	OG
Howard Richards	OG-OT
Herbert Scott	OG
Glen Titensor	OG-C
Tom Rafferty	C-OG
Robert Shaw	C
Too Tall Jones	DE
Harvey Martin	DE
Don Smerek	DE
Bruce Thornton	DE-DT
Larry Bethea	DT-DT
John Dutton	DT
Randy White	DT
Bob Breunig	LB
Guy Brown	LB
Anthony Dickerson	LB
Mike Hegman	LB
Angelo King	LB
D.D. Lewis	LB
Danny Spradlin	LB
Benny Barnes	DB
Michael Downs	DB
Ron Fellows	DB
Dennis Thurman	DB
Everson Walls	DB
Charlie Waters	DB
Steve Wilson	DB
Glen Corano	QB
Gary Hogeboom	QB
Danny White	QB
Tony Dorsett	HB
James Jones	HB
Robert Newhouse	FB
Timmy Newsome	FB
Ron Springs	FB-HB
Doug Donley	WR
Tony Hill	WR
Butch Johnson	WR
Drew Pearson	WR
Doug Cosbie	TE
Billy Joe DuPree	TE
Jay Saldi	TE
Rafael Septien	K
Dextor Clinkscale	achilles injury
John Fitzgerald	knee injury
Randy Hughes	shoulder injury
Bill Roe	ankle injury

1982

NAME	POSITION
Jim Cooper	OT
Pat Donovan	OT
Phil Pozderac	OT
Kurt Petersen	OG
Howard Richards	OG-OT
Herbert Scott	OG
Glen Titensor	OG-C
Steve Wright	OG-OT
Brian Baldinger	C-OG
Tom Rafferty	C-OG
Larry Bethea	DE-DT
Too Tall Jones	DE
Harvey Martin	DE
John Dutton	DT
Don Smerek	DT-DE
Randy White	DT
Bob Breunig	LB
Guy Brown	LB
Anthony Dickerson	LB
Mike Hegman	LB
Angelo King	LB
Jeff Rohrer	LB
Danny Spradlin	LB
Benny Barnes	DB
Dextor Clinkscale	DB
Michael Downs	DB
Ron Fellows	DB
Rod Hill	DB
Monty Hunter	DB
Dennis Thurman	DB
Everson Walls	DB
Glen Corano	QB
Gary Hogeboom	QB
Danny White	QB
Brad Wright	QB
Tony Dorsett	HB
James Jones	HB
Robert Newhouse	FB
Timmy Newsome	FB
George Peoples	FB
Ron Springs	FB-HB
Doug Donley	WR
Tony Hill	WR
Butch Johnson	WR
Drew Pearson	WR
Doug Cosbie	TE
Billy Joe DuPree	TE
Jay Saldi	TE
Rafael Septien	K
Robert Shaw	knee injury
Norman Wells	knee injury

1983

NAME	POSITION
Jim Cooper	OT
Pat Donovan	OT
Phil Pozderac	OT
Chris Schultz	OT
Howard Richards	OT-OG
Kurt Petersen	OG
Herbert Scott	OG
Brian Baldinger	OG
Tom Rafferty	C
Glen Titensor	C
Jim Jeffcoat	DE
Too Tall Jones	DE
Harvey Martin	DE
Larry Bethea	DT
John Dutton	DT
Don Smerek	DT
Mark Tuinei	DT
Randy White	DT
Bob Breunig	LB
Anthony Dickerson	LB
Mike Hegman	LB
Bruce Huther	LB
Angelo King	LB
Scott McLean	LB
Jeff Rohrer	LB
Michael Walter	LB
Bill Bates	DB
Dextor Clinkscale	DB
Michael Downs	DB
Ron Fellows	DB
Rod Hill	DB
Dennis Thurman	DB
Everson Walls	DB
Glen Corano	QB
Gary Hogeboom	QB
Danny White	QB
Gary Allen	HB
Tony Dorsett	HB
Chuck McSwain	HB
Robert Newhouse	FB
Timmy Newsome	FB
Ron Springs	FB-HB
Doug Donley	WR

1984

NAME	POSITION
Tony Hill	WR
Butch Johnson	WR
Drew Pearson	WR
Doug Cosbie	TE
Billy Joe DuPree	TE
Cleo Simmons	TE
Jim Miller	K
Rafael Septien	K
John Warren	K
James Jones	knee injury

NAME	POSITION
Jim Cooper	OT
John Hunt	OT
Phil Pozderac	OT
Howard Richards	OT-OG
Dowe Aughtman	OG
Kurt Petersen	OG
Herbert Scott	OG
Brian Baldinger	OG
Tom Rafferty	C
Glen Titensor	C-OG
Jim Jeffcoat	DE
Too Tall Jones	DE
John Dutton	DT
Don Smerek	DT
Mark Tuinei	DT
Randy White	DT
Bob Breunig	LB
Billy Cannon	LB
Steve DeOssie	LB
Anthony Dickerson	LB
Mike Hegman	LB
Eugene Lockhart	LB
Jeff Rohrer	LB
Jimmie Turner	LB
Vince Albritton	DB
Bill Bates	DB
Dextor Clinkscale	DB
Michael Downs	DB
Ron Fellows	DB
Carl Howard	DB
Victor Scott	DB
Dennis Thurman	DB
Everson Walls	DB
Gary Hogeboom	QB
Steve Pelluer	QB
Danny White	QB
Gary Allen	HB
Tony Dorsett	HB

Name	Position
James Jones	HB
Chuck McSwain	HB
Norm Granger	FB
Timmy Newsome	FB
Ron Springs	FB-HB
Harold Carmichael	WR
Doug Donley	WR
Tony Hill	WR
Kirk Phillips	WR
Mike Renfro	WR
Waddell Smith	WR
Fred Cornwell	TE
Doug Cosbie	TE
Brian Salonen	TE
Jim Miller	K
Rafael Septien	K
John Warren	K
Chris Schultz	knee injury

1985

NAME	POSITION
Jim Cooper	OT
Phil Pozderac	OT
Chris Schultz	OT
Crawford Ker	OG
Kurt Petersen	OG
Howard Richards	OG-OT
Broderick Thompson	OG
Glen Titensor	OG
Tom Rafferty	C
Mark Tuinei	C
Kevin Brooks	DE
Jim Jeffcoat	DE
Too Tall Jones	DE
John Dutton	DT
David Ponder	DT
Don Smerek	DT
Randy White	DT
Vince Albritton	LB
Steve DeOssie	LB
Mike Hegman	LB
Eugene Lockhart	LB
Jesse Penn	LB
Jeff Rohrer	LB
Brian Salonen	LB
Bill Bates	DB
Dextor Clinkscale	DB
Michael Downs	DB
Ricky Easmon	DB
Ron Fellows	DB
Victor Scott	DB
Dennis Thurman	DB
Everson Walls	DB
Steve Pelluer	QB
Danny White	QB
Gary Hogeboom	QB
Tony Dorsett	HB
James Jones	HB
Robert Lavette	HB
John Williams	HB
Todd Fowler	FB
Timmy Newsome	FB
Gordon Banks	WR
Kenny Duckett	WR
Leon Gonzales	WR
Tony Hill	WR
Karl Powe	WR
Mike Renfro	WR
Fred Cornwell	TE
Doug Cosbie	TE
Mike Saxon	K
Rafael Septien	K
Dowe Aughtman	shoulder injury
Brian Baldinger	knee injury

1986

NAME	POSITION
Jim Cooper	OT
Phil Pozderac	OT
Howard Richards	OT
Brian Baldinger	OG
Crawford Ker	OG
Nate Nelson	OG
Glen Titensor	OG
Tom Rafferty	C
Mark Tuinei	C
Jesse Baker	DE
Kevin Brooks	DE
Jim Jeffcoat	DE
Too Tall Jones	DE
Bob Otto	DE
Kurt Ploeger	DE
John Dutton	DT
David Ponder	DT
Don Smerek	DT
Randy White	DT
Steve DeOssie	LB
Mike Hegman	LB
Garth Jax	LB
Eugene Lockhart	LB
Jesse Penn	LB
Jeff Rohrer	LB
Vince Albritton	DB
Bill Bates	DB
Michael Downs	DB
Ron Fellows	DB
Cornell Gowdy	DB
Manny Hendrix	DB
Johnny Holloway	DB
Victor Scott	DB
Everson Walls	DB
Regie Collier	QB
Paul McDonald	QB
Steve Pelluer	QB
Danny White	QB
Tony Dorsett	HB
Robert Lavette	HB
Herschel Walker	HB
Todd Fowler	FB
Timmy Newsome	FB
Gordon Banks	WR
Tony Hill	WR
Karl Powe	WR
Mike Renfro	WR
Mike Sherrard	WR
Thorntor Chandler	TE
Doug Cosbie	TE
Mike Saxon	K
Rafael Septien	K
Norm Granger	hamstring injury
Brian Salonen	groin injury
Kurt Petersen	knee injury

1987

NAME	POSITION
Brian Baldinger	OT-OG
Dave Burnette	OT
Steve Cisowaki	OT
Kevin Gogan	OT
Phil Pozderac	OT
Jon Shields	OT
Mark Tuinei	OT
Sal Cesario	OG
Crawford Ker	OG
Nate Newton	OG
Gary Walker	OG
Bob White	OG
Jeff Zimmerman	OG
George Lilja	C
Tom Rafferty	C
Joe Shearin	C
Mike Zentic	C
Jim Jeffcoat	DE
Too Tall Jones	DE
Ray Perkins	DE
Don Smerek	DE-DT
Randy Watts	DE-DT
Kevin Brooks	DT
John Dutton	DT
Mike Dwyer	DT
Walter Johnson	DT
Danny Noonan	DT
Mark Walen	DT-DE
Randy White	DT
Ron Burton	LB
Steve DeOssie	LB
Chris Duliban	LB
Harry Flaherty	LB
Mike Hegman	LB
Jeff Hurd	LB
Garth Jax	LB
Dale Jones	LB
Eugene Lockhart	LB
Jesse Penn	LB
Jeff Rohrer	LB
Victor Simmons	LB
Russ Swan	LB
Kirk Timmer	LB
Vince Albritton	DB
Jimmy Armstrong	DB
Bill Bates	DB
Anthony Coleman	DB
Michael Downs	DB
Ron Francis	DB
Alex Green	DB
Tommy Haynes	DB
Manny Hendrix	DB
Bill Hill	DB
Bruce Livingston	DB
Victor Scott	DB
Everson Walls	DB
Robert Williams	DB
Paul McDonald	QB
Steve Pelluer	QB
Loran Snyder	QB
Kevin Sweeney	QB
Danny White	QB
David Adams	HB
Alvin Blount	HB
Tony Dorsett	HB
Robert Lavette	HB
Herschel Walker	HB
Darryl Clack	FB
Todd Fowler	FB
E.J. Jones	FB

Name	Position
Timmy Newsome	FB
Gerald White	FB
Gordon Banks	WR
Ron Barksdale	WR
Cornell Burbage	WR
Vince Courville	WR
Kelvin Edwards	WR
Kelvin Martin	WR
Mike Renfro	WR
Chuck Scott	WR
Sebron Spivey	WR
Rich Borreson	TE
Thornton Chandler	TE
Doug Cosbie	TE
Steve Folsom	TE
Tim Hendrix	TE
Kerry Brady	K
Roger Ruzek	K
Buzz Sawyer	K
Mike Saxon	K
Luis Zendejas	K
Kurt Petersen	knee injury
Robert Smith	arm injury
Glen Titensor	knee injury
Brian Salonen	groin injury
Ray Alexander	wrist injury
Mike Sherrard	broken leg

1988

NAME	POSITION
Bob Brotzki	OT
Kevin Gogan	OT
Daryle Smith	OT
Mark Tuinei	OT
Dave Widell	OT
Crawford Ker	OG
Nate Newton	OG
Glen Titensor	OG
Jeff Zimmerman	OG
Tom Rafferty	C
Bob White	C
Jim Jeffcoat	DE
Too Tall Jones	DE
Kevin Brooks	DT
Danny Noonan	DT
Mark Walen	DT-DE
Randy White	DT
Ron Burton	LB
Garry Cobb	LB
Steve DeOssie	LB
Garth Jax	LB
Eugene Lockhart	LB
Ken Norton	LB
Sean Scott	LB
Vince Albritton	DB
Bill Bates	DB
Michael Downs	DB
Ron Francis	DB
Manny Hendrix	DB
Billy Owens	DB
Victor Scott	DB
Everson Walls	DB
Robert Williams	DB
Charles Wright	DB
Steve Pelluer	QB
Scott Secules	QB
Kevin Sweeney	QB
Danny White	QB
Mark Higgs	HB
Herschel Walker	HB-FB
Darryl Clack	FB
Todd Fowler	FB
Timmy Newsome	FB
Ray Alexander	WR
Cornell Burbage	WR
Kelvin Edwards	WR
Everett Gay	WR
Michael Irvin	WR
Kelvin Martin	WR
Thornton Chandler	TE
Doug Cosbie	TE
Steve Folsom	TE
Roger Ruzek	K
Mike Saxon	K
Jeff Hurd	knee injury
Jeff Rohrer	back injury
Rod Barksdale	knee injury
Mike Sherrard	leg injury

1989

NAME	POSITION
Kevin Gogan	OT
Mark Tuinei	OT
Dave Widell	OT
Crawford Ker	OG
Nate Newton	OG
Mark Stepnoski	OG-C
Jeff Zimmerman	OG
Tom Rafferty	C
Bob White	C
Willie Broughton	DE
Jim Jeffcoat	DE
Too Tall Jones	DE
Tony Tolbert	DE
Jon Carter	DT
Dean Hamel	DT
Danny Noonan	DT
Garry Cobb	LB
Jack Del Rio	LB
Onzy Elam	LB
David Howard	LB
Eugene Lockhart	LB
Ken Norton	LB
Randy Shannon	LB
Jesse Solomon	LB
Ken Tippins	LB
Vince Albritton	DB
Scott Ankrom	DB
Bill Bates	DB
Eric Brown	DB
Ron Francis	DB
Manny Hendrix	DB
Issiac Holt	DB
Ray Horton	DB
Tim Jackson	DB
Tony Lilly	DB
Everson Walls	DB
Robert Williams	DB
Troy Aikman	QB
Babe Laufenberg	QB
Steve Walsh	QB
Paul Palmer	HB
Kevin Scott	HB
Curtis Stewart	HB
Darryl Clack	FB
Daryl Johnston	FB
Broderick Sargent	FB
Curtis Stewart	FB
Junior Tautalatasi	FB
Ray Alexander	WR
Cornell Burbage	WR
James Dixon	WR
Bernard Ford	WR
Michael Irvin	WR
Kelvin Martin	WR
Derrick Shepard	WR
Thornton Chandler	TE
Steve Folsom	TE
Keith Jennings	TE
Mike Saxon	K
Roger Ruzek	K
Jeff Hurd	knee injury
Mark Walen	knee injury

1990

NAME	POSITION
Louis Cheek	OT
Kevin Gogan	OT
Mark Tuinei	OT
John Gesek	OG
Dale Hellestrae	OG-C
Crawford Ker	OG
Nate Newton	OG
Tony Slaton	OG
Mark Stepnoski	OG
Jeff Zimmerman	OG
Lester Brinkley	DE
Jim Jeffcoat	DE
Danny Stubbs	DE
Tony Tolbert	DE
Willie Broughton	DT
Dean Hamel	DT
Jimmie Jones	DT
Danny Noonan	DT
Mitch Willis	DT
Willis Crockett	LB
Jack Del Rio	LB
Dave Harper	LB
David Howard	LB
Eugene Lockhart	LB
Ken Norton	LB
Randy Shannon	LB
Vinson Smith	LB
Jesse Solomon	LB
Vince Albritton	DB
Bill Bates	DB
Michael Brooks	DB
Ron Francis	DB
Kenneth Gant	DB
Manny Hendrix	DB
Issiac Holt	DB
Ray Horton	DB
Stan Smagala	DB
James Washington	DB
Troy Aikman	QB
Babe Laufenberg	QB
Cliff Stoudt	QB
James Dixon	HB-WR
Emmitt Smith	HB
Timmy Smith	HB
Tommie Agee	FB
Alonzo Highsmith	FB
Daryl Johnston	FB
Rob Harris	WR
Michael Irvin	WR

Name	Position
Kelvin Martin	WR
Dennis McKinnon	WR
Derrick Shepard	WR
Alexander Wright	WR
Robert Awalt	TE
Steve Folsom	TE
Jay Novacek	TE
Mike Saxon	K
Ken Willis	K
Scott Ankrum	knee injury
Keith Jones	knee injury

1991

NAME	POSITION
Nate Newton	OT
Mark Tuinei	OT
Erik Williams	OT
John Gesek	OG
Kevin Gogan	OG
Dale Hellestrae	OG-C
Alan Veingrad	OG-OT
Mark Stepnoski	C
Tony Hill	DE
Jim Jeffcoat	DE
Danny Stubbs	DE
Tony Tolbert	DE
Tony Cassillas	DT
Jimmie Jones	DT
Leon Lett	DT
Russell Maryland	DT-DE
Danny Noonan	DT
Darrick Brownlow	LB
Reggie Cooper	LB
Jack Del Rio	LB
Dixon Edwards	LB
Godfrey Myles	LB
Ken Norton	LB
Mickey Pruitt	LB
Vinson Smith	LB
Vince Albritton	DB
Bill Bates	DB
Larry Brown	DB
Kenneth Gant	DB
Manny Hendrix	DB
Issiac Holt	DB
Ray Horton	DB
Stan Smagala	DB
Donald Smith	DB
James Washington	DB
Robert Williams	DB
Troy Aikman	QB

Name	Position
Steve Beuerlein	QB
James Dixon	HB-WR
Curvin Richards	HB
Emmitt Smith	HB
Tommie Agee	FB
Ricky Blake	FB
Daryl Johnston	FB
Alvin Harper	WR
Michael Irvin	WR
Kelvin Martin	WR
Derrick Shepard	WR
Alexander Wright	WR
Robert Awalt	TE
Jay Novacek	TE
Alfredo Roberts	TE
Mike Saxon	K
Ken Willis	K
Michael Brooks	knee injury

1992

NAME	POSITION
Mark Tuinei	OT
Erik Williams	OT
John Gesek	OG
Kevin Gogan	OG-OT
Dale Hellestrae	OG-C
Nate Newton	OG
Alan Veingrad	OG-OT
Frank Cornish	C-OG
Mark Stepnoski	C
Charles Haley	DE
Tony Hill	DE
Jim Jeffcoat	DE
Tony Tolbert	DE
Tony Cassillas	DT
Chad Hennings	DT
Jimmie Jones	DT
Leon Lett	DT
Russell Maryland	DT-DE
Bobby Abrams	LB
Dixon Edwards	LB
Robert Jones	LB
Godfrey Myles	LB
Ken Norton	LB
Mickey Pruitt	LB
Vinson Smith	LB
Bill Bates	DB
Larry Brown	DB
Thomas Everett	DB
Kenneth Gant	DB
Clayton Holmes	DB

Name	Position
Issiac Holt	DB
Ray Horton	DB
Kevin Smith	DB
James Washington	DB
Robert Williams	DB
Darren Woodson	DB
Troy Aikman	QB
Steve Beuerlein	QB
Derrick Gainer	HB
Curvin Richards	HB
Emmitt Smith	HB
Tommie Agee	FB
Daryl Johnston	FB
Alvin Harper	WR
Michael Irvin	WR
Kelvin Martin	WR
Jimmy Smith	WR
Jay Novacek	TE
Alfredo Roberts	TE
Lyn Elliott	K
Mike Saxon	K

1993

NAME	POSITION
Ron Stone	OT
Mark Tuinei	OT
Erik Williams	OT
John Gesek	OG
Kevin Gogan	OG-OT
Dale Hellestrae	OG-C
Nate Newton	OG
Frank Cornish	C-OG
Mark Stepnoski	C
Charles Haley	DE
Jim Jeffcoat	DE
Tony Tolbert	DE
Tony Cassillas	DT
Chad Hennings	DT
Jimmie Jones	DT
Leon Lett	DT-DE
Russell Maryland	DT
Bobby Abrams	LB
Dixon Edwards	LB
Robert Jones	LB
Godfrey Myles	LB
Ken Norton	LB
Darrin Smith	LB
Matt Vanderbeek	LB-DE
Bill Bates	DB
Larry Brown	DB
Thomas Everett	DB

Name	Position
Joe Fishback	DB
Kenneth Gant	DB
Chris Hall	DB
Brock Marion	DB
Elvis Patterson	DB
Kevin Smith	DB
Dave Thomas	DB
James Washington	DB
Robert Williams	DB
Darren Woodson	DB
Troy Aikman	QB
Jason Garrett	QB
Derrick Gainer	HB
Derrick Lassic	HB
Emmitt Smith	HB
Tommie Agee	FB
Lincoln Coleman	FB-HB
Daryl Johnston	FB
Alvin Harper	WR
Michael Irvin	WR
Kevin Williams	WR
Tyrone Williams	WR
Kelly Blackwell	TE
Scott Gabraith	TE
Joey Mickey	TE
Jay Novacek	TE
Jim Price	TE
Lyn Elliott	K
John Jett	K
Eddie Murray	K
Clayton Holmes	knee injury
Jimmy Smith	appendix
Alfredo Roberts	foot injury

1994

NAME	POSITION
Larry Allen	OT
George Hegamin	OT
Ron Stone	OT-OG
Mark Tuinei	OT
Erik Williams	OT
Dale Hellestrae	OG-C
Derek Kennard	OG
Nate Newton	OG
Mark Stepnoski	C
Shante Carver	DE
Charles Haley	DE
Jim Jeffcoat	DE
Tony Tolbert	DE
Chad Hennings	DT
Leon Lett	DT

Name	Position
Russell Maryland	DT
Hurvin McCormack	DT
Darrick Brownlow	LB
Dixon Edwards	LB
Robert Jones	LB
Godfrey Myles	LB
Jim Schwantz	LB
Darrin Smith	LB
Matt Vanderbeek	LB
Bill Bates	DB
Larry Brown	DB
Joe Fishback	DB
Kenneth Gant	DB
Clayton Holmes	DB
Brock Marion	DB
Kevin Smith	DB
Darren Studstill	DB
Dave Thomas	DB
James Washington	DB
Darren Woodson	DB
Troy Aikman	QB
Jason Garrett	QB
Rodney Peete	QB
Lincoln Coleman	HB
Emmitt Smith	HB
Blair Thomas	HB
Tommie Agee	FB
Daryl Johnston	FB
Cory Flemming	WR
Alvin Harper	WR
Michael Irvin	WR
Kevin Williams	WR
Scott Gabraith	TE
Jay Novacek	TE
Chris Boniol	K
John Jett	K
Derrick Lassic	knee injury

1995

NAME	POSITION
Kevin Williams	WR-KOR-PR
Deion Sanders	WR-LCB-KOR-PR
Edward Hervey	WR
Michael Irvin	WR
Cory Fleming	WR
Billy Davis	WR
Mark Tuinei	LT
Ron Stone	LT-LG-RG-RT
George Hegamin	LT-RT
Nate Newton	LG
Michael Batiste	LG-C-RG-RT
Derek Kennard	C
Dale Hellestrae	C-PC-KC
Larry Allen	RG
Erik Williams	RT
Jay Novacek	TE-H
Kendell Watkins	TE
Eric Bjornson	TE-H
Troy Aikman	QB
Wade Wilson	QB
Jason Garrett	QB
Daryl Johnston	FB-PC-KC
David Lang	FB
Emmitt Smith	RB
Sherman Williams	RB
Dominique Ross	RB
Tony Tolbert	LE
Hurvin McCormack	LE
Oscar Sturgis	LE-PC
Russell Maryland	LT
Chad Hennings	LT-RT
Darren Benson	LT
Leon Lett	RT-RE
Charles Haley	RE
Shante Carver	RE
Dixon Edwards	SLB
Godfrey Myles	SLB-MLB-WLB
Darryl Hardy	SLB
Robert Jones	MLB
Jim Schwantz	MLB-WLB
Darrin Smith	WLB
Robert Bailey	LCB
Larry Brown	RCB
Alundis Brice	RCB
Brock Marion	FS-KOR
Charlie Williams	FS
Greg Briggs	FS
Darren Woodson	SS
Scott Case	SS
Bill Bates	SS
John Jett	P-H
Chris Boniol	K-P

PHOTOGRAPHY CREDITS

★

Special thanks to the *Fort Worth Star-Telegram* photography staff for a generous contribution to this book

The publisher is especially grateful to Bob Lilly for his photographs from
Bob Lilly: Reflections
Copyright 1983, Bob Lilly and Sam Blair

AP Wide World Photos contribution was critical to a complete presentation

Photographs by John Maziotta provided by the Dallas Public Library

Thanks to Al Panzera for the use of his excellent photographs

Vernon Biever

Dallas Cowboys Weekly

Dallas Cowboys Cheerleaders

The Green Bay Packers

The San Francisco 49ers